THE DEATHS OF CINDY JAMES

NEAL HALL

The Deaths of Cindy James

M&S

An M&S Paperback Original from
McClelland & Stewart Inc.
The Canadian Publishers

An M&S Paperback Original from McClelland & Stewart Inc.

First printing January 1991

Copyright © 1991 by Neal Hall

Canadian Cataloguing in Publication Data

Hall, Neal
The deaths of Cindy James

ISBN 0-7710-3784-8

1. James, Cindy, 1944–1989. 2. Coroners –
British Columbia – Vancouver. 3. Murder –
British Columbia – Vancouver. 4. Offenses
against the person – British Columbia – Vancouver.
I. Title.

HV6535.C33V35 1991   364.1′523′092   C91-093038-4

"Who By Fire" copyright © 1974 Leonard Cohen.
Used by Permission. All rights reserved.

Front cover photos: Roy Makepeace (l)
Back cover photos: Roy Makepeace; *The Province* (Vancouver)

McClelland & Stewart Inc.
The Canadian Publishers
481 University Avenue
Toronto, Ontario
M5G 2E9

To the memory of my parents, Les and Kitty Hall,
whose ashes have settled in Okanagan Lake.

Contents

Acknowledgements

My sincere gratitude for all those who consented to interviews and shared their thoughts for this book, including police officers and officials who spoke on a not-for-attribution basis.

In particular, I would like to thank Dr. Roy Makepeace for sharing his complete files, including calendars, related correspondence, legal documents and photographs that he meticulously kept over the years.

I would also like to extend my sympathy to the members of the Hack family, as well as Cindy's friends and colleagues, for having to re-live their often painful, private memories.

I'm grateful to my astute editor, Brian Scrivener, for providing concise, efficient and thoughtful criticism. He also offered deft, intelligent cuts that improved the manuscript.

My appreciation also to James Adams, my editor at McClelland and Stewart, not only for his support, but also for prompt and timely feedback as the writing progressed.

And my gratitude to my literary agent, Helen Heller, for her hard work and perseverance.

I offer my thanks to my friend Blake Williams for his help reproducing the photos, to my colleague Peter Wilson for his encouragement to embark on this project, to writer Eric Nicol for his behind-the-scenes encouragement of McClelland & Stewart publisher Doug Gibson to support a book on this sad and unusual case, and to my editors at *The Vancouver Sun* and the staff of the B.C. coroners service for their cooperation.

Finally, I would like to offer special thanks to my wife, Jackie Haliburton, and my children, Eli, Rachael and Becky, for their patience and support during the considerable time I spent away from them, first covering the Cindy James story as it unfolded and subsequently writing this document.

I would note that the intent of this book was not to exploit Cindy's troubled life or the cherished memories of her those who loved and cared for her, but to shed light on the complexity of her problem for the benefit of others like her, hoping they will be recognized sooner and spared a similar ordeal.

Any errors or omissions in this work are, of course, solely the responsibility of the author.

And who by fire, who by water
Who in the sunshine, who in the night time,
Who by high ordeal, who by common trial.
Who in your merry, merry month of May,
    who by very slow decay
and who shall I say is calling?

And who in her lonely slip, who by barbiturate
who in these realms of love, who by something blunt,
Who by avalanche, who by powder,
who for his greed, who for his hunger
and who shall I say is calling?

And who by brave assent, who by accident
who in solitude, who in this mirror
Who by his lady's command, who by his own hand
who in mortal chains, who in power
and who shall I say is calling?

LEONARD COHEN,
"Who By Fire"

ONE

The Body

THE CARS and trucks driving along Blundell Road at 1 p.m. on June 8, 1989, slowed and merged into one lane to pass the street crew digging up the pavement. It was a sunny day in the Vancouver, B.C., suburb of Richmond, at least 25 degrees Celsius, hot for the West Coast of Canada where it seems to rain more than half the year. A mother in a mini van loaded with children headed to the local mall. Blue-suited businessmen checked their wrist-watches as they crawled by the obstruction. Trucks loaded with lumber passed on their way to construction sites. Richmond was expanding rapidly. Single-family homes, condominium developments and shopping malls were sprouting up all over the flat, alluvial delta that had been farmland not so many years before.

Gordon Starchuk was operating a jackhammer in the middle of the 8100-block Blundell that day. He was part of a Richmond street crew, sent about noon to investigate a depression in the pavement. It was one of those sudden, irksome dips that drivers like to blame on civic bureaucrats.

As Starchuk stepped back to let the backhoe dig, he was distracted by a nagging sensation – he had to take a leak. Without a portable toilet, it was always a hassle trying to find somewhere convenient. He looked up and down the busy four-lane thoroughfare. There was no gas station close by, only middle-class homes whose occupants would not welcome a worker with dirt-caked boots knocking on the door, asking to use the bathroom. But on the north side of the street, Starchuk spied an abandoned house. It was about 20 metres down the road, right next to an empty, overgrown lot. Perfect.

As Starchuk waded through the waist-high grass, he was careful not to brush against the prickly thistles whose purple, globular heads were beginning to bloom. The smell of moist loam filled his nose as he entered the shade of the west side of the brown-and-white bungalow, where a stand of cedar and deciduous trees provided a natural alcove, secluded from the view of passing motorists.

As he stood in the bush, he suddenly sensed he was not alone. Someone was lying in the cool shade of the trees, on a bed of twigs and blackberry brambles. Probably just a homeless bum taking a nap, he thought. Until he stepped closer, noticing the painted fingernails, the maroon pants and . . . the buzzing flies. A helluva lot of flies. Christ, it's a woman. A dead woman.

He had never seen a corpse before, but he was pretty sure he recognized this one. Her face had been splashed in every newspaper for the past two weeks, with her tale of torment reported in great detail.

Starchuk forgot all about his bladder. He ran to the street, waving his arms to draw the attention of his buddies.

"There's a body back there," he shouted over the noise of the machinery. "Call somebody! Call the cops!"

"What? Are you sure?" asked the crew foreman, Dave Fontaine.

"Yeah," Starchuk said, fighting a rising sense of nausea. "I think it's that nurse who went missing."

Don Vinish shut down his backhoe, wondering what Starchuk was so excited about. "What's this about a body?"

"Back there," said Starchuk, pointing to the trees.

Vinish thought Starchuk was kidding, except his face looked dead serious. Another worker, who could not hear what was being said, thought Starchuk had found a leaking gas main. Fontaine suggested Starchuk sit in the truck; he was obviously in shock and looked as if he might faint. Vinish and another couple of workers went into the bush to have a look. It was probably just somebody passed out, sleeping it off.

They halted within two metres of the body. It was a corpse, all right, lying on its side in a contorted position. The woman's hands and feet were tied behind her back with . . . what was it? Not rope or string, but black cord of some kind. Vinish noticed the woman's face. It was black as a beetle's shell.

"Looks like she's been beaten," he said in a hushed voice, as though discussing the departed at a funeral.

The men, shaken by the sight, came out of the bush silently, wrapped in their private thoughts. As they headed toward the foreman's truck, Fontaine asked if she was dead.

"Definitely," Vinish replied.

Fontaine got on the two-way radio to notify the works yard. "Could you send police out to No. 3 and Blundell?" he asked. Seconds later, the works yard called back. "You've got to have a reason for calling the cops," Fontaine was told.

"We've found a body," he replied.

"Oh. I guess that's a good enough reason."

Richmond gets only a handful of homicides each year, mainly the domestic-dispute variety. A husband and wife get in an argument, tempers flare and someone ends up dead – usually the wife. Kitchen knives and hunting rifles are the popular weapons. The suburb's most serious crime problems are burglary and car theft, not murder. Its crime rate is nothing compared to neighbouring Vancouver.

Vancouver, separated from Richmond by the muddy Fraser River, has the highest per capita crime rate in the country. The city, with its surrounding suburbs, including Richmond, has about 1.4 million residents and is the economic and cultural hub of the province of British Columbia.

The Port of Vancouver is one of the busiest in the country, and B.C., with its thousands of kilometres of uninhabited coastline and close proximity to the U.S. and Asia, is a drug smuggler's haven. And along with the drug trade come all the disturbing spinoffs – gang-style slayings, street prostitution and one of the largest concentrations of heroin and cocaine addicts in Canada.

Tourists like Vancouver because it's clean, green and not anywhere as mean as major U.S. cities. Snow-capped mountains provide a stunning northern backdrop to the silhouette of downtown office towers. The city core is surrounded by sandy swimming beaches facing a bay filled with sailboats and windsurfers, even in winter. But the city's laid-back lifestyle and temperate climate have their downside – they attract a transient, desperate population that exists by scrounging out of dumpsters and sleeping year-round in downtown alleys, under bridges and in wooded parks scattered throughout the region.

Despite Richmond's residential and commercial boom, it still lacks both inner-city blight and urbane sophistication. Vancouver City has a population of 450,000 and is home to internationally acclaimed restaurants, old-money hotels, upscale shopping districts and a vibrant nightlife. Richmond, with about 120,000 citizens who commute to the big city to work and play, is a decidedly safer place to bring up kids. But Richmond gets some spill-over from Vancouver's burgeoning crime scene: it has earned a reputation as a great place to dump a body. Canada's most notorious serial killer, Clifford Olson, buried three of his child victims amid the shadows of Richmond's stretches of unpopulated bush and tranquil blueberry fields. When the call came from the municipal works yard about a body at No. 3 and Blundell, police initially assumed that they had another Vancouver murder victim on their hands.

What had been a fairly lazy summer afternoon at the Royal Canadian Mounted Police detachment in Richmond changed the moment the call came in at 1:08 p.m. The police dispatcher jotted notes as she listened calmly to the person on the other end of the line. A patrol officer was immediately sent to verify the report of a tied-up female corpse found in the bush at No. 3 and Blundell.

Constable Joseph Primeau arrived at the scene at 1:10 p.m. The workers told him they had not touched the body or disturbed anything around it. Primeau secured the crime scene by asking the street crew to stand on the sidewalk while he radioed for backup officers and serious-crime investigators. He removed a notebook from his pocket and began recording everyone who entered and exited the scene.

Identification squad officers arrived minutes later. It was their job to tag possible evidence, photograph the body and surrounding scene, and help cordon off the area with yellow tape to keep out the curious, including the media, who began swarming outside the house after hearing the call over police scanners.

Three plainclothes officers arrived at 1:34, followed shortly afterward by another plainclothes investigator, Constable Jerry Anderson, who took charge of the scene.

Anderson went into the bush to confirm what he already suspected – Cindy James, missing for two weeks, had finally turned up dead. He stood over the body. It was Cindy, all right. No doubt about it.

Anderson's sigh was mixed with remorse and disappointment at the sight. The burly, soft-spoken investigator had worked long and hard on Cindy's case. He had hoped it would never come to this.

The decomposing body lay on its right side, fully clothed in maroon pants and a long-sleeved, high-collared, frilly pink blouse. An old-fashioned burgundy shoe was on her right foot. The other chunky-heeled shoe was lying about half a metre from the corpse. There were small cuts on the back of her blouse, as well as on the front and sides. Partially lying on a blue coat, she had a Lorus watch on her left wrist, and, on closer examination, was

wearing pantyhose and a bra. There had been blood staining the front of the blouse between the right collarbone
and breast, but there was no underlying wound.

Anderson had met Cindy the previous October. She had
been attacked outside her home, she said, and Anderson
was the chief investigator. The perpetrator was never
found, but Anderson learned that Cindy had a long history
of victimization. Before moving to Richmond, she had
complained repeatedly to Vancouver police that someone
was making her life a living hell. There were almost 100
incidents spread over the last seven years, including obscene phone calls, threatening letters, arson attempts and
five sadistic assaults.

Pathologist Sheila Carlyle pronounced death upon arrival at the scene. After discussing quietly with Anderson
the possible scenarios leading to Cindy's death, Carlyle
got down to the grim task of examining the minute detail
of the final act of a life.

For pathologists and homicide investigators, a death
scene is sacred. Once clues are disturbed, history cannot
be recreated. But the clues at this scene were sparse. A
McDonald's cup was suspended in the bushes nearby
while a soft-drink straw was later found beneath the body.
Both were tagged as evidence and would be examined in
the lab. Carlyle noted a puncture wound on the inside of
the right arm, at the elbow. It appeared to be a hypoder-
mic needle injection site. A maggot stuck its head through
the hole in the skin, a sign that a colony had infested the
tiny wound. Carlyle made a mental note of the size of the
maggot's head, about two millimetres.

A special light was used to examine the body for foreign hairs and fibres, which were collected with sticky
tape, placed in small sealable bags and tagged as exhibits.
In some murder cases, a single hair can link a suspect to
the victim and provide a murder conviction.

The body was in an advanced state of decomposition,
Carlyle noted. The skin was drying and cracking – a condition known as mummification – and the corpse was
skeletonizing in some spots. Carlyle peered at one of the

woman's fingers, which appeared scratched to the bone by a finger of the other hand, the result, perhaps, of some involuntary action as the woman lost consciousness.

Carlyle suggested to police that the cause of death appeared to be strangulation from the black nylon stocking tied around the victim's neck. A second black stocking had been used to tie the woman's arms and legs behind her back.

Officers photographed, videotaped and sketched the scene before the corpse was placed in a body bag and taken by Pacific Body Removal to the morgue at Royal Columbian Hospital, in the nearby suburb of New Westminster. There it was locked by Anderson in a refrigerated, stainless-steel crypt until the autopsy, which would be performed the next day.

For homicide investigators, securing a body maintains "continuity of evidence." If the case gets to court, police will have to testify that the body was not tampered with. A sharp defence lawyer always looks for any lapse in continuity so he can free his client on a technicality, or at least create a reasonable doubt in the minds of jurors that police were sloppy.

With the body and evidence secure, investigators now faced the task of answering the question: Who killed Cindy James?

Anderson realized it was not going to be a simple answer, especially after police thoroughly combed the scene for clues. There was, for instance, no syringe anywhere in the vicinity (during previous attacks, Cindy claimed she had been injected with drugs by unknown tormentors who stalked her for nearly seven years). In fact, there was no sign at all pointing to a suspect.

Officers began knocking on the doors of residents in the neighbourhood, but no one had seen or heard anything out of the ordinary. Police also interviewed a man who was living in a blue van behind the abandoned house. Vasily Ufimstev, who spoke with a Russian accent and seemed of limited intelligence, explained he had been there for three weeks. That would mean he had been living within five metres of the body for at least a week, assuming James was not killed elsewhere and her body dumped.

The squatter was not aware of the body until police and the media arrived. Ufimstev had erected a corrugated-metal fence along the rear, west side of the house to keep local kids from coming in the back yard. The kids using the "party house" would come by at night and bang on the side of his van to harass him, but the fence put an end to that, the man said. Police noted the squatter cooked his meals on a firepit near the makeshift fence, less than two metres from the body. Yet Ufimstev had noticed no foul odour.

Inside the house, the walls had been smashed and spray-painted with obscenities and what appeared to be satanic references. "Devil" was sprayed in big red letters, along with "666" and what looked like a pentagram – a circle with a star inside it. A swastika was splashed on another wall. Police thought it was probably just the handiwork of local punks and likely not related to Cindy's death, but inquiries would be made among local teenagers to find out who used the house. One neighbour mentioned that skinheads hung out in the building, which was slated for demolition.

After leaving the scene, Anderson phoned James's father, Otto Hack, who lived in Sidney, a small community on Vancouver Island, a two-hour ferry ride from the mainland. The officer explained in a low, sympathetic voice that a woman's body had been found and, although the identity could not be positively confirmed until the autopsy, he believed it was Hack's daughter.

"In my mind I have no doubt it's Cindy," Hack told a reporter later that evening. After weeks of uncertainty, he felt relieved that at least he knew what happened to her. The military training of the former Royal Canadian Air Force Lieutenant-Colonel served him well – Hack betrayed no emotion as he spoke.

Shortly after noon the next day, Cindy's crypt was unlocked, the body removed. Carlyle, known as a thorough pathologist with a sharp analytical mind, methodically conducted the autopsy in the morgue in the presence of Anderson and RCMP Corporal Jack Henzie, who tagged exhibits for lab analysis. Also present were Coroner Mike Olifkey and Gail Anderson, an entomologist from Simon Fraser University, who collected insect samples to be incubated in a lab to try to pinpoint exactly how long the body had been lying beside the abandoned house. Before touching the body, ultra-violet and laser lights were used again to examine for foreign hairs and fibres. An RCMP Ident officer videotaped the autopsy as it began.

Anderson emphasized he wanted to preserve the black nylon around Cindy's neck and the one binding her hands and legs behind her back. He assisted Carlyle by gently removing the ligatures, which seemed loose, perhaps due to dehydration of the body. The nylons were carefully reconstructed on a piece of plywood to preserve how they were found on the body. Anderson planned to have them examined by a knot expert.

Clothing was removed a piece at a time. Carlyle noted the top button of the blouse appeared to have popped off; it was missing. The collar line was cut, apparently by a sharp instrument, and there was a tear up the seam of the blouse above the right wrist. Oddly enough, there were no underlying wounds corresponding to the many cuts and tears on the front and back of the garment.

On closer examination of the apparent injection site on the right arm, Carlyle noted the surrounding tissue was bruised. She opened the skin to reveal a maggot colony in the vein. Insect samples were taken.

Due to the drying and mummification of the body, Carlyle had difficulty drawing a sufficient blood sample for testing – only 20 cc. Usually a body this size, 44 kilograms, would yield about a litre. The toxicology lab would not have much to work with, she thought.

Carlyle's original opinion that strangulation was the cause of death did not bear out under closer, microscopic examination. There was an absence of hemorrhaging of the neck blood vessels, usually an indication of strangulation. The brain was normal and there was nothing unusual about the internal organs. After inspecting the chest, Carlyle determined that the blood staining the blouse stemmed from the oozing of body fluid during decomposition, not from injury to the body. And there was no apparent bruising in the pelvic area that would suggest sexual assault.

At the end of the autopsy several hours later, Carlyle could not offer police a definitive cause of death.

"We're going to have to wait for the toxicology tests to see if there were drugs in her system," she said.

Anderson dreaded the thought. He knew drug tests could take months, while the family and media would keep pressing police for an immediate answer.

TWO

Final Days

THE DEMISE of Cindy James may have brought her peace, but her friends and family were infuriated by the seeming sadistic finality of her death scene. And while they could not have imagined it at the time, stories of Cindy's hellish life and bizarre death would soon horrify and fascinate hundreds of thousands across Canada.

For many, it was incomprehensible that the terror had gone on unabated for so many years. "Why could police never catch the culprit?" people would ask again and again as the stranger-than-fiction details of Cindy's living nightmare began to emerge in the media. It would take almost a year to unveil the answer to that perplexing question.

Five days before she went missing, Cindy James wrote a letter to her youngest sister, Melanie Cassidy, who lived in Whitehorse, capital of Canada's sub-arctic Yukon territory. The letter, received by Melanie on May 26, 1989, the day after Cindy disappeared, contained no hint that she suspected death was imminent. Cindy was actually optimistic that she may have found a solution to catch whoever had been terrorizing her for years.

"This is just a wee note on this beautiful paper to say hi!, hope all is well with you and thanks for the interesting mail you've sent in the last while," Cindy wrote in her slightly back-handed writing style. "I've been busy in the garden whenever I can, getting it slowly in shape. We've had some really nice weather lately.

"I'm still getting harassed from time to time by someone trying to break in here, but I think we've come up with a solution if it doesn't cost too much. Gord [Lalonde, husband of Cindy's friend Dorene Sutton] is going to wire in a sensor for me, so hopefully we'll know when someone enters the back yard and we can quietly call the police while he is busy doing his thing. I'm really hopeful we might actually catch him soon. Wouldn't that be wonderful! I could actually start living a normal life again. I've almost forgotten what that feels like. The police have been pretty useless so it would be wonderful to hand him over on a silver platter.

"Well, I must bath and get ready for Marion to pick me up. Hope to hear from you soon. Love, Cindy."

"Marion" was Marion Christensen, Cindy's former boss. They had worked together at the Children's Foundation, a facility for emotionally disturbed children, during the 1960s and had remained friends after Cindy left to become team co-ordinator of Blenheim House, a day-treatment centre for pre-school children with emotional and behavioural problems. Marion had always admired Cindy's patience, sense of humour, warmth and sincerity. She saw Cindy regularly, about twice a week, and often chatted with her on the phone to keep in touch, to make sure Cindy was okay.

Christensen called Cindy after lunch on Thursday, May 25, just hours before James was to go missing, to say she and her husband Wally would be on Vancouver Island for a few days. Cindy, now working at Richmond General Hospital, sounded very happy on the telephone as she explained she was about to begin a five-day break. Some of that time would be spent with friends and attending a birthday party for Adrian, the eight-year-old son of her friend Dorene Sutton, whom Cindy once referred to as "the sister I never had."

Cindy mentioned to Christensen that there had been a series of attempted break-ins at her house in recent weeks, after many months without a single incident. "She seemed to feel pressure was building up and something was going to happen," recalled Christensen, who knew how the cruel, painful attacks had forced Cindy to venture rarely from her house, her refuge. "It was frightening to myself, just hearing about the insistence to get at her."

Shortly after the call, Cindy went to The Bay in a Richmond mall for a cosmetic makeover, something she had talked about doing for some time. She had a facial skin problem, which had been spawned years before when she began taking birth-control pills. She wanted advice on the proper makeup for her condition. The cosmetician spent more than an hour helping Cindy choose suitable shades of eyeshadow and lipstick, showing Cindy how to apply them and properly cleanse her skin.

She arrived at Richmond General a few minutes before 4 p.m. to pick up her paycheque. Tammy Carmen, a hospital payroll clerk and Cindy's next-door neighbour, told her she was not allowed to hand out cheques until 4 p.m., so Cindy went for coffee with a nursing friend, Diane Yong.

Yong told Cindy her makeover looked great. The two women discussed their travel plans for the near future. Yong was preparing to go to Hong Kong while Cindy spoke of going to Africa to visit her brother Roger, who was the manager of the Canadian High Commissioner's office in Nairobi, Kenya. Cindy expressed that her life was going great and everything was quiet – there had been four break-in attempts in a month followed by two weeks of her alarm being silent. Cindy said, in fact, it had been too quiet for too long. She was worried that "something big" was going to happen. Before parting, Cindy and Diane arranged to get together for dinner the following evening.

As Cindy picked up her paycheque, Tammy Carmen told Cindy how good her makeover looked. She recalled that Cindy was quite "bubbly."

Everyone who knew Cindy agreed she was the happiest she had been in years.

Cindy spent the rest of the afternoon shopping for Adrian's birthday present. Earlier, she had phoned her friend Agnes Woodcock and asked, "What do I buy for an eight-year-old?" She had also arranged for Agnes and her husband Tom to play bridge and stay overnight that evening. The Woodcocks were among Cindy's dearest friends. They loved her as if she were their own daughter and had given her plenty of support in times of trouble, often staying with her for weeks on end when Cindy feared being alone.

Agnes, 69, had retired from her job as a bus driver at Blenheim House, where Cindy had been director, and had driven an Easter Seal bus for 10 years before that. Agnes was always cheerful, positive and quick to laugh at a joke. She seemed always to have a smile on her face, which was encircled in straight grey hair that she wore in a blunt cut that hung to her shoulders. Tom, 83, was Agnes' second husband, the former chief officer of B.C. Ferries until he retired. The couple had nine children between them. When people first met Tom Woodcock they thought he was gruff and indifferent, but he was really hearing impaired, a work-related condition.

The Woodcocks arrived shortly after 10 p.m. at Cindy's modest, well-kept house on Claysmith Road, a quiet residential street in suburban Richmond. One of the features Cindy had liked when she bought the place was that it had no back alley. She hated the thought of someone lurking in a dark lane, watching her.

Agnes tooted her horn as she pulled her 1979 Mercury Monarch into the driveway. Usually Cindy would appear at the window and wave, but this time there was no response. Also, Cindy's car, a blue 1981 Chevrolet Citation, wasn't in the driveway or anywhere in the immediate vicinity of her home. Agnes knocked at Cindy's front door. Again no response. Tom got out of the Mercury and went with Agnes around to the back door. There was no response as they knocked. Before leaving, the couple decided to check with Cindy's downstairs tenant, Richard Johnston, to see if he knew anything.

The Woodcocks were worried. Cindy James had suffered all manner of physical and mental torture for almost seven years. Three years earlier, they themselves had barely escaped from a late-night blaze ignited by a firebomb thrown through Cindy's basement window while they were staying overnight with her.

"Do you think she had car trouble?" Agnes asked Johnston. She knew that Cindy sometimes would take her car in to get it fixed when she had several days off. As far as Johnston knew, Cindy's car was working fine. She had driven away at about 4:00 or 4:30 p.m., saying she was going to deposit her paycheque and do some shopping. He had not seen her since.

Agnes and Tom got back in their car and sat for several minutes, waiting, thinking Cindy might drive up any second. It was not like her to be late. Agnes thought about her last phone conversation with Cindy – she said she would definitely be home by dark. Agnes had looked at her watch while talking on the phone, noticing it was 8:50 p.m. and already dark.

Feeling that something had happened to Cindy, the Woodcocks decided to go home and call the police. On their way, Agnes decided to swing by Blundell Centre, at No. 2 Road and Blundell, where Cindy usually did her banking.

"There's her car," Agnes said, pulling into the lot so her headlights illuminated Cindy's blue Chevy parked in front of the Bank of Montreal. They got out and looked inside, noticing several bags of groceries on the front seat.

Everything seemed normal. Agnes, however, sensed something amiss: Cindy's car was parked some distance from the bank in a relatively empty lot. "Every time I went with her she pulled right up to the bank," Agnes recalled.

"She would wait sometimes for somebody to pull out, even, so she was facing the bank, right at the curb."

Agnes told Tom not to touch the car. "Let's just go tell police it's here."

It was almost 11 p.m. when the Woodcocks arrived at the Richmond RCMP station about a kilometre away. They climbed the cement stairs, opened the glass door and told the woman behind the counter they wanted to report their friend missing.

"How long has she been missing?" the woman asked.

"I'm not sure. A couple of hours."

"Sorry," the woman said. "Police only investigate if someone's been missing 24 hours." She turned and disappeared around a partition behind the counter.

Frustrated by the woman's apparent indifference, Tom and Agnes stood outside the building for a few moments, collecting their thoughts, then returned inside. Agnes told the woman their missing friend, Cindy James, "has a file here and Constable Anderson told me to report anything suspicious, any little thing."

"Sorry, Anderson's off duty and won't be in until the morning," the woman replied, again walking away. Once more outside with Tom, Agnes said, "I don't feel right about this. We should talk to somebody other than the girl." Entering the building a third time, Agnes could see the woman sitting behind the partition, watching them in a convex mirror as they approached the counter.

"What do you want now?" the woman said curtly, clearly losing her patience. Agnes asked to talk to a police officer. The woman explained that all the officers were busy in the jail cells at the moment.

"We'll wait," Agnes said. They sat on a bench waiting for 20 minutes until an officer arrived. After briefly explaining Cindy's history and Anderson's request that police be contacted right away if anything suspicious happened, the officer said he would attend to the matter.

A patrol car was dispatched to the mall to investigate. The officer got out and shone his flashlight on the outside of Cindy's car. Noticing a drop of blood on the driver's door, he radioed for backup. Looking around, he noticed Cindy's bank card and deposit slip were lying less than a metre under the car, nearest the driver's side. The officer was careful not to touch the vehicle until Ident members arrived to check for prints. The blood on the car suggested a struggle. Cindy James, it appeared, had been abducted.

Const. Jerry Anderson was off duty the night Cindy disappeared. He was at home, still up, when the phone rang at 12:30 a.m. James was missing, he was told. Her car had been located with blood on the driver's door.

"What do you think?" the officer asked Anderson.

"I think we should treat it very seriously. I'll be in to the office in a few minutes." After a briefing at the office, Anderson phoned Cindy's father to give him the disturbing news.

Anderson, a plainclothes investigator, had truly liked Cindy and felt he had gained her trust in recent months. In a letter she had written May 15 to the head of the detachment, complaining about rudeness displayed by officers investigating her complaints, Cindy had singled out Anderson "for his patience, unfailing professional conduct and his exemplary investigation of this case. . . . He is the only member of the RCMP I feel I can trust and be comfortable with. He is an excellent example of how a police officer should act and I am confident he is doing all he can to resolve this case."

Anderson put on his holster before driving to the shopping centre to examine Cindy's car. The Ident crew found no prints. Police began searching the area, even checking dumpsters, looking for traces that would lead them to Cindy. Police dogs would continue searching through the night, without success.

A few minutes before 1 a.m., a Richmond Mountie called Agnes Woodcock just as she was getting undressed for bed. She was asked to meet him at Cindy's house so that he could use her key to check inside. She arrived 15 minutes later and was surprised when the officer told her he already knew the code to disarm Cindy's burglar alarm. "She told me not to give it out to anyone, not even police," Agnes recalled.

Before opening the door, the officer said, "I understand there's a dog in there. Will he bite?"

"Oh, no. Heidi won't even know you're there. She's deaf and almost blind," Agnes replied. Heidi was a little dog, a "Heinz 57" variety that Cindy's ex-husband had bought her 16 years earlier as a Christmas present.

Everything appeared perfectly normal inside Cindy's home, which was filled with more than 80 well-tended house plants. A deck of playing cards and scorepad were on the table, awaiting the bridge game. The only thing unusual was the fact that the drapes were open. Agnes knew Cindy always closed them before it got dark; she did not want anyone to be able to monitor her movements inside the house. As the officer locked the door, Agnes asked for her key back, but police wanted to keep it and would let Agnes in when she needed to feed the dog.

Cindy's car was towed at 2:30 a.m. to the police impound lot, where it was locked in a storage bay until it could be examined closely in daylight. Anderson suggested two officers pay a visit to Cindy's ex-husband, Dr. Roy Makepeace.

Constables Robert Boal and Kevin Strand arrived at 3:16 a.m. at Makepeace's condominium near Kitsilano Beach in Vancouver. The uniformed officers bypassed the intercom system, entering the building as another resident unlocked the front door to let himself in. Police would later learn that they would have to ring the intercom using Morse code to let Makepeace know it was a friend at the door, not a foe.

As the officers knocked at the door of the doctor's top-floor one-bedroom suite, Makepeace looked out the peephole, noticing two men in Mountie uniforms, but he was suspicious and would not open the door. Instead, he phoned the building manager, who came and asked the men to show identification. They were reluctant to do so. Only when the manager tried kicking them out did they show their badges, and Makepeace let them in.

"You guys back off, in the other room. I want some distance," Makepeace told the officers as they entered. They moved into the living room so he could get a better look at them. The room was stacked with books, papers and magazines that indicated Makepeace was a sailing and firearms enthusiast. Pictures of his ex-wife were hanging on his walls.

Tall and balding, Makepeace had the shocked look in his eyes of a deer caught in the headlights of a car on a mountain highway. He was a large-boned man, slightly overweight and he spoke with a throaty South African inflection that people often mistook for a British accent. Standing in the hallway, close to the bathroom, Makepeace was wary about a police visit so late at night. Once he realized the RCMP officers were legitimate, he moved into the room.

"Look. Do you see this mark," Makepeace said, pointing to a black scrape on the living room wall nearest the front door. "It's from a rifle." As he spoke, he reached behind the bathroom door and pulled out a .303 rifle. "Now don't go saying I pulled a gun on you. I'm going to pull it out butt first," he said. "You can see the safety catch is on, okay?"

Makepeace said he kept a gun by his side in his apartment because "that's how scared I am." He explained that there had been some suspicious things happening lately and he was nervous, feeling uncertain about whom he could trust.

He was asked if he could account for his whereabouts during the last 24 hours. Makepeace explained that he and a woman friend had cycled to Richmond that afternoon for the opening of Bridgepoint Market, a farmer's-style market for the condo crowd. While at the market, he bought a stool for gold-panning. It was in the trunk of his car, he explained.

After that, they had cycled back to Vancouver, picked up his car and went for dinner. Later he installed a stereo system at the home of his woman friend in Deep Cove, a small community on an inlet about a 30-minute drive northeast of Vancouver. He said he left his friend's place about 11:30 p.m. and arrived home sometime after midnight. His friend would confirm his whereabouts. She later did.

"So you were in Richmond yesterday evening?" one of the officers asked while the other, using the excuse to look at the rifle, checked the rest of the small suite. From the bathroom, he could see Makepeace's bed had been slept in and he was alone.

Makepeace wanted to know what was going on, why they were there. When told police had found his ex-wife's car and she was missing, he let out a sigh of exasperated sadness. "My God, she's dead," he said, shaking his head, his eyes slightly misty. "She's dead."

Makepeace mentioned he had a strange tape police might be interested in hearing – two messages he had received on his answering machine last October 11 and 12. The first one sounded like "Cindy dead meat soon." The other, in the same hoarse, menacing whisper, said, "More smack, more downers, another grand after we waste the cunt. No more deal." He explained he had sent a copy of the tape to his lawyer, but not to Vancouver police, in whom he'd developed a deep distrust.

Initially, Makepeace explained, he thought the first one said, "Sunday. Dead meat soon." He thought it was a threat against him, making reference to two strange characters he had noticed lurking in front of his building the Sunday before the calls. The two men had appeared startled when they noticed he was watching them from his car, he said. He thought they might be the same two men who had attacked and harassed Cindy years earlier. But with repeated plays of the message, a friend of Make-peace pointed out that the voice was saying Cindy, not Sunday.

Makepeace spent several minutes looking for the tape among the clutter. Unable to locate it, he said he would contact police when he had.

In their report of the visit, officers Boal and Strand noted that Makepeace could account for his whereabouts on May 25 and they did not find his behaviour suspicious.

Later that day, Richmond police began knocking on doors of residents near the mall, widening their search to a one-and-a-half-block radius of the shopping centre. RCMP subsequently began a wide-scale search of Rich-mond, using a helicopter that took aerial photos of the shopping centre where Cindy's car was found. Police also searched Richmond's shoreline with the aid of a Cana-dian Coast Guard hovercraft. Officers were assigned to check the dikes surrounding Richmond, most of which lies below high-tide level. Vancouverites often joke that as the Greenhouse Effect causes global warming and the melting of the polar ice caps, Richmond will be first to be submerged by the rising tides.

Police checked Vancouver International Airport, lo-cated on Sea Island in Richmond, to make sure Cindy had not caught a flight out of town without telling anyone. They could find no evidence that she had. Cab companies were contacted, but there were no fares the previous night from the vicinity of Blundell Centre. Bus drivers whose routes traversed the area were contacted, but no one could recall picking up a passenger matching Cindy's descrip-tion. Throughout the day, police talked to every store owner and clerk who had been working at Blundell Centre the day Cindy went missing. Many of them recognized her from a photo but none recalled seeing her May 25. Like

the residents police interviewed in the surrounding neighbourhood, no one at the mall saw or heard anything suspicious that day. Cindy, it seemed, had vanished.

Anderson arrived at the police compound at 5:30 p.m. on
May 26. RCMP Corporal Henzie, the other investigator
assigned to the case, was already there with a member
from Ident, who photographed the contents of the car as it
was searched. Before disturbing anything, the interior and
exterior were closely checked for any hairs and fibres.

The car's heater had been on, it was noted, set to the
"defrost" position. The transmission lever was in "park,"
and Cindy's hospital parking pass was on the dashboard.
The car ashtray was closed and contained six Cameo butts,
Cindy's brand. The fuel tank was almost half full. The AM/
FM cassette deck contained a Herb Alpert tape. Cindy
liked "easy listening" music. It helped calm her nerves.

Found between the front seats of the car were a number
of Bank of Montreal "quick deposit" slips and envelopes.
In the glove compartment, among maps and papers, was a
pad of paper with the words "KDV 784 Small, silver
(grey)" scrawled on it. Presumably it was a note Cindy
made of the licence plate of a suspicious vehicle. The pad
did not appear to have been used recently, since it was
buried at the bottom of the glove compartment. The licence number would be checked anyway; no B.C. car
would be found matching the plate and description. Also
in the glove box was a Sofrex hand-held emergency
alarm.

Anderson was familiar with Cindy's "panic button."
Ozzie Kaban, a private investigator Cindy had hired to
protect her after she was first attacked in 1983, had given
it to her to use in emergencies. The silent alarm would
notify Kaban's security firm that Cindy was in trouble; a
Kaban employee would then call police. Cindy carried it
in her purse wherever she went and she usually held it in
her hand while getting out of her car at night.

She had last used it in October 1988 when police found her unconscious in her car, her naked legs dangling from the open driver's door. Her hands had been tied behind her back and duct tape was plastered over her face to prevent her from breathing. As in previous attacks, she was found with a black nylon stocking tied around her neck. Cindy had gone into a coma that time, but survived.

Her black purse was on the front passenger seat between two brown paper Safeway bags, with another two bags of groceries on the floor. The purse contained $2.77. On the back seat were two blue Sears bags containing a croquet set and some wrapping paper, obviously the gift for Adrian. The receipts showed the croquet set was bought at 12:33 and the wrapping paper at 12:43. There was no receipt for the groceries. In the days to come, Mounties would go to the Safeway at Blundell Centre and run the groceries through the till, but they would not find a sales total in the computer for May 25 that matched the cost of the groceries in Cindy's car. It was puzzling.

The car's back seat was removed to gain access to the trunk. It was empty. As with previous investigations of Cindy's complaints, there did not seem to be a single fingerprint or shred of solid evidence that would lead police to a suspect. One of the few clues was Cindy's deposit slip. It showed she deposited her paycheque at 7:58 p.m. Maybe another bank customer used the automatic-teller machine around the same time and saw her, Anderson thought.

Police contacted the Bank of Montreal and examined the computerized records, interviewing everyone who used the machine within 15 minutes before and after Cindy. One woman, Tracey McLean, had used the machine shortly before 8 p.m. As she left the parking lot, she recalled a blonde woman had almost driven into the side of her car. "I saw her jump and turn away." The blonde parked in the middle of the lot, away from other cars. She was wearing a pink top and her hair was about shoulder length, McLean thought. Police showed her a photo of Cindy, but she was not positive it was the same woman.

Barry Leroy used the bank machine at 8:01 p.m. A Bank of Montreal manager, he had just arrived home from Calgary and needed some cash to run a few errands and pick up some take-out chicken for dinner. He recalled driving into the parking lot and seeing a blonde walking diagonally across the lot, heading in the direction of the corner of Blundell and No. 2 Road. He watched her walk maybe five or 10 paces, but did not see her leave the lot. She was wearing dark slacks and what appeared to be a blue jacket. He recognized the photo of James but was not sure it was the same person. "I only saw her for 10 or 15 seconds," he explained. Anderson later arranged a hypnosis session for Leroy, hoping to enhance his memory of the woman. The only detail gained during hypnosis was a more specific description of the woman's clothing – she was wearing a boot-style shoe. He could not recall seeing anyone in the six or eight other cars parked in the lot.

Police interviewed Cindy's tenant, Richard Johnston, who said he talked to her about 2:30 p.m., when she mentioned she was going to do some shopping. He saw her leave at 4 p.m. and she had never returned.

Johnston had not known Cindy long. He sold life insurance and first contacted Cindy in September 1988 after finding her name in the "lost customer" file; she had missed the payments for two or three years on a policy she taken out in the 1960s. He sold her a new $15,000 life-insurance policy and did not hear from her again until January 1989, when she phoned to ask if he would be interested in renting her basement suite.

"She said she would feel safer with a guy, a man around the house," Johnston said. Shortly after moving in at the end of February, Cindy told him she had had some problems in the past, and was recovering from post-traumatic stress disorder. She discussed a few details of past incidents, but was vague in pinpointing the source of her problems.

"Who have you burnt in the past?" Johnston asked her. It did not seem normal. Obviously she had crossed somebody. "She really couldn't give me an answer why someone would want to do this to her." Experience had taught Cindy not to be too open about discussing anything. She did not know whom she could trust, especially since several Vancouver police officers never believed her.

Johnston did not realize what he was getting into at the time. He had to disarm the burglar alarm whenever he came inside his suite – there was a 10-second delay to allow him to open the door and turn it off. He never expected the alarm to go off in the middle of the night as much as it did.

It started a few days after he moved in, when Johnston was awakened about 3 a.m. by someone turning the doorknob of the basement door leading to his suite. About a month later, on April 8, 1989, there was an attempted break-in through Cindy's kitchen window at the back of the house. The same thing happened May 10, when Johnston heard the alarm ring. That time, someone forced a window and left a threatening note. "Cindy was really, really shaken. I'd never seen someone with so much terror in her eyes," Johnston recalled.

Police investigated each of the incidents and they handled things nicely, Johnston thought. But he had expressed his concerns to Cindy about the harassment. "I moved in thinking it was a nice quiet neighbourhood," he told her. "I don't want to live under these conditions."

A few days before Cindy went missing, Johnston had brainstormed with her, trying to come up with a solution to her obvious security problem. They came upon the idea of a motion detector or a heat sensor, which could be installed at the back of the house, about a metre off the ground and aimed at the back door. It would alert Cindy to any intruder. Johnston even offered to pay for it, but Cindy said she would buy it and have an electrician friend install it.

A few days after Cindy went missing, Johnston contacted Anderson and said a man had phoned his office to elicit details about Cindy's life insurance policy. Since the man claimed to be Cindy's father, the secretary who took the call began providing information, then stopped when she remembered staff were not permitted to give out policy information over the phone. She told the caller – he sounded like an older man with a slight British accent – to visit the office personally to discuss the matter. Cindy's father later denied making the call. It was another detail that would baffle the police.

Another strange event happened around the same time. On the fuel tank beside the abandoned house where Cindy had been found, someone spray-painted a cruel message: "Some bitch died here." An orange line was painted from the tank to the spot where her body had been found, and a body was outlined on the ground in orange spray-paint.

After Cindy's disappearance, her father, Otto Hack, a neatly trimmed man in his sixties, served as the media spokesman for the family, detailing for reporters how his daughter had first been attacked in 1983 by two men in her garage, where she was stabbed, strangled and left for dead. Police never found her attackers.

Over the years, she had been beaten, strangled and left to die five times, but police could never find the perpetrators. She had also been terrorized with dead cats left in her yard on four occasions, sometimes with threatening notes attached.

The resulting widespread media coverage brought a flood of public sympathy for the family and Richmond RCMP received hundreds of "tips." One person reported a sighting of Cindy at a bus depot in Tofino, a small fishing village on the west coast of Vancouver Island. Another claimed to have seen her riding in a car in Kelso, Wash., just south of the Canada-U.S. border. There were also suggestions that satanists may have kidnapped Cindy and subjected her to ritual death rites, or that her murder involved witchcraft or voodoo. Each tip was investigated, but none provided any concrete leads.

On May 29, Anderson met with Cindy's parents to discuss avenues to be investigated. Otto Hack suggested that, as a former military man, he could muster 500 soldiers from the Canadian Armed Forces base in nearby Chilliwack to conduct a foot search, concentrating on abandoned lots and houses. Anderson's superior officer, Sergeant Hugh Campbell, declined the offer, saying police dog masters were asked to search those areas and he felt the army would only duplicate the police effort. The refusal of Hack's offer would later come back to haunt police.

The discovery of Cindy's body June 8, 1989, occurred precisely two weeks after she had been reported missing. It also happened to be Makepeace's sixty-third birthday.

On June 9, Ozzie Kaban was in Oklahoma attending a convention when he got a call from his son, who had read in the newspaper that Cindy had been found. Kaban had spent years investigating the case, assisting police, doing his own private surveillance of her home and installing elaborate electronic security systems to try to catch those he believed had injected fear in her life for so long. Cindy had wanted to get a gun for protection before she disappeared, but Kaban advised against it, knowing she was not trained to use firearms, which could have proven dangerous to herself and her friends.

After catching the first flight home, Kaban attended the morgue June 10, a day after the autopsy. While examining Cindy's corpse and taking photos, he noticed blotching on her left side, which he thought was post-mortem lividity, a phenomenon caused by blood settling in the body immediately after death. If his assumption was correct, the fact that police found Cindy on her right side indicated she had been killed elsewhere and her body dumped. She had been probably kept in a cool place for some time before being moved, he thought.

He also felt the "parching" of Cindy's skin odd, since he had noticed the site where she was discovered had been shady and moist. Besides, Kaban wondered, how could the body have been in the bushes, 20 metres from the sidewalk, for two weeks and no one smell it or see it? Wouldn't the corpse have been nibbled at by rats, birds and other animals in the area? It did not add up. Kaban passed along his suspicions to Peter Leask, the lawyer hired by Cindy's family. In the meantime, he would continue his own investigation.

June 12 would have been Cindy James's forty-fifth birthday, usually a time of cards, cake and candles. Instead, family members gathered at the Richmond Funeral Home, preparing for Cindy's memorial service June 14.

Police used a hidden video camera to record the faces and licence plates of everyone who attended the funeral. Notably absent was Cindy's ex-husband.

In his address to the more than 200 mourners, Pastor Ralph Mayan said: "No one can imagine the pain and heartache Cindy must have experienced in those years that culminated in her murder." James's death was a grim reminder of the hatred and violence that are often the "order of the day in this society."

Long-time friend Wally Christensen told mourners that Cindy's life had been "snuffed out" for no apparent reason and the "greatest horror" was that the person responsible was still "loose in the community." He remembered James as warm and caring, with a bright smile and infectious laugh, who had devotedly worked with special-needs children, often under trying circumstances. Her move back to nursing after 17 years away from the profession, Christensen noted, was a testament to her strength and perseverance.

"To us she was love and beauty personified," Otto Hack sadly told the gathering.

Although police officially said they were investigating a homicide, privately officers were saying they believed Cindy was the author of her own misfortune. That hunch made headlines next day in *The Province*, Vancouver's morning tabloid newspaper. Cindy's friends and family were incensed. Cindy had told them that some of the officers who investigated her case over the years didn't believe her. And now this. "My daughter was murdered," Otto Hack insistently told reporters, impatience tinging his voice.

The bizarre twist to an already baffling case stirred the emotions of two women columnists at Vancouver's two daily newspapers.

"It is that sad, sad photograph of nurse Cindy James that unsettles me," Nicole Parton wrote June 15 in the afternoon paper, *The Vancouver Sun*. "The downcast mouth, the dark shadow under one eye. Was she punched? And then a second, faltering thought – did she punch herself? . . . I look at that picture and see the face of a woman whose spirit died before she did. . . . What happened to Cindy James? Not only in death, but in life?"

Patricia Graham, columnist for *The Province*, wrote the next day: "I have spent hours thinking of Cindy James . . . and still I feel disgust and anger, sadness and regret that we let her down so badly. . . . can it be that Cindy James died because she was a difficult person, too difficult to either protect or believe?"

Twenty days after Cindy James was found, Cpl. Henzie phoned Otto Hack to inform him that preliminary drug tests showed the presence of the sedative flurazepam in Cindy's body. In fact, the officer explained, it appeared to be an overdose level. He added there was also an indication that a similar sedative was present in the body, along with the opiate morphine. Police offered no interpretation to the preliminary drug tests.

Hack asked if police were investigating the possibility that Cindy's death was a satanic or occult ritual murder.

"No," Henzie replied, "but we'll look into it."

On July 11, the family was asked to attend a meeting at the RCMP detachment. Otto Hack, his wife, Tillie, and their son Doug were greeted by Anderson, along with Henzie and coroner Olifkey. The mood was tense and Anderson quickly got to the point of the meeting. "I can no longer consider foul play was involved in Cindy's death," he said. "The investigators believe Cindy took her own life, either by suicide or accident."

The family, outraged, stormed out of the station. RCMP were steadfast in their refusal to elaborate further – no reason would be disclosed as to what led to the decision, the commanding officer of plainclothes investigators told reporters. "It will all come out at the coroner's inquest," Staff-Sgt. Ron deRoon said, adding cryptically, "Sometimes there's a difference between knowledge and evidence."

THREE

Cindy's Nightmares

H*ER BREATH came in sharp bursts as she ran from the dark figure chasing her down the alley. Suddenly, she felt his boney fingers clasp her neck, the pin prick in her arm, something being tied around her wrists and ankles. Her face was being covered by something rough. She choked, unable to breathe, unable to see. The pain, the horrible things he was doing. Everything was dark, so dark...*

In the final years of her nightmarish life, Cindy James often awoke in the dead of night shrieking in terror. She dreaded going back to sleep, fearing her horrible nightmares would return. Those close to her were not surprised by her dreams, considering the hell she had been through. Although her nightmares were intensified by the horror of the attacks and harassment, they were spawned sometime in her early childhood, long before the problems she reported to police.

She was born Cynthia Elizebeth Hack on June 12, 1944, in the town of Oliver, located about 300 kilometres east of Vancouver. At the time of Cindy's birth, her parents ran an orchard. Later, her father taught high school in Vancouver.

Cynthia, as she was called then, was a sweet, happy little girl with beautiful blond hair, a quiet manner and an eagerness to please her parents. The Hacks would eventually have six children, three boys and three girls. Cindy was the second oldest. Her brother Doug was a year older, her sister Marlene two years younger and her brother Roger five years younger than Cindy. The youngest children, Melanie and Ken, were born 16 and 17 years after Cindy, forming a "second family" for the Hacks.

Her father, Otto Henry Hack, was born in Posin, Poland. Her mother, Mathilda (Tillie) Monk before she was married, came from the Prairie province of Manitoba. Otto and Tillie had met after their families had settled in the Okanagan Valley, which is known for its clear blue lakes and lush, irrigated orchards set amid arid rolling hills spotted with sage and Ponderosa pines.

Tillie never completed high school and devoted her life to being a mother and a housewife. Cindy became her little helper as the other children were born. Melanie, Tillie recalls, called Cindy "mommy." The Hacks were devout Christians, attending Lutheran church on Sundays and reading chapters of the Bible every night after dinner, with father Otto leading the family discussion afterward.

A strict disciplinarian at home and at school, Hack occasionally would spank Cindy with a leather strap. Later in life, Cindy would express resentment of her father's authoritarian style. She also felt angry that her parents never gave her enough praise.

When Cindy was five years old, her father joined the Royal Canadian Air Force just before the outbreak of the Korean War. She attended her first elementary school at the Sea Island military base in Richmond. Eager to be perfect, she was a straight-A student. During her formative years, the family would pull up roots many times, moving to a new base to coincide with military transfers and promotions. By the time Cindy reached high school, where she skipped Grade 11, her father was stationed at Air Defence Headquarters in St.-Hubert, Quebec. She was quite shy and reticent among her classmates, which Cindy felt was misinterpreted as aloofness. Every time the Hack family moved, Cindy regretted leaving behind the friends she had made. She also felt her parents strongly discouraged her from bringing friends home.

A few years before her death, Cindy wrote: "I was afraid of my father and no matter how I tried, it seemed I never succeeded in winning praise or approval. . . . I grew up often feeling my parents would separate. My father was very difficult to communicate with and ruled the household in the same way he ruled his subordinates in the Air Force."

Cindy felt her mother was always the mediator in the family; she and her brothers and sisters would approach their dad through their mother if they wanted him to reconsider a decision. Cindy described her mother as a warm, outgoing person who was unhappy in the marriage but feared being on her own.

Cindy's parents, however, recall nothing out of the ordinary that would cause Cindy to be so resentful toward them. Otto says he and his wife were firm but fair. They deeply loved each of their children, although Otto would admit Cindy was "sort of" his favourite. And though he occasionally drank with his fellow officers on Friday night and came home tipsy, he did not see it as a drinking problem, just regular military-style carousing. Tillie agreed with her husband.

Cindy and her sister Marlene Weintrager, now an Ottawa nurse, were closest, sharing a double bed until six months before Cindy moved away to begin nursing school. They also shared their private thoughts and fantasies. As little girls, they dreamed of growing up, meeting a handsome man, living in a big house, having lots of kids and living happily ever after. While their lives did not exactly turn out that way, Marlene remembers their childhood as happy, normal. "We camped with our parents a lot, that was the highlight."

Her father, Marlene said, believed in the maxim that children should be seen and not heard. Sure, he would tell them, "Shut up. I don't want to hear from you right now," but in that, she admits, her parents probably were no different than most who were raising kids in the 1940s and 50s.

One of the earliest nightmares she shared with Cindy was of snakes slithering out of the basement woodbox. It stemmed from a time when the girls, aged three and five, had been sent downstairs by their parents. With the door closed, the basement was a dark, scary place. They imagined that snakes lived in the woodbox and would crawl out to wrap their scaly coils around them.

Over time the snakes in Cindy's dreams became large, cloud-like hands that would come up from under the bed to grab and smother her. By the time she reached adulthood, her dreams became darker and more malevolent. In one of her recurring nightmares, she would be chased by two Dobermans and fall into a pit. As she tried to climb out, the dogs would snap and bite at her hands. Then a figure would appear, dressed all in black, standing at the top of the pit, laughing.

Marlene recalled one traumatic episode when Cindy was about seven years old that may have caused her to feel abandoned by her mother and father. Cindy had come down with scarlet fever while her parents were out of town for a month picking apples in the Okanagan. The wife of an officer at the Sea Island base was looking after the kids, a rather "nasty" woman, Marlene remembers. Cindy became extremely ill, spending a week in hospital, and upon her return home she was put in quarantine. The woman told the kids that their parents had been contacted and told Cindy was sick, but they did not wish to cut short their trip. Cindy and Marlene cried for days until their parents came home.

Marlene believes one of Cindy's biggest problems during childhood was her reluctance to speak up for herself. If Cindy was unhappy about something, she would keep it to herself, internalizing her grievances. Because she was quiet, she didn't socialize much. However, when the Hack family moved to Ottawa following Otto's promotion to Air

Force Squadron Leader, Cindy, in her final year of high school, Grade 13, had a boyfriend she deeply loved. She did not dare tell her parents that they were secretly engaged. Cindy became wildly upset when she learned her father was going to be transferred to Europe. She pleaded with him to let her stay in Ottawa to study nursing at university. Her parents felt Cindy, at 17, was too young to be on her own.

"I want you to break off with that boy," Otto demanded at the time. Cindy cried, trying to reason with him for a few minutes. "Break off with him!" her father said, raising his voice to let her know it was not a request. Marlene remembers Cindy cried for about half an hour, dried her tears, then went to break off with her fiancé.

Cindy's parents told her she could attend nursing school at Vancouver General Hospital. It was not the academic world she longed for, but it was considered a top-notch program at a growing, major metropolitan hospital. Cindy's parents had relatives in the Vancouver area, as well as the Okanagan, who could keep an eye on her. Before his transfer to Europe, Otto made sure Cindy was safely settled in Vancouver, carefully checking the references of a woman who ran the boarding house where Cindy first lived.

"Of course, we knew boys were attracted to her and she was attracted to boys," Otto recalled. "But we were not leaving her there where the fox could get in the henhouse."

Cindy blossomed both physically and intellectually during her first year of nursing school. She turned heads wherever she went on the wards at Vancouver General. She also enjoyed her new-found freedom without tight parental control. She had an affair with a young resident doctor at VGH and was deeply distressed when he was killed in a car crash in 1963. She did not have a serious boyfriend again until her third year, when she met another resident physician at the hospital, Dr. Roy Makepeace.

Makepeace was an intelligent, charming man who helped her in the fall of 1965 on a project for a study group attended by nurses in training and doctors doing their residency. Each member of the group would deliver a research paper on a timely topic or provide a synopsis of an article in a leading medical journal. Cindy's project was on the medical and historical aspects of "Free Love," especially how the birth-control pill had brought about a sexual revolution. Makepeace showed her how to research a topic and access a library's abundance of knowledge, which Cindy found intellectually liberating.

Makepeace was married at the time and father of two children. His wife, Lois, worked as a medical secretary at VGH. He and his wife had come to Canada in 1954 to escape the mounting racial tension in their homeland, South Africa. Canada, they felt, would be a good place to raise kids and provide new opportunities. The couple's first daughter, Marion, had been born in December of the year they arrived in Canada. Another daughter, Gwen, was born two years later, in March 1956.

Makepeace came from a British-Scottish background. His father, Royal Victor Makepeace, was born in Wales and emigrated to South Africa with his family as a child. The senior Makepeace married Elizabeth McClelland in 1922 at Port Elizabeth, South Africa, where Roy was born four years later.

Roy, an older brother and a sister grew up during the Great Depression of the 1930s. Roy's father was a South African aviation pioneer. An air-force pilot decorated in the First World War, he became the first manager of the Johannesburg municipal airport in 1934. With the outbreak of the Second World War, he was appointed a sub-director of the South African Air Force, in charge of choosing and designing airports throughout South Africa. Following in his father's footsteps, Roy joined the Air Force during the Second World War and was decorated for service in Italy and Egypt. After the war, he attended Rhodes University in South Africa, where he obtained a B.Sc. in Psychology and Zoology. The following year, 1949, he earned an honours post-graduate degree, with

distinction, in Psychology. In 1950, he accepted a temporary one-year post as the head of the psychology department at South Africa's Fort Hare University College and
married his first wife, Lois. In those days, Makepeace was
a slim, dashing young man who sported a thin moustache
and slicked-back black hair.

After arriving in Canada, Roy was unable to find a job,
so he tried his hand at farming in the Fraser Valley, near
Vancouver. He eventually landed a job as a personnel officer at Vancouver city hall, where he stayed for two years.
He returned to South Africa in 1957 to study medicine at
University of South Africa, where he also received his
industrial psychologist certificate in 1960. Graduating
from medicine in 1962, he served a two-year medical
internship in neurology and surgery at hospitals in Cape
Town. His internship completed, he re-emigrated to Canada with his family in 1964 and did a four-year psychiatric residency at Vancouver General Hospital, where he
met and fell in love with Cindy.

By the time Cindy graduated as a registered nurse in
May 1966, she and Roy had decided to get married. After
graduation, Cindy had to move out of the nurses' residence, so Roy rented a little house in Burnaby, a bedroom
suburb of Vancouver, where they lived together. They did
not dare tell their colleagues. Roy was still married, a
resident physician living with a nurse 18 years his junior
who worked in the children's unit at the same hospital.
Roy had already been warned by his superiors that he had
been seen kissing a young nurse (Cindy) in his car while
dropping her off one night at the nurses' residence.

Fearing scandal, Roy kept his clothes and all his possessions locked in a closet at the Burnaby house, hiding
the evidence of their co-habitation in case colleagues
dropped by unexpectedly. Cindy called Roy "Mickey," an
extended version of MIC, their verbal shorthand for Man
In the Closet.

Roy and Cindy had planned to get married right away,
in June, since both their birthdays were in that month, four

days apart. Cindy dreaded the thought of her parents finding out she was living "in sin," especially with a married
man only six years younger than her father. So she put off
telling her parents until Roy got his divorce.

At that time, one of the few grounds for a speedy divorce was adultery. On May 7, 1966, Cindy and Roy spent
the night at the Royal Oak Motel, where a private detective took photos of them in bed together. Lois Makepeace,
who had agreed to divorce Roy so he could marry Cindy,
filed a divorce action three days later, naming Cindy as the
"adulteress." Cindy's parents never knew about the scene
of the adultery, but when Cindy's father heard she planned
to get married, he fiercely opposed it on the grounds the
man was not only much older, but a divorcé as well.

The divorce, giving Makepeace's wife a support pay-
ment of $150 a month and sole custody of the children,
was not finalized until December 5, 1966. Four days later,
Roy and his 21-year-old bride were wed in a courthouse
civil ceremony, with Cindy's brother Doug and his wife,
Barb, as witnesses.

Cindy hesitantly wrote to her parents shortly before the
impending marriage to tell them the date. Stationed at that
time in Metz, France, the Hacks were terribly upset by the
news, which arrived a few days before the wedding. They
tried to persuade Cindy to postpone the wedding until
January 1967. They were planning to fly back to Canada
then for their silver wedding anniversary from Metz,
where her father had become the mayor of the Canadian
military community of 20,000.

Cindy and Roy found this unacceptable. They were nervous about working in the same hospital along with Roy's
ex-wife; it was awkward and embarrassing. Cindy was
also worried her parents would try to sabotage the wedding. Roy felt the parents were more upset about not being
able to throw a big wedding party for their own relatives
than about missing the nuptials.

On December 8, a day before the wedding, Otto wrote
a letter "in confidence" to his son Doug, who was study-

ing mathematics at Simon Fraser University, located on Burnaby Mountain overlooking Vancouver.

"I write this with sad heart and heavy hand. In fact, I'm prompted to write only because of your mother's extreme mental shock following Cynthia's announcement of her marriage. Never before in our 25 years together have I seen your mother so disturbed and heartsick, and I, too, must confess am extremely disillusioned.

"It is not that we object to the marriage, for we don't know the man nor the circumstances that led to this sudden decision. What really hurts is the fact that our own child, and the oldest daughter at that, decides to get married without seeking our counsel and, most significantly, without sharing with us the joy of the momentous event. Your mother and I have for years discussed and planned the joy-filled wedding day we would help arrange for our first daughter, as has been the custom for centuries; and now, suddenly and shockingly, we are not even given the opportunity to participate in the occasion! Your mom just keeps brooding on where our parental responsibility failed to secure enough confidence and trust for our child to share with us a decision that is so final and vital. God knows!, we would have borrowed the money and moved heaven and earth to have shared those important moments with our daughter. However, we were cruelly denied that opportunity, and that type of history never repeats itself."

The letter went on to ask Doug if he could gather the relatives together for a silver wedding anniversary party – a surprise for his mother – during their scheduled visit in January. "That is, if she doesn't break-down and we have to cancel our trip – she hasn't been without tears for three days!" Hack wrote. "I think the only thing that can mitigate your mother's . . . feeling of rejection is a genuine demonstration from others who are close to her."

Seven days later, on December 14, Tillie Hack wrote to Cindy and Roy, saying she was still trying to get over the shock of the wedding. "It is still hard to think that you couldn't wait until the 14th when father and I will be in

Vancouver, as we mentioned in our telegram. In fact, at first we were going to cancel the trip, we were so mad and hurt that you couldn't have let us know a little sooner or given us a little more time. Do you know you didn't even ask if we could or would be able to come? We feel now we must have really failed you all the time we were in France. Please forgive us for being so hurt, we really wanted to be there so very much, and I'll admit I cried until I was sick and your father took it very hard also. He said he'd have gladly cashed our bond to give our first daughter a lovely wedding. As you will remember Cynthia, all his sisters died and he was so happy when you were born.

"We pray that you will have a long and happy life to-gether and you have my blessing. Father will have to speak for himself as he said 'Roy will have to be a damn fine man before I accept him as my son-in-law.' (You know your father, Cynthia.) He feels (and so do I) that Roy being so much older than you, you should have realized how we'd feel." She ended the letter wishing them a very Merry Christmas.

Despite an inauspicious beginning, Roy and Cindy's early years of marriage were extremely happy. "We had a mar-riage made in heaven," Roy recalls, adding his wife was intelligent, gentle and a natural beauty. Cindy, however, did not like the attention her looks attracted and some-times felt men were following her.

"I thought it was the perfect marriage," said Marlene, who first met Roy in 1967. He had sent her a train ticket – she was living in Montreal at the time – and put her up in a hotel for the night so he could meet Marlene while attend-ing a medical symposium in Toronto. "I liked him a lot."

So did Cindy's youngest sister, Melanie, who was only in her early teens when, in 1975, she moved back with her family to B.C. "I got along really well with him," she said. "We had a lot of fun together."

The newlyweds struggled financially for the first few years. Roy was making only $234 a month working 20-hour days as a resident physician and having to pay his ex-wife $150 a month in support. But his talent had earned the recognition of his superiors: in 1968, he was awarded the Vera and Dudley Myers Prize for the post-graduate resident showing the best ability and promise in the field of psychiatry. After completing his residency, he did not seek employment as a psychiatrist. He had failed an oral exam for certification as a psychiatrist in 1968. During the exam, Roy had an argument with one of his colleague-examiners and said he did not want to join the psychiatry "club" that still held nineteeth-century views.

Still, Makepeace was hired to teach psychiatry at the University of British Columbia. Two years later, he was appointed acting head of the Division of Social Psychiatry, one of the top five positions in the Psychiatry department.

In 1972, he left teaching and took a job in occupational medicine at B.C. Hydro, the provincial gas, electric and transit utility. The Crown corporation had about 12,600 employees at the time. Two years later, he was appointed director of health services at Hydro, a position he would hold until 1985 when he took early retirement as Hydro slashed its post-recession payroll to about 5,500 employees.

Meanwhile, Cindy proved to be an adept nurse, but she was more interested in child psychiatry. After two years at VGH she left nursing to work as a nurse-therapist at Laurel House, a day-treatment centre for autistic children. From there, she worked for three years with emotionally disturbed patients at the Children's Foundation. In 1975, she was hired as the founding director of Blenheim House, a new facility located on the corner of 41st Avenue and Blenheim Street in Vancouver.

Cindy loved her job there, where she divided her time between administration and therapy. The only aspect she did not enjoy about the job was firing or disciplining employees. She hated "being the heavy."

The facility employed 10 staff: a family psychiatrist, child psychiatrist, three child-care counsellors, speech therapist, psychiatric assessment worker, bus driver, secretary-receptionist and Cindy, who worked with a group of six pre-school children. Some of the kids were hard to handle, hyperactive, and had problems interacting with other children. They were often aggressive and acted out their hostility, or they would be reticent, withdrawn. It was the job of Blenheim House staff to try to tone down the children's behaviour or draw them out so they could be integrated into kindergarten the next year.

Although Cindy loved kids, she never had any of her own. The children of Blenheim House filled that need. They were like her little family. The staff worked together as a non-hierarchal team. "That's why it worked so well," said Dr. Alan Cashmore, a psychiatrist at Blenheim House and friend of Cindy. "One of her duties was to keep the team working harmoniously."

Blenheim House was a key part of Cindy's life "and we were very dependent on her," Cashmore recalled. Cindy was considered extremely competent by staff and well-liked by the children. Cindy was marvellous with kids. "Warm, caring, firm when she had to be," Cashmore recalled. She was also popular with the children's families.

As their marriage progressed, Roy and Cindy's dual incomes gradually eased them over the hump of financial struggles. The couple used a chunk of their increasing disposable income to buy a small boat for weekend excursions.

Roy soon discovered Cindy had a phobia about water. She said it stemmed from her childhood, when she had been thrown in the water and forced to swim. The experience had frightened her. She even refused to swim in a metre-deep wading pool at Vancouver's Aquatic Centre. Still, Cindy made an effort to go boating, just for Roy. Her main activities aboard the boat were cooking and suntanning. She could hardly wait until the boat was at anchor, so they could put ashore.

Cindy's brother Doug and his wife, Barb, spent a lot of time with Roy and Cindy. The foursome played bridge, bought property together in the Gulf Islands, and Doug would often go boating and fishing with Roy. "We were great friends," Doug said. "It was a really enjoyable time of life."

In his basement workshop, Roy extended his four-metre-long power boat to almost five metres one year. He thought a larger boat would help ease Cindy's fear. In 1977, Roy purchased his dream boat, a nine-metre "Catalac" catamaran that he bought for $110,000 from a shipbuilder in England. He had the double-hulled yacht shipped to Vancouver aboard a freighter. It was a gorgeous vessel, with sleek lines and a roomy cabin. Roy named her *Peacemaker*.

During the maiden voyage November 11, 1977, Roy, Cindy and another couple sailed to Saltspring Island overnight. On their return across the gulf to Vancouver, they were caught in a full gale, winds gusting to 50 knots, which was terrifying for all aboard, even Cindy's little dog Heidi, which cowered spread-eagled on the floor of the cabin.

Despite the episode, Cindy continued to go sailing, somewhat begrudgingly, as she would really rather be gardening.

Cindy tended her garden at their home at Granville and West 41st, in Vancouver's upper middle-class Kerrisdale area, with the same kind of care and patience as she displayed in her therapy with the pre-school children at Blenheim House. She spent years nurturing and rearranging bedding plants and flowering trees so they would blossom into beautiful bursts of cobalt violet, Prussian blue and cadmium yellow, like small Monet paintings. She marvelled at the juxtaposition of colour, shapes and textures she could create with the plants. The garden was an outlet for her artistic side. She also loved the gratifying, therapeutic results of working the soil with her hands, and was fascinated by the seasonal cycle of decay and renewal. It lifted her spirits to watch the dormant plants come alive each spring.

In a sense, Cindy's garden was her sanctuary, a small, reassuring haven where she would retreat as conflict arose in her marriage. Her garden was the one part of her world over which she had complete control, to shape and order to her satisfaction.

By the fall of 1981 the Makepeace marriage had soured. While Cindy spent most of her spare time in the garden, Roy was aboard the *Peacemaker*, often in mixed company in close quarters. Tempers would flare when Cindy's jealousy erupted. Roy denied Cindy's suggestion that one woman sailing companion was other than a friend. But as he and Cindy began to socialize separately, the gap between the couple widened.

The couple began to drift apart, starting August 29, 1978, at the end of a week-long sailing trip up the coast to an inlet called Desolation Sound, with Cindy's youngest brother and sister, Ken and Melanie, aboard. Sailing toward Vancouver, Cindy was making soup below deck when Roy encountered choppy seas and had to change tack abruptly, causing the soup to spill. An argument ensued, but it didn't end there. Cindy kept bringing up the incident after they got home, Makepeace recalls. Unable to take Cindy's needling any longer, he lost his temper and slapped her face. Cindy's brother and sister heard the commotion coming from the upstairs bedroom. They would later relate the incident to other family members, who would shake their heads in sympathy for Cindy.

Makepeace said Cindy warned him that a repeat episode would end the marriage. To appease her, he promised in future to cruise using the motor only, and never to hoist the sails while she was aboard the boat.

This arrangement went smoothly until a three-week boating trip to the Gulf Islands in July 1981. Roy and Cindy had motored to Thormanby Island, about 70 kilometres northwest of Vancouver, in Georgia Strait. While fishing for salmon on the fourth day, the motor's drive-shaft snapped and Roy had to break out the sails in order to reach Buccaneer Bay, where they were staying at a cabin owned by a psychiatrist friend.

Night was descending and rough seas mounted higher. At one point, the boat came precariously close to an out-crop of rocks as Roy swung the sails. Terrified, Cindy refused to go any further once they dropped anchor for the night. Her brother Doug, who lived on nearby Saltspring Island, had to take a water taxi to Buccaneer Bay the next day to help sail the boat back to Vancouver. Cindy made the return trip by water taxi and drove Doug's car home.

Extremely distressed by the incident, Cindy vowed never to set foot on the boat again. But years later, she would tell a story of the trip to Thormanby Island that was far more terrifying than that narrowly averted boating mishap. It would be the turning point in their relationship.

If Cindy was unhappy in her marriage, it was not yet affecting her performance at work. On May 4, 1981, in Cindy's annual evaluation, staff described her as "warm and nurturing, yet firm with children in the program . . . a model in setting and maintaining clear limits with both children and parents. . . . " The conclusion was that Cindy was providing staff and clients of Blenheim House with "a superb standard of leadership."

In early 1982, Cindy told Sue Fisk, a Blenheim House speech pathologist, that she was leaving Roy. No precise explanation was given, only that it was a "bad marriage."

On July 1, after 16 years of marriage, Roy and Cindy began a trial separation. Cindy moved into a rented home in East Vancouver while Roy stayed in their home at 1415 West 41st, which they referred to as the "big house." They divided their possessions "down the middle," with Cindy getting the gardening tools and supplies, all the plants, pots and grow lights, their dog Heidi, her mother's Royal Albert dishes, all the Hummel figurines, half the crystal, a king-size bed, alarm clock and bedlight.

Roy took his Zulu shield, a treasured photograph from Capetown, all construction tools, a South African book-shelf and all boating books and magazines.

There were no arguments. It was over and they were going to try living their own lives, no strings attached, although they would still "date." As Roy said, "It was an amicable separation until all [the] nonsense came on."

The stress of parting with Roy, however, triggered a reprise of Cindy's earlier terrifying dreams. In her recurring nightmare in which she was chased by Dobermans and fell into a pit, the black-clad figure at pit's edge began to take on a familiar face. It was Roy. As the dogs snapped at Cindy's fingers, he laughed as she tried to claw her way out.

FOUR

The Terror

C INDY HAD never really lived alone before her separation. She had gone from her family home, to a
boarding house, to nurses' residence, and then to living
with Roy all her adult years until the marriage break-up.
After moving into the rented main floor of a house at 334
East 40th, she felt vulnerable, especially at night. The
break-in rate ran high in the tidy, working-class neighbourhood in Vancouver's East End. Although a young un-
married couple rented the basement suite, Cindy never felt
as safe as she had at her old home, where Roy continued
to live.

She missed the big house, the homey feeling of its cozy
breakfast nook and the little glass greenhouse in the back
yard, with its two-metre-high wood fence and large shade
trees providing a sense of privacy and privilege. Her new
home, a one-storey stucco bungalow, looked forlorn compared to the two-storey house she and Roy had bought
seven years earlier. They had agreed to put the property
on 41st up for sale, so she felt assured that once it sold, she
would have enough money to buy her own house.

On October 7, 1982, three months after she and Roy
had separated, Cindy received an obscene and threatening
phone call. It would mark the beginning of a reign of
terror that would only end seven years later – with her
death.

The man repeatedly used Cindy's first name, describing in graphic terms how he was going to sexually mutilate her. She slammed the receiver down, then the phone rang again. This time there was no voice on the other end, only the haunting sound of slow, steady breathing coming from somewhere in the night.

The following evening, she got another call. "You're dead, Cindy," a male voice said.

The next day, about mid-afternoon, another silent call. The same breathing routine. Later that night, the phone rang again. "Don't think pulling the drapes means I don't know you're in there, Cindy," the man said in a hoarse whisper. She had closed the drapes about 10 minutes before the call.

On October 11, another breathing call. During the afternoon of the 12th, she picked up the phone and heard a man's menacing whisper. "I'll get you one night, Cindy." Fed up with this harassment, she called police.

The officer who attended suggested she make a list of any strange calls and phone police if she heard any suspicious noises outside her house. He also advised Cindy to get an unlisted number. After the officer left, she got another obscene call that night. Since it sounded like the same man, she told him she had contacted police and her line was being tapped.

"You fucking bitch," he snarled, "I'll get you."

A man called the next day before 11 a.m. "So you think calling the police will keep you safe. Just wait. I've got my zipper open, I'm taking out my throbbing. . . . "

Disgusted, Cindy hung up. About midnight the same evening, she heard someone fiddling with her back door. Police investigated but found no trace of a prowler.

On October 15, someone smashed Cindy's back window and entered the house while Cindy was out. The back door was found unchained, unlocked and ajar. The front door was also unlocked, but closed. Nothing had been taken or disturbed. Cindy could have understood it better if something was stolen. She wondered how long the person had been inside her house. Long enough to have a good look around and examine her things? What were they looking for? Had the person been scared off?

Four nights later, Cindy came home to find someone had entered her home again. This time it was with a key, which was later found on the floor by her bed.

Agnes Woodcock was with Cindy as they stood in shock, staring at the open back door.

"Don't go in, Agnes," Cindy said. "We'll run next door."

"The guy next door," Agnes later recalled, "knew she had had some problems. He had said, 'If there's any trouble, come and get me.' He was a great big guy. He went into the house and searched everywhere. He said, 'There's nobody here now, you can come in.' We went in and I went into the back bedroom and the next thing I heard was this awful scream. I thought, 'Oh my God. He's in there with her.' I ran to the bedroom and she was sobbing on the bed. Her pillow was slashed to shreds. We went to the neighbour's and called 911."

Cindy shivered with fright, knowing an intruder had pulled back her eiderdown quilt and meticulously slashed her pillow more than a dozen times. The parallel cuts looked like they had been done with a razor, maybe a scalpel. It bothered her that nothing else had been disturbed or stolen. What was the slashed pillow supposed to mean? Was it a message? A warning of some kind? She had no idea who would do such a thing. Or why.

Constable Pat McBride, dispatched to investigate, listened sympathetically as Cindy explained about the earlier events – the prowler fiddling with the back door, the first break-in and the flurry of obscene and threatening calls from a man who spoke in a low, hoarse whisper. She had changed her phone number but still the whispering and silent calls continued. "No-talk calls," McBride wrote in his notebook. He advised Cindy to change her locks and install deadbolts. The only other assistance he could offer was to request that his fellow officers patrol the area more frequently.

On October 20, the downstairs tenants notified police that they had heard something suspicious upstairs after Cindy had left for work. Police investigated but found nothing amiss.

As a friendly gesture, McBride dropped by Cindy's house a few days later to install dead-bolt locks. The eight-year police veteran had recently separated from his wife and was looking for a place to rent for a month until an apartment came up December 1. Cindy told him he was welcome to sublet a room, since she had three bedrooms. She said she would feel safer having a man around the house, especially a policeman.

On October 29, Cindy found an obscene note on her back porch. Police dusted it for fingerprints but none were found.

McBride moved in three days later. He found he enjoyed Cindy's company and they quickly became good friends, eating meals together and sharing living expenses. Pat paid for food, telephone and utilities during his month-long stay. They also went out together on weekends.

McBride asked Cindy about the man who had been making the strange calls. He thought it might be a "weirdo" living in the neighbourhood, since he had checked and found a woman two doors down the block who had reported getting a number of "nuisance" calls. He also examined police reports of neighbourhood break-ins, looking for similarities. He convinced Cindy to get an unlisted number.

On November 14, after Cindy had changed her phone number, another late-night call rocked the house. A week later, she found a bizarre note on her car windshield: it was a picture of a blonde woman cut from a magazine with cut-and-paste letters making a collage of phrases that radiated a foreboding, ominous energy. The woman's eyes appeared to be scratched out with sharp blade. Was it the same blade that had been used to slash the pillowcase?

McBride questioned Makepeace, who had been dating Cindy at least once a week since the separation, but the doctor was not a man who seemed suspicious. Instead, he seemed a reasonable guy and a well-respected professional. Not the sort of man who would submit a person to mental torture.

Then again, McBride knew some estranged husbands could sometimes behave in strange ways.

Cindy's next-door neighbour said she observed a strange man around Cindy's house on three occasions. She first saw him knocking at the front door, another time leaving by the front door. It was not, she said, Dr. Makepeace; she knew what he looked like. McBride also eliminated the landlord as a suspect after talking to him. Another neighbour living behind Cindy's house said he had surprised a man in his back yard one night between 9 and 10 p.m. The man had broken the gate hinge running away. The only description he could provide was that the suspected prowler had been wearing a red jacket.

On November 27, three days before McBride was to move to his own apartment, someone crept silently onto the back porch and poured water over the outside light, which was kept on all night.

By this time, the neighbourhood had been classified by police as needing "special attention," meaning officers should patrol the area more frequently and keep their eyes open for possible prowlers. McBride would often cruise by Cindy's house or drop in for coffee and doughnuts while he was working the night shift. He dropped in for coffee the night of November 28 and everything seemed fine. Later that evening, he was alerted to a problem at Cindy's house: her phone line was dead.

McBride arrived to investigate with his partner, Constable Andy Richards. They examined the phone lines, which entered the house about two metres from the ground. The lines had been cut in five places – once at the junction box and several times where the line ran along the house. The TV-cable line was also cut, but the phone

line for the downstairs tenants was undisturbed. Cindy
explained she had received a whispering call about 30
minutes before she discovered the line dead.

McBride and Richards checked inside the house to
make sure it was secure and nothing had been disturbed.
McBride even checked his own bedroom, where he was
surprised to find a small pair of wirecutters on top of his
toolbox. He could not remember leaving them out, but it
was possible he had. Suspiciously, he eyed what appeared
to be black-plastic wire insulation on the wirecutters. Was
it possible Cindy had cut the wires? McBride thought not.
The wirecutters were too small to cut the lines, and even if
they had been used, they likely would have broken during
the attempt. Besides, Cindy knew nothing about electron-
ics. She certainly would not be able to tell the difference
between the upstairs and downstairs phone lines.

McBride felt that whoever cut the lines was planning to
return that night, so he and his partner maintained surveillance of the house until 7 a.m., with McBride watching
from inside the house while Richards sat in an unmarked
police car.

Again, no fingerprints were found, leading McBride to
wonder if the suspect was perhaps aware of his involvement with Cindy. Maybe the person even had knowledge
of police procedures. Based on Cindy's description of the
male caller's low, slow pattern of speech, McBride thought
it likely that the suspect was disguising his voice.

The cutting of the phone lines prompted Cindy to remember another strange incident that had taken place
before police got involved. While she was standing on the
back porch in September, a man had startled her when he
entered her back yard uninvited.

Cindy asked: "Are you looking for me?"

"Where's Jimbo?" the man replied. He was in his
twenties, with a slim, muscular build and straight, greasy
brown hair.

"I don't know anybody by that name," Cindy said. The
man insisted she did and got quite annoyed. When she

noticed a big roll of money in the man's hand, he nervously stuffed it in a pouch of his jacket. He then asked if she wanted to get "laid." He said he had a lot of money and would pay for it.

As Cindy turned to retreat to her house, the man came forward a couple of steps. "Hey," he shouted, "you haven't seen me!" Cindy shook her head and closed the door, thinking it was just some neighbourhood creep.

Cindy never liked going into much detail about the incidents that were happening to her, especially the obscene calls and threats. She found it embarrassing. "She said she was a very private person and didn't want her life dragged out in public," McBride recalled. His relationship with Cindy intensified after he moved out. They dated, went dancing and out to dinner. Roy was also still in the picture and occasionally they would double date – Pat, Cindy, Roy and his woman friend.

Roy also was concerned with his wife's safety. Cindy told her doctor that early one morning in December 1982, Roy's car had been stopped by police in the lane behind her house. Police had noticed it circle the block and then park with the headlights out. Roy told the officers he was there to protect Cindy and was waiting for the "mafia goon" who had been harassing her to show up. Police told him to go home.

"Roy told me about it the next day," Cindy recalled some years later. "He was furious, disparaging of police and contemptuous of their incompetence. He warned me that I'd better stop using the downstairs laundry room as someone could easily slip in there when my back was turned, slit my throat and I might not be found for days. He was getting worked up again so I told him to stop talking like that. It didn't help and it was just scary. He got really angry and said I wouldn't laugh when it happened . . . he'd warned me it was a jungle out there and I wouldn't survive on my own. He offered me another chance to move back with him and when I refused, he stormed off making all kinds of dire predictions of what would happen."

Later in December, Roy called Cindy, suggesting they get together on their wedding anniversary "for old times' sake." Cindy would later recount to her doctor that Roy "sounded so lonely, I couldn't say no. The evening went quite well, although I was tense and cautious about saying the wrong thing. He was quiet during dinner and sad, saying he was dreading the coming holidays alone. I finally found myself inviting him to spend Christmas with me at my parents', as a friend only."

Just before Christmas, Cindy received another threatening note in the mail: "Merry Christmas" said the greeting, with a photo of a blonde woman, her throat slashed with red ink, pasted on the card.

This is getting very weird, Cindy thought.

Cindy and Roy spent the four-day Christmas weekend, Friday through Monday, at her parents' house on Vancouver Island. The mood was strained but everyone tried to act happy, as if everything was the way it used to be. Cindy gave Roy a Texas Instruments calculator; he gave her a Lorus wristwatch. When she returned home December 29, she found another threatening cut-and-paste note in her mail. Nervous about being alone in her house, Cindy decided to stay with friends for the next seven days.

The notes and phone calls continued through January, prompting McBride to ask the phone company to tap her line. The callers, however, rarely stayed on the line long enough for a full trace, which takes between one and three minutes. One silent call was traced January 6 to the 73 exchange, the Kitsilano area of Vancouver. Another call was made the following night, but the phone company could only say it did not come from the 73 exchange or the 26 exchange, the southwest side of Vancouver closest to Richmond. Another silent call on January 14 was traced to the 26 exchange.

Late on the afternoon of January 15, McBride was visiting Cindy when she got another "no-talk" call. McBride listened in. He could hear a woman's voice on a public address system in the background. Again, the caller did not stay on the line long enough for a full trace, but the partial trace showed it came from the "27" exchange in Richmond. Vancouver's airport was located there and often had public announcements about flights, McBride reasoned. Cindy had talked to her ex-husband only five minutes beforehand, so McBride ruled him out. Dr. Makepeace lived near 41st and Granville, so it would have taken him at least 10 minutes to get to the airport, or anywhere in Richmond for that matter.

If McBride had ever doubted Cindy in the past, this call reaffirmed his belief she was not "staging" incidents to attract attention to herself. It galvanized his belief that the harassment was very real. Still, he could not figure out who would want to do this to such a warm, sweet woman.

Near the end of January, Cindy phoned Roy to suggest they go for dinner. They went to a restaurant on West 41st that served steak-and-kidney pie. Cindy mentioned she had an appointment to look at a house, so Roy drove her there. The place was dingy and depressing. The landlord also would not allow dogs, so Cindy would not have been able to keep Heidi. Feeling sorry for her, Roy suggested she move back into their house on 41st until it was sold. "I'm just a bachelor. I can find an apartment somewhere," he said.

Cindy immediately agreed to the proposed idea, but insisted that the locks be changed. Roy agreed to move on two conditions: if Cindy took responsibility for any realtor "open houses" and if he could continue to have access to the garage and basement, where he kept his tools and boating supplies.

Before Roy dropped her at home, Cindy asked him to stop the car – she bought two newspapers so they could both scan the want ads for apartments. Thirty minutes after Roy got home, Cindy called. She suggested he look at a suite at 2084 West 44th, not far from their house. Roy looked at the place the next day. It was a basement suite, a bit dark, but he said he could live with it. He took the place, which was available at the end of the month.

On January 27, as Cindy was packing boxes preparing to move, her tormentor struck again. This time, he went for blood.

Agnes Woodcock called Cindy from home about nine that night. There was no answer, which was odd. Agnes had arranged to stay the night at Cindy's house to keep her company, easing her friend's fear of being alone.

Woodcock got in her car and arrived at Cindy's about 9:30 p.m. She knocked at the front and the back doors, without any response. As she stood on the back porch trying to decide what to do, she heard moaning coming from the yard. She walked down the stairs and saw Cindy slumped in the basement stairwell. Her arms and legs had been slashed, and a black stocking was tied around her neck. It was so tight Agnes could not get her fingers under it. She pounded on the basement door. The downstairs tenant threw open the door. After seeing the stocking around Cindy's neck, he ran to get a knife. He cut off the nylon and helped Woodcock move Cindy inside, sitting her on the couch. Cindy's blouse was ripped off on one side and the cut through her jeans seemed deep. Her pant-leg was soaked in blood.

Dazed, gasping for breath, Cindy could not speak. Later, she explained she was moving boxes into the garage and tried turning on the garage light.

"Oh my God, the light's out," Cindy thought aloud. Then someone, she said, grabbed her from behind. The man fled the garage before she got a look at him. That was all she remembered.

"She didn't want to talk about the attacks or anything after they were over," Woodcock explained. "She would say, 'I wish he'd leave me alone. I just want to disappear and live my own life.'"

Woodcock was extremely sympathetic and supportive of Cindy. She did not press her for more information. She thought Cindy would tell her everything when and if she was ready.

An ambulance and police arrived minutes later. Constable Val Woollacott found Cindy upset and disturbed. "She wasn't totally all there, as far as being coherent," he recalled, adding that there was no smell of alcohol on her breath.

After Cindy had been taken to hospital, the officer interviewed one of the downstairs tenants, Wendy Hampton. She said she had heard a knock at the back door earlier, before Agnes pounded on the door, but she did not open it, fearing what might be lurking outside.

Woollacott checked the garage and saw a blood smudge on a cardboard box. He thought it looked like a thumb print. There were no obvious signs of a struggle. Boxes and wood were stacked neatly in the garage. The light operated normally. There was a chair directly below a wooden overhead crossbeam, where the dust had been disturbed, leading Woollacott to believe Cindy may have been planning to attempt suicide. Still, maybe the assailant placed the chair in the spot. It was not until later, after he had filed his incident report, that Woollacott learned the police inspector at the scene, Ron Foyle, had moved the chair to examine the wiring on the crossbeam, making sure the garage light had not been tampered with. Foyle had disturbed the dust while checking the wiring.

Woollacott found Cindy's back door unlocked and he noted blood stains on the bathroom counter. The blood was still wet and had not coagulated. There also appeared to be a fine spray of blood on the sink and mirror. The officer later phoned Dr. Kwok-Sum Chan, who examined Cindy at the emergency ward of Vancouver General Hospital. Chan said there was an obvious strangulation mark on her neck and bruises on her right forehead. There were two lacerations on the upper left arm, and multiple cuts to the back and shoulder. About 14 cuts in all, possibly made by a razor or a scalpel. There were two relatively serious cuts on the back of the shoulder, but for the most part the cuts to the back and arms were short, superficial wounds. The longest cut was a shallow 10-centimetre incision on the leg, just above the ankle. The parallel nature of most of the cuts on her back seemed to suggest there had not been a struggle.

Woollacott never asked Cindy about the blood in the house. He would leave that to the detective assigned the case. Woollacott, who had been with the force three years, wrote in his report that he believed the incident had been an attempted suicide.

Still, it was titled "attempted murder" when the case was assigned to Detective David Bowyer-Smyth, a tall, lanky veteran with 26 years of service on the force. He began the investigation with an open mind. One thing an experienced officer learns: never jump to conclusions without knowing all the facts. A smart suspect can often "stage" crime scenes to distract investigators and lead them down the wrong investigative path. Over the years, investigators become highly trained observers. A veteran cop has a "sixth sense" and can pick up on little signs – nervousness in facial expressions, tone of voice, eye movements – that ring alarm bells.

At 5:15 p.m. the night after the attack, Bowyer-Smyth interviewed Cindy James at the Oakridge police detachment in South Vancouver, a low-slung building in a quiet residential area. Greeting Cindy at the front counter, he led her to a small, stark room with bare, colourless walls, furnished sparsely with a table and a couple of chairs. Overhead the flourescent lights hummed faintly as the detective, pen in hand and pad of paper at the ready, asked Cindy to recall the details of the incident.

Cindy explained she was packing boxes. "I went out to the garage the first time. I put on the light and got three boxes. I pulled the door almost shut. I left the light on because I knew I was going back for more boxes. After about five minutes, I went back to the garage from the house. I pushed the door open, took a few steps into the garage. I realized the light wasn't on, it was dark. I turned to leave and I was grabbed by my right arm. I said, 'Oh my God, it's happening.' He said, 'Shut up.' It was a deep, low, male voice."

She felt a pin prick on her right shoulder. No, change that to the left shoulder. The man moved his right arm around her right side and across her chest.

"Keep quiet or I'll cut your face," the man hissed. Cindy could feel something on the left side of her neck. "I could cut your throat but I won't – it's too quick," said the man, bringing his left hand around in front of her. He was holding a knife.

She knocked it aside with her left arm. "You fucking cunt," he cursed.

Thinking he was going to go for her face, Cindy brought her left arm over her face and bent to the right. She felt a searing pain as he cut her back, whispering: "Keep quiet. Don't make me cut you." Cindy felt something go around her neck. The man tightened it from behind as he let go of her body. She kicked backward twice, hitting his shins.

"I couldn't breathe," she told Bowyer-Smyth, who nodded silently. "I grabbed at the object at my throat to pull it away. I tried to talk."

"Keep quiet! Don't make any noise!" said the man, pushing Cindy to the concrete floor, where she struck her head. She tried kicking him again and he cut her on the leg. Before the man left, closing the door behind him, he leaned close to Cindy, telling her, "It will take a long time to die."

Cindy recalled she could not get the stocking off her neck and was having trouble breathing. Feeling her way in the dark garage, she found the door, stumbled across the yard to the back basement door and banged on it. Next thing she could remember, Agnes Woodcock found her.

Asked to describe the suspect, Cindy said she did not get a look at his face; she could only see his shape in the darkness. But she remembered he was wearing tight gloves and blue running shoes. When the man pulled her against him, she could feel his chin in the back of her head. "That would make him about five-foot-ten," she said.

Cindy mentioned she felt a "slight sting" on her right arm during the attack. The detective examined Cindy's arm. On the inside at the elbow, he saw what appeared to be a needle mark. She gave Bowyer-Smyth some background on when her problems began but she had no idea who her attacker was. She did not suspect it was her husband or anyone connected to her work. She had no known enemies, she said. When she and Roy were married, they never had any break-ins or similar problems.

Cindy signed her statement. Not fully satisfied with this, Bowyer-Smyth pressed for further details and asked Cindy if she would be willing to take a polygraph test "to cover all the bases." She said she had no problem with that. A date was arranged for February 11.

The detective, meanwhile, met with Cindy's husband on February 7. "You know, being an estranged husband, you're inevitably on the suspect list," Bowyer-Smyth explained.

"That I can imagine for myself," Makepeace replied, denying that he had any involvement in the harassment of Cindy. He said he had worked late at B.C. Hydro the night of the attack, staying until about 9 p.m. working on a memo to his boss regarding the health factors of video display terminals in the workplace. After leaving work, he had dinner at a White Spot restaurant a few kilometres from Cindy's house. By the time he got home, the 10 o'clock news had already started. He signed his statement and was getting up to leave when Bowyer-Smyth asked Makepeace if he would take a polygraph. "Fine, you organize it and tell me when and where," he said.

When Makepeace arrived for the appointment a few days later, the police polygraph operator read him his rights, telling him anything he said could be used against him. The officer then went through a questionnaire, asking Makepeace if he was taking any kinds of drugs or medication.

"Yes, I'm taking medication," Makepeace said, explaining he took Inderal and Isordil pills for angina, a cardiac problem, that had started in 1981.

"I'm sorry," the officer said, "I can't test you." He explained that not only might drugs falsify the test, voiding the results, but also the test was very stressful. It was against his ethical code to administer it if it might be a health risk.

Bowyer-Smyth was unhappy with this development. Without a polygraph, he had no way of verifying Makepeace's statement.

"I was very surprised," Makepeace later recalled. "It wasn't that important to me at the time. I was perfectly willing to take the test."

On February 10, Bowyer-Smyth interviewed one of Cindy's close friends and colleagues, Rena O'Donnell. She had worked with Cindy for years and they often had dinner together after work.

"Do you think Cindy may have been responsible herself for any of these incidents?" Bowyer-Smyth asked.

"Definitely not," O'Donnell replied. "She confided in me about her personal life and problems."

"Did she discuss her relationship with her husband?"

"Yes," O'Donnell said, noting that, prior to separating, the Makepeaces often vigorously disagreed. At the same time, Cindy was protective of her husband.

The day after the O'Donnell interview, Cindy took her polygraph test. She was asked if she had inflicted the wounds on herself the night of January 27, and if she tied the stocking around her neck.

She "failed" the test, but she was extremely nervous throughout and seemed under duress, which Bowyer-Smyth knew may have affected the results. A second polygraph was arranged for the next week. Again, Cindy "failed." She went up to the polygraph operator, Sergeant

Vic Farmer, and said, "Vic, I'm sorry, I'm sorry." Farmer thought she was highly emotional when retelling the story of the attack, which may have influenced the results. He could not determine if Cindy was lying or withholding information by not telling the whole story.

Bowyer-Smyth again urged her to tell him everything she knew. Cindy said she might have more information but needed more time to consider it. A few days later, she decided to make another statement. She told Bowyer-Smyth she had omitted some information in previous interviews because she feared for the safety of herself and her family. She wanted the entire investigation "shut down, concluded." The detective told her that was not possible, considering the serious nature of her case.

After considerable persuasion, Cindy gave a verbal statement but would not sign it. She stated again that she was afraid for herself and her family. Again she related sketchy details of what happened during the attack. It would not be until much later that Cindy would recall the full story.

FIVE

The Full Story

YEARS LATER, Cindy was able to push aside her fear to reveal what she believed really happened in the first attack, explaining why she had been reticent to tell Bowyer-Smyth all the details – she was afraid of threats made to hurt her mother and sister if she told the "pigs." This account, similar but more detailed than what she told Bowyer-Smyth, is drawn from Cindy's own notes that police would later find in her home.

Cindy recalled that Pat McBride had been helping her pack for several nights around the end of January 1983, but she did not feel she was getting enough done since his visits meant stopping for coffee and chatting. She had to have all her houseplants and crystal boxed up that night of January 27 so they could be moved after work the next day. After dark, she realized she needed more boxes from the garage but she was nervous about going out for more. She wished McBride would have come over after all. Nervous and suspicious of every sound she heard, she took a two-milligram Ativan pill, a tranquilizer, to calm down and get up the courage to go to the garage.

Suddenly, there was a knock at the back door. Startled, she anxiously walked to the door and peeked through the curtain. There was Pat McBride, wearing his familiar blue jacket and a toque, standing, seemingly, with his back to the window, looking toward the yard.

Cindy felt a mixture of relief and annoyance that he had come over against her wishes. She opened the door, teasing him that he could not stay away, when she realized she had made a horrible mistake: it was not Pat.

The man pulled down his toque, a ski mask to cover his face, and lunged toward her. Cindy tried slamming the door but he stuck his foot in and swung the door open. She raced for the bathroom, which had a lock on the door, but he caught her before she could close it.

The attacker smashed his fist across Cindy's head, knocking her down. She got up and faced him in the doorway just as Heidi came running out of the bedroom, snarling. He had a knife in his right hand and it seemed he was going to stab the dog.

"No!" Cindy shouted, trying to grab his hand. He booted Heidi, who yelped as she hit the wall. The assailant swung around at Cindy with the knife. She lifted her hand to protect her face and the knife caught her in the shoulder.

Cindy hunched over the bathroom counter, waiting to be stabbed in the back. "Oh my God, just make it quick," she thought. Then the man grabbed her by the hair and one arm. He said he had a friend outside who wanted to see her.

He pulled her across the kitchen and out the back door. Cindy tried closing the door shut with her hand as she went by, so Heidi would stay inside. She hoped someone would see them outside so she could scream, but her throat was so dry she was not sure she could make any sound. At first she thought he was going to take her to the laundry room. She panicked, remembering what Roy had said. Instead, he pulled her across the back porch and down the stairs. Oh no, she thought. "They've got a car . . . they can take me anywhere and I'll never be found."

Cindy tried to pull away, but the masked man knocked her to the ground, pulled her by the hair and put the knife to her throat. "One more fucking sound bitch and you're dead meat," he said. He took her to the garage door and flung her inside, where another man was waiting. The first man told him, "Don't fuck around too long with the bitch. I'll go finish the dog."

Cindy tried to scream, "No, please don't hurt her," but the second man grabbed her upper right arm. She felt a sharp pain in her right shoulder. "Please God, this isn't happening," she thought. A foot kicked the door shut, enveloping the garage in darkness.

The man reached around from behind to pin her right arm to her chest, his right hand clamping on her left arm. Cindy frantically tried to pull away. "Please don't let him hurt me," she pleaded.

"Shut up, fucking bitch, don't make me cut you," he said several times as he flicked his knife, cutting her left arm. She also felt a sharp cut on her neck, below her left ear. "See this knife?" he asked. "It would be so easy to slice your throat but that would be too quick. You were warned to get rid of the fucking pigs and you didn't. You're going to die real slow, cunt."

He released her arm, then roughly squeezed her left breast. Cindy felt his arm move in front of her and she jerked back her head and flung up her arm. As she tried pulling away, she heard him grunt. She thought she had hurt him. Maybe he had stabbed himself with the knife. But then she felt a sharper jab in her left shoulder blade, and he clamped his right arm across her chest and arms again.

Her attacker repeatedly stabbed at the back of her neck as he whispered, "Fucking cunt. Know what it feels like to be fucked with a knife? I'll cut your fucking pussy off. It'll feel real good while I stick it up your fucking cunt and twist it around, see where it comes out."

The man ran his hand down Cindy's body, between her legs, then clamped his arm across her chest again.

"You're dead, bitch," he whispered. "Maybe we'll have some fun with your mother and two sisters next. The blonde sexy one, she looks like she'd be good."

Cindy started babbling, "Oh God, please leave them alone. I'll do anything you say. Please don't hurt them. I won't tell anyone. I won't tell anyone anything. I promise. I swear I won't tell."

"It's too fucking late, cunt," he said as she felt something tighten around her neck. Unable to breathe, Cindy was shoved to the ground. The right side of her head hit the concrete floor and she thought her head was going to burst from the pain. She began kicking and flailing. Sharp jabs spiked her arm and leg. She felt like an animal, cowering on the ground, not thinking anymore, just hearing herself screaming inside her head.

Suddenly, the door was flung open. "Get the fuck out," the first man said. "One more time. If she's not dead, we'll get her again."

Once more, it was all dark. Cindy tried pulling at the thing around her neck but she was getting dizzy. Her thought bubbles rose slowly from the floor where she lay. "Not enough air. Have to get out. Get help. They might be waiting out there. It might be a trick. Don't move. Oh God, I'm going to die here in the dark. Don't know the way out. Crawling over stacked wood and boxes. Can't find the door. My head's going to burst open from the pressure . . . I'm going to die in here. Oh, mommy, please help me. I'm so scared. I don't want to die."

She fell against a garage cupboard and found the door, but she wondered if the men were lying in wait for her on the other side. "Have to get out of here," she thought. She staggered across the lawn but kept falling over. "Want to sleep," she thought. She fell down the basement steps and tried to pound on the door.

"No one coming," she thought, her consciousness fading. "No one home. . . . Can't pound anymore. I'm going to die. Just let go." She heard someone screaming far, far away.

The next thing Cindy remembered was being wrapped in a blanket, sitting on a couch. She felt dizzy, nauseous, cold. So cold. Dripping blood on the carpet. "All the people's mouths are moving but they make no sense," she thought. "So cold, so cold. I wish they'd go away. Don't think. Just try to get warm."

After Cindy was released from the emergency ward, she stayed for two nights at the home of her colleague, Dr. Carl Rothschild. Her friends moved her belongings back to the house on 41st. She kept asking them to check Heidi, but the dog was all right.

The first few weeks after Cindy moved back to the big house were a blur of raw emotions, terror and the fear of being alone. She cried often and would let no one touch her. She kept insisting she wanted to return to work and regain some normalcy in her life.

Based on police reports from the scene, Bowyer-Smyth initially thought he was investigating an attempted suicide, but Cindy's fuller version of the attack changed his opinion. The new information explained the blood in the bathroom.

Bowyer-Smyth spent many hours researching known sex offenders and criminals who lived in Cindy's neighbourhood or within close proximity. He came up with a photo lineup, which he showed to Cindy on March 10, 1983. She recognized none of them, but then, she said, she never got a good look at her attackers.

The majority of the people Bowyer-Smyth interviewed thought highly of Cindy and believed she was truthful. The woman was generally cheerful and upbeat. She was a well-regarded administrator-therapist at a psychiatric facility and worked closely with psychiatrists, who believed Cindy was telling the truth. Unfortunately, there was no conclusive evidence to point to a suspect.

Bowyer-Smyth declared Cindy's attempted-murder file inactive a month later, although he would continue investigating new incidents as they arose. The detective concluded his report with the ambiguous comment: "The victim may know more than she has revealed, perhaps even the identification of the suspects."

Back in the big house, Cindy was wary about the lingering memories there but looked upon the move as only a temporary measure. She would continue to look for a house to buy.

On February 8, the threatening cut-and-paste letters that had been sent to her old address on East 40th began to be delivered to her new home.

Two months later, the phone calls started again. Mc-Bride was present when Cindy received several of the calls. During a call on April 14, a male voice asked, "Are you afraid?"

On April 22, Cindy and Roy discovered the back yard floodlamps had been unscrewed and smashed on the concrete.

A look of terror swept over Cindy's face. It was all starting again. It was time to move.

Although her friends and family advised her that she would be safer in an apartment or condominium, Cindy was stubborn. She was determined she was going to live a normal life and not hide. She also wanted a house with a garden and a yard for Heidi. She found a little stucco bungalow at the corner of West 14th and Blenheim, which she moved into April 30. It was a nice tree-lined street populated by upper-middle-class families, lots of kids and Volvo station wagons. Cindy also got an unlisted phone number. After the move, Cindy took a vacation to Jakarta, Indonesia, to visit her older brother Roger, who was stationed there with Canada's External Affairs department.

Before her departure in June, she sent Roy a card. He had given her $300 cash and a keepsake to wear on the trip: an Egyptian hieroglyphic pendant on a chain. "Dearest Roy," she wrote. "I just want you to know I'll be holding you close in my thoughts while I'm away. Remember our little mice? Well, I feel rather as I did then. I'll miss you Roy. I wish our paths had been such that we were taking this one together. Take care of yourself Royboy and if I don't come back, remember, I've always loved you."

Cindy returned from the two-week trip refreshed and relaxed. It seemed to be just the tonic she needed, and July and most of August passed without any obscene notes or menacing phone calls. On August 22, however, a letter addressed to Cindy arrived at work. It was found in the outside mailbox by Blenheim House secretary Denise Perkins, who was first to arrive every morning.

There was no mistaking who it was from. Magazine letters spelling "CINDY" were pasted haphazardly on the outside of the envelope. Inside, the jumble of cut-and-paste phrases read: "Welcome Back. Death. Blood. Love. Hate." Cindy ripped it up. Whoever was behind this was not going to get the best of her.

Similar letters, which Cindy destroyed without opening, began arriving at Blenheim House regularly. Cindy stayed overnight at Blenheim House on September 13 to see if she could catch the person dropping the letters in the outside mailbox. But nothing happened. Another letter was found September 20 by O'Donnell. On October 11, two more letters arrived by mail. Yet another arrived by mail the next day. It appeared to be a full-time obsession.

On October 15, Cindy heard Heidi barking in the night and in the morning she was horrified to find a different sort of threat left in her yard: a dead cat with a rope around its neck. A nearby note read: "You're next."

Almost two weeks went by before the next incident: someone trampled all her bedding plants, pulled out her shrubs and dumped her potted plants. Cindy had spent many hours after moving in, almost all her free time, trying to get the garden just the way she liked it. Someone knew Cindy well enough to know what would really hurt her. Two weeks later, Cindy found another dead, strangled cat at her back door.

At this time, Pat McBride's relationship with Cindy was winding down. According to Cindy, he had asked her to marry him, but she was not ready to make that kind of commitment. Nonetheless, McBride remained concerned for Cindy's safety and felt she should be under electronic surveillance. He suggested Cindy contact Ozzie Kaban, who ran a well-known Vancouver security firm that provided private investigation as well as security systems.

Kaban was hired November 14 as a security consultant and to provide protection, if needed. At a hefty 120 kilograms, Kaban resembled a clean-shaven Raymond Burr. He had done a two-year stint as an auxiliary RCMP officer before starting his own company, which had a small army of about 60 employees at the time. A large part of Kaban's business was private and corporate surveillance using the latest technology – laser beams, ultrasonic sensors and infra-red detection devices. He once boasted that the $45,000 system he installed in the $7-million home of Vancouver stock promoter Murray Pezim involved almost four kilometres of wiring. Kaban also provided bodyguards for celebrities, movie stars and dignitaries visiting Vancouver. One of his favourite snapshots was of himself with Frank Sinatra, Dean Martin and Sammy Davis, Jr., taken on a dock beside a float-plane during a Rat Pack fishing trip to B.C.

Kaban's first impression of Cindy was that of "a very frightened lady." He also knew Cindy had little cash to spend on a sophisticated alarm system, so he offered a solution to fit her budget: he gave her an aerosol spray can of oil-and-jalapeno-pepper dog repellent to use if she was attacked again, and he equipped her home with a two-way radio link to his 24-hour dispatch system in case her phone lines were cut. Kaban assured Cindy that he was going to try to "catch the sucker" who was terrorizing her.

On November 22, another dead cat and note were found at Cindy's home. Kaban sent an employee to investigate. This cat, however, had not been strangled. It had been hit by a car.

The incidents continued regularly during the following two months, usually about once a week but sometimes every few days. There seemed to be no pattern. A threatening note was left on her back porch when she was out for the evening. No-talk calls were received at Blenheim House. On New Year's Eve, 1983, Cindy's basement bedroom window was found smashed. Nine days later, Cindy returned home from work to find her back porch lights unscrewed. The next night, Heidi began barking after 2 a.m. and Cindy heard a loud thump at the back of the house. She tried the phone – the line was dead. There was another loud noise at the front of the house, followed by a thump at the back. Cindy cowered until all was quiet. She locked herself in her room until 7 a.m., then went to work and called Kaban, who found the phone lines cut, a basement window broken and a threatening letter left in the back.

Days later, Cindy heard a noise like metal hitting the front door, followed by the doorbell chiming. She checked the front and back. No one there. On January 24, the doorbell rang at 3 a.m. and she found a letter in her mail slot, which Cindy turned over to Kaban. The jumbled cut-and-paste words read: "Blood Terror Love Death."

The next day, Bowyer-Smyth paid Cindy a visit to talk to her about recent events, which she was reporting to Kaban but not to police. She said she felt the Vancouver police department had little interest in her case. McBride had told her that. She mentioned that the guy looking for Jimbo back in September 1982 reminded her of the shadowy figure in the garage when she was attacked the previous January. He spoke in a whisper, but she could not say for certain that it was the same person. The other man who took her to the garage spoke in a low, gruff voice. She assumed he had made some of the earlier phone calls.

As far as suspects, she told Bowyer-Smyth she remembered a man who worked briefly as a child counsellor at Blenheim House from July 1978 to August 1979. He was going through a lot of personal problems at the time and was not doing a proper job. He was angry and resentful when Cindy fired him. He told another staff member he hated Cindy's guts. The last time Cindy had seen him was July or August 1983, when he drove by Cindy's house and honked his horn. Cindy talked to him and he was friendly. He said he had just bought a house up the street from her.

The only other person she had a run-in with was a real estate salesman who kept asking her out. He showed up the day Cindy had moved into the rental property on East 40th in the summer of 1982. Rena O'Donnell was there. The man had been drinking and wanted Cindy to go to a party with him. She refused. He phoned the next day, apologized, then asked her out. Again, she refused. He phoned twice more in the next few weeks, then she never heard from him until August or September 1983, when he pulled up in his car at Cindy's house and again requested a date. She declined once more and had not seen him since.

Cindy told Bowyer-Smyth she had not seen Pat Mc-Bride for about two months, although he phoned a couple of times a week. With the harassment starting up again, she did not want him involved. "I thought it might jeopardize his job," she said.

She reiterated that she did not suspect her husband. She and Roy still went out about once a week to dinner or a movie. Just two weeks previously they had seen *Terms of Endearment*. Theirs was a friendly, platonic relationship.

SIX

The Interrogation

FIVE DAYS after Bowyer-Smyth's visit, Cindy Makepeace was attacked for the second time. It would be
more baffling than the first.

At 5:10 p.m. on January 30, 1984, Ozzie Kaban was
notified by his dispatch office that strange noises were
coming from a client's home at 14th and Blenheim. Arriving at 6:05, he rapped on the front door. When no one
answered, he went around to the back. Sensing something
was wrong – he spotted Cindy's canister of dog repellent
on the back porch – he peered through an opening in the
curtains. All he could see was a blonde head of hair on the
floor. With both the front and back doors locked, he radioed his office to call police, then booted the back door
open, breaking the night latch off the frame. Cindy's keys
and purse were on the kitchen floor, which was smeared
in blood.

Cindy was lying in a twisted position on the hallway
floor, face down, fully clothed, with a paring knife stuck in
the back of her hand. Impaled by the knife was a blood-
stained note that read, "Now You Must Die Cunt," in the
familiar cut-and-paste style.

Kaban felt Cindy's body. It was cold and clammy.
Thinking she was dead, he called for an ambulance.
While waiting for its arrival, Kaban looked at Cindy and
tried to figure a likely scenario. She was probably stabbed

in the kitchen and crawled to the hallway to use the two-way radio, smearing blood as she went.

The ambulance paramedics immediately cut a black nylon tied around Cindy's neck. Kaban had not noticed it. She was rushed to hospital, where she was tested for possible brain damage, then released after midnight.

During a later interview with police, Cindy said she had arrived home from work after 5 p.m. and was coming up the back porch with her can of repellent in one hand and her keys in the other. She was just opening the back door to let Heidi in when a man came through the back gate.

"Hi," he said, sounding friendly. She thought it was a neighbour. As he bounded up the stairs Cindy noticed something in his hand. He struck her over the head. That's all she could remember.

Ozzie Kaban had a long talk with Cindy after the attack. He felt she was withholding information and wanted her to level with him. "Unless you're willing to tell me the truth, there's no use working for you."

"There would be times I would spend two or three hours talking to her. . . . I was frustrated, no question about that," Kaban recalled. "I think she fired me three or four times and I quit three or four times."

Cindy told Kaban she was too frightened to tell what happened – her attacker warned her not to tell anything to anyone, particularly the police, or he would inflict "damage" on Cindy and her family.

Kaban's persistence, however, paid off. She told him her attacker had a moustache, brown eyes and a blue nylon jacket. "You should relay this to police," Kaban urged. He also suggested Cindy take another lie-detector test to redeem herself in the eyes of the authorities.

Two days later, with Kaban's anger about withholding information echoing in her mind, she offered Bowyer-Smyth more information about her husband. "He used to be fascinated with the witch doctors in South Africa – the way they would say you would die, and you would die just by the power of suggestion. They used voodoo dolls."

She went on to explain that between July and September 1982, just after they had separated, Roy wanted her to come back to him. The only way she would return, she said, was if they both agreed to see a marriage counsellor. Roy got angry at this suggestion and a vigorous argument ensued, Cindy explained.

Near the end of June 1983, a couple of days before Cindy left for Jakarta, she and Roy were having a drink on her back patio. He was saying the trip would be good for her: she could do some thinking about their relationship and maybe they could get back together when she returned.

Cindy, however, told him that even if they went to a marriage counsellor it was probably best if they went their separate ways.

"You don't trust me," he said.

Cindy jumped up. "No, I don't Roy," she shot back. She got angry and told him to get away from her. "And I don't want you to come back."

After she had returned from Jakarta, Cindy said, Roy had seemed more depressed than angry. Most of his anger stemmed from his frustration at work – he hated bureaucracy and did not have patience with those he felt were fools, she explained. Roy warned Cindy about the kinds of things that could happen to her. Being female and alone she was very vulnerable, and it was unsafe to be alone.

On February 3, Bowyer-Smyth interviewed Cindy once more. She was staying at the Bayshore Inn, a luxury hotel on Vancouver's inner harbour where Kaban had his headquarters. He often lodged clients in hotel rooms if they needed protection and used a nearby apartment as a "safe house."

Bowyer-Smyth wanted to clarify who had keys to Cindy's home. "It is my understanding that your dead-bolt key was on a ring with the rest of your keys inside, near the rear door by your purse on the floor. That key is brass. Also on the floor near the purse was this key, which is aluminum." He said he had learned that Agnes Woocock also had a key.

"Who installed the dead-bolts and supplied the keys?"

Pat McBride had installed them, Cindy told him. He had purchased them from a lock company. A man from the company came to the house with the locks and keys and Pat installed them. "Pat gave me two brass keys . . . he said they were the only keys. This was at the first part of May '83. Near the end of June I gave Agnes Woodcock one of the keys so she could look after my plants and she stayed at my place. I took the other key with me when I went to Jakarta. After I returned, I phoned Agnes and told her I needed her key for my parents who were coming. Agnes said she had another key cut. I got a key from Agnes and later my mother returned it to me. I thought I only had one spare on a ring." Cindy had accounted for all the keys.

Later that same day, Bowyer-Smyth contacted Dr. Makepeace by phone, telling him he would like to discuss Cindy's problems, not at the moment, but in the near future. Makepeace said he had been trying to get in touch with his wife for days and had been unable to reach her; he had phoned Cindy's employer and was told she had been attacked. Bowyer-Smyth confirmed it, but provided no details. Cindy was safe, he said.

The detective next interviewed Adrei Danyliu, the B.C. Hydro manager who was in charge of overseeing Makepeace's department. Danyliu explained that in the early summer of 1983, Makepeace confided in him "with a spontaneous outburst of tears" that Cindy was being subjected to a "diabolical campaign of terror." Makepeace had gone into details of phone calls, letters and the attack of January 1983, Danyliu said.

Bowyer-Smyth, wishing to probe deeper into Makepeace's background, contacted Interpol, which in turn contacted police in South Africa, who began to make inquiries.

On February 8, nine days after the second attack on Cindy, Bowyer-Smyth received confirmation that Makepeace had a firearm registered in his name: a Browning

.22-calibre handgun. Detectives had also made discreet inquiries among people Makepeace knew and associated with. Police also sought permission for a warrant to search Makepeace's home. The application, however, was turned down on February 10 by the Attorney-General's department; Crown counsel felt there was not enough concrete evidence to implicate Makepeace as a suspect.

Thinking now that direct confrontation might be the only way to get the truth, Bowyer-Smyth phoned Makepeace on February 14, asking if he could come into the Oakridge police detachment to talk about Cindy.

"Sure," Roy said. "I'll knock off at 4:30 p.m. and be been there by 5."

He was greeted by Bowyer-Smyth and introduced to another plainclothes officer, Bob Law, the sergeant in charge of the city's south-side detectives. Makepeace was led to a small interview room, where he took a seat on a wooden chair. The venetian blinds on the one window were closed.

"What do you think this is all about?" Bowyer-Smyth asked calmly and sympathetically, his facial expression offering concern as he spoke.

"I don't know. You tell me," said Makepeace, baffled.

The officers explained, in vague detail, that Cindy had been attacked for a second time. She said that two men had hit her over the head.

Makepeace told the officers that he believed the Mafia were behind Cindy's problems. Cindy, in her line of work, often had children removed from families. Maybe she had some child removed from a Mafia family.

Both Law and Bowyer-Smyth stared emotionlessly at Makepeace. They were watching for tell-tale signs – nervous twitches, avoidance of eye contact – but the doctor seemed fairly cool.

Law, who had yet to speak a word, leaned forward in his chair and said: "Well, you know, Dr. Makepeace, would you be interested in what I think about it?"

"Yeah, I sure the hell would," replied Makepeace, anticipating some enlightenment about what was happening to Cindy.

"Well, Dr. Makepeace, I think you're very clever, but you're not going to get away with it," Law said in a no-nonsense tone.

Makepeace laughed nervously. Law's face, however, showed he was not joking. He stared unblinkingly at Makepeace, waiting for a reply.

"Don't laugh, Dr. Makepeace," Bowyer-Smyth chimed in. "I have some evidence here that you might be interested in." He pulled out a few sheets of paper and flashed them briefly before Makepeace. "Do you recognize this handwriting? Well, Cindy doesn't know we've got these papers."

"Very interesting, but what are these papers?" Makepeace asked, recognizing Cindy's handwriting.

"Well, . . . let me read a couple of excerpts here: 'And when he started to beat on me . . . and he hit me on the head with an ashtray and when I hid under the bed. . . .' "

"Yeah, go on," Roy said, shifting in his chair, which suddenly seemed extremely hard. Feeling his blood pressure rise, he loosened his tie.

"How do you explain this?" Bowyer-Smyth asked.

"Christ, I've got no explanation for that whatsoever," Makepeace replied.

"Well, that's not good enough for us, Dr. Makepeace."

Makepeace denied that he was involved in Cindy's problems in any way. "I hit Cindy once or twice, maybe three times during our marriage, but with a flat open hand when she verbally abused me. I didn't beat her. I haven't touched her since we separated. I've never pointed a loaded gun at her head, which you tell me she told you in a flood of tears. Cindy really said that?"

"Bullshit," said Law. "Don't give us this crap."

Makepeace jolted upright. He was a doctor and not accustomed to being treated this way. His blood pressure leapt. He was outraged, realizing that he was not just a suspect but the one and only suspect, or so it appeared.

Law and Bowyer-Smyth continued to question Makepeace. "Cut the crap," they told him. "Be straight with us. The game's up, Dr. Makepeace."

The interrogation went on for close to six hours. At its end, Makepeace had not uttered one incriminating statement. Law and Bowyer-Smyth told him he was free to leave.

Just before Makepeace left the room, Bob Law looked him square in the eye. "You and Cindy tell totally different stories," he said. "One of you is lying, and I'm going to find out which one."

SEVEN

Banished

POLICE, of course, could not rule out the possibility of Makepeace's involvement in Cindy's troubles. Particularly at the onset of investigations, ex-spouses are invariably considered prime suspects in certain crimes. But did Makepeace have any compelling motive?

At the same time, investigators wondered if a complete stranger, some nut-case, had latched onto Cindy. Was he torturing her for twisted pleasure? Suppose Cindy had another side no one knew about. The notes, the phone calls, the black stockings – they all had sexual overtones. Was she having kinky sex with a secret lover? Or was she involved in the drug scene, being blackmailed, maybe, by a drug addict, perhaps someone she knows?

Bowyer-Smyth and Bob Law had spent many late nights in the office, tossing around scenarios, suspects, possibilities, trying to make sense of Cindy's ever-thickening file. Continually in their minds was the suspicion that Cindy was faking the incidents, trying to draw attention to herself. Did she have a cop fetish? It was not unusual that an officer would attend a report of a break-and-enter and be met by a woman dressed in a flimsy negligee, interested in more than her stolen TV set. It was one of the hazards of the job, and women officers got the same come-ons as their male counterparts.

Cindy, however, just did not come across that way. There was nothing to suggest she was playing games. She appeared totally honest and sincere. She also seemed to lack the sophistication and technical expertise to carry out the complex variety of incidents reported to police.

This led to a spin-off theory: was there an accomplice involved? McBride himself came under suspicion. The harassment of Cindy had started right around the time he came on the scene. His colleagues even went so far as to administer a polygraph test to McBride before ruling him out.

In a lighter moment, one policeman suggested that Cindy's little dog Heidi was orchestrating the terror.

A homicide case was easier to comprehend. Somebody gets killed and you find the person who did it. It takes digging, determination, maybe years to solve, but the ground rules were always the same. Only the players and circumstances changed.

Every theory had the same problem. There was a lack of concrete evidence to prove it. Why could police never find a single tell-tale piece of evidence, one tiny fingerprint that would lead to a suspect? Cindy's case had a confounding elusiveness, a dream-like quality that seemed to drift out of reach.

Still, Cindy was not claiming aliens from outer space had landed and attacked her. Everything that happened – and her explanations of what occurred – was plausible, consistent with how twisted criminal minds operate.

One day, frustrated by too many late nights on the case, Law shook his head wearily. "I think I'll try to get the film rights to this one."

Two days after the interrogation of Makepeace, Bowyer-Smyth went back to interview Danyliu, Makepeace's supervisor, who said Roy had displayed a lot of stress when relating his lengthy questioning by police. Roy had also mentioned he was seeing a psychologist, Danyliu said.

Kaban contacted Bowyer-Smyth around the same time to tell him that Makepeace had phoned Otto Hack to arrange a meeting, but Hack had put him off. Cindy, meanwhile, was staying with her sister Melanie in Victoria, the province's capital on Vancouver Island.

On February 17, 1984, Makepeace sent a four-page letter to Cindy, telling her how shocked he had been to hear of the second attack, which he said he had learned about almost a full week after it took place.

"At least three of my predictions appeared to be correct," he wrote, "in spite of contrary opinions voiced by some others: that is, he would persist; when he traced you [to your new home] he would study the new situation . . . to identify all visitors, cars, workplaces, habits of shopping, coming and going. When he strikes again it will be like a whirlwind coming out of the woodwork."

Makepeace told Cindy that during his interrogation, police revealed a variety of statements and facts that shocked him more than the attack itself, including the police belief that "I am not only a suspect . . . but the only suspect." By spending all their time investigating him, police were being diverted from doing adequate surveillance "which would have apprehended the party responsible by now!" He also noted police were doing damage to his reputation "by interrogating my social network and my business superiors."

He went on to itemize the things police said she had told them about him during and after their marriage. "Either the law-enforcement people are lying in order to pressure me into some kind of confession, phoney or otherwise, in order to cover their own incompetence to produce genuine results . . . or your psychopathology is far deeper and more pervasive throughout your personality than has ever been realized by anybody, including myself. If you have made these claims, and still stand by them, then I can only reply that your sanity is at stake; in fairness to yourself, you should absolutely ensure that you submit to the finest psychiatric care that your parents can afford."

Makepeace's letter informed Cindy that he had retained a top-notch lawyer, who advised him not to discuss anything further with police unless formal charges were laid, and only to communicate with Cindy "in the presence of a witness whom I trust."

He added: "I cannot blame you for being in your present emotional state. I can only reiterate that you must take every opportunity to get well, and the hell with pride and vanity. . . . We are all caught up in the agony of this protracted affair. So far there's only one person laughing; let us resolve to close ranks and pull together so that he won't laugh any more!"

He signed the letter, "With Love, as always, From Your Husband and Next-of-Kin who has always stood by you in troubled times, Roy."

The next day, Makepeace decided to fire off a letter to Bowyer-Smyth, responding to the police allegations, "in the spirit of cooperation." He repeated his willingness to undertake a polygraph test "if your qualified operator is prepared to waive his avowed ethical code regarding not testing clients who routinely use prescriptions drugs such as Isordil (anti-spasmodic) and Inderal (anti-arrhythmic agent)."

In the eight-page, typewritten letter, Makepeace explained he was very tired, had been having trouble sleeping since the interrogation, and was seeing a "senior" psychiatrist. Once again, he reiterated his denial that he was involved in Cindy's "problems."

He did admit that he slapped Cindy two times during the marriage. "I have always deplored such violence, which degrades both parties involved," he wrote, "even though . . . it is provoked by persistent and vehement verbal abuse. In a later and more rational discussion, Cindy held the view that verbal abuse is fair game and that there is never any justification for physical violence no matter what the provocation might be. I can only reply that the world at large disagrees; it takes two to tango, and both parties are equally responsible to discontinue any trends that commonly lead to violence."

Lapsing into his role as social scientist, Makepeace suggested that Cindy's fear of him and her irrational anger were "deep-seated" within the "substrate" of her personality, and had existed since childhood. He offered the theory that his estranged wife's unresolved fear and anger were strongly repressed into her subconscious mind and should be explored by a therapist, not by police. He further noted that Cindy had a "total inability to come to terms with the concept of death." Cindy was not even able to watch a public-service TV advertisement for life jackets in which a child drowns.

He also wrote that Cindy may be experiencing guilt stemming from a number of things in the marriage. He explained that birth control pills aggravated "and maybe initiated" her facial skin disorder, so he had had a vasectomy to discontinue her use of the pill. The vasectomy, Roy noted, led to a "gross reduction in mutual gratification in sexual matters," which served as "a vortex to suck in any and all other dissatisfactions, tensions, feelings of lowered self-worth, etc. . . . Not forgetting that the vasectomy also negated all future choice whether to have children."

He recommended police not delve into that territory, but leave it to highly trained professional therapists, "especially when the patient is so fragile after a repeated attack by a malevolent intruder."

In closing, Roy wrote: "I feel that a maximal, unrelenting effort at surveillance of both Cindy's house, her work site and of myself should be made. . . . I would welcome the implementation of any such comprehensive plan to tighten surveillance all around until the malevolent individual perpetrating this bizarre persecution of Cindy is apprehended, identified and put away."

After finishing the letter, Roy had second thoughts about sending it to Bowyer-Smyth. He had had enough of the police. He wrote "cancel now" in the margin beside his offer of allowing surveillance of his home and his phone line, then sent the letter to Cindy's father with a hand-written covering note.

It read: "My feeling is that Cindy requires far more protection from investigators (as I do, myself) than she is capable of realizing in her present situation. . . . I have come to the conclusion that with 'friends' like them [the police] nobody needs any enemies; you've got your hands full already! . . . I feel that these people are entirely out of their league on matters of personality disturbance, etc., and I emphasize here that it is not only Cindy's life that is at stake, but her long-term mental health!"

On February 20, Kaban contacted police to advise that Cindy was going to visit her mother on Vancouver Island and she wanted to return to work the following week. Bowyer-Smyth advised Cindy not to have any contact with her estranged husband.

Once Cindy returned to Vancouver, she moved into Kaban's "safe house" apartment in the West End, a densely populated area of Vancouver dominated by high-rise apartment buildings. But Cindy wanted to return home. On March 1, Kaban's firm installed a two-way radio for emergencies and a burglar alarm system in her home at 3293 West 14th. Vancouver police also installed a "silent sentry" that was connected via phone lines to the communications centre of the police station, where it would be monitored by the police dispatcher. Cindy phoned Roy and told him to stay away and not communicate with her. Then she moved back home March 2.

Bowyer-Smyth, who eventually received a copy of the letter Makepeace sent to Otto Hack, phoned Cindy's husband and tried to take him up on his written offer to take another polygraph. Makepeace stated he did not wish to have any contact with police and referred the detective to his lawyer, George McIntosh. He later wrote a letter to Bowyer-Smyth, saying, "our client, Dr. Makepeace, will not be taking the polygraph test. I point out that Dr. Makepeace elected not to take the test based entirely on my advice. My advice was based, in turn, on the fact that Dr. Makepeace continues to be under the medication which you described to me as the basis for the test not having been administered at an earlier stage."

Cindy sent a terse, business-like letter to Roy on March 12, explaining that her employee benefits were changing; another company was taking over her medical and dental plan coverage. She enclosed the forms and asked him to fill them out.

On March 14, Cindy's parents went to the Oakridge police substation to discuss their daughter's case. They were concerned that Makepeace had phoned Melanie to ask her to come to Vancouver to attend the symphony with him.

Later that morning, Otto Hack phoned Roy and arranged to meet him for coffee at 10:30 at a doughnut shop less than a block from Makepeace's home.

The meeting started out quite friendly as they exchanged information about Cindy's case. Makepeace also recounted to Hack that he had watched a recent CBC television show, *the fifth estate*, which had featured an interview with Cecil Kirby, a former contract killer employed by organized crime in Canada until he had turned police informant. Maybe, Roy suggested, a Mafia type like Kirby could be behind Cindy's attacks.

As he got up to leave, Hack informed Makepeace that, from now on, any contact with the family had to be made through him alone. Makepeace was surprised, but agreed to the request. He mentioned that his boat was moored on Saltspring Island and he planned to go sailing with Cindy's brother Doug in the summer.

"Yeah, but that's a few months away," Hack said. He hoped that the case would be resolved before then, and intimated that an arrest was imminent.

"Christ, Otto, they think that's me!" Roy said. "They think they're going to arrest me!"

He tried to emphasize that everyone was cutting him off and he was the only truly effective resource person Cindy had. As Hack paid the bill, Makepeace said, "Otto, this is really serious. I'm not at all sure that I haven't seen my wife alive for the last time already." Hack took a step backwards, his face turning ashen grey as he stared at his son-in-law.

Roy did not realize it at the time, but his meeting with Otto Hack marked the end of virtually all communication with Cindy and her family. He was the main suspect, and was now being banished from her life until police could resolve the matter.

Later that day, Makepeace detailed his Mafia theory in a letter to Cindy's father. He wrote that Cecil Kirby, the underworld hit man, revealed a "mentality and modus operandi that fits Cindy's case well." As examples, he quoted Kirby saying his victims "'never see a face; they never know what hit them. . . . I feel nothing at all. It's just a job to be done.'"

Kirby, Makepeace noted, said he charged $1,000 for beating someone up and $10,000 for a contract killing. Roy suggested a mother may have taken out a "revenge contract" on Cindy because she had been involved in a Family Court case to remove a child from a home. He noted "both series of harassments appear to have commenced around August each year," which, he suggested, may be some kind of anniversary date – either the child's birthday or when the child was removed from the home. He urged police to check the Blenheim House files for relevant cases.

He also offered an "alternative (less likely) scenario" that might go further back, before Cindy was hired at Blenheim House. "Suppose Cindy was the only person who ever really got emotionally close to a very disturbed 10-year-old male kid, say, 15 years ago; he would be about 25 years of age right now. Like Johnny Guitar, who became a habitual criminal and was apparently stabbed to death by a cell mate not too long ago. Maybe the cell mate and/or other inmates not only got fed up with Johnny, but also got fed up hearing about this 'Cindy' person that he mentioned . . . too often. Now that Johnny's dead they can't get to him any more, but any one who's free now can take out their frustrations on Cindy, like a sort of displaced revenge."

In closing, Roy wrote that he was angry at police, whom he felt had pressured Cindy "unduly in a 'captive' situation and, I believe, she is developing a hostage mentality like Patty Hearst. It is not just for her physical danger I fear! You are the only one who has access to her; you are the only one that can keep a watchful eye on this aspect. I have been cut off as a resource person to her. I know she will miss it!"

Two days later, Makepeace wrote his estranged wife a more wistful letter. "Hi Chicky," it began. "Last night I heard [pan flutist] Zamfir and the Vancouver Symphony Orchestra in the Orpheum. It was magnificent. Unfortunately, I had an empty seat next to me and they were first-class seats (at $26.50 apiece!) as you can see from your unused ticket . . . I thought of you every minute, and I cried back home. It's lonely without my soul-mate at that type of very special performance; I greatly miss our weekly visits. . . .

"I guess you were under orders to keep bluffing me that there had been no contact from the Mafia in the latter half of 1983. Not very smart, though, because I could have blundered right into something vicious, totally unsuspecting, when going to the garage in your absence, as I have done at times. . . . " He went on to expound the theory that somehow Cindy had tampered with a Mafia family's child. "This is one of three things the Mafia does not tolerate and they plan to take revenge; 'equivalent misery' is the name of the game." There were definite similarities, he maintained, between her campaign of terror and a typical Mafia pattern. "Remember how the big burly guy was 'taken out' in *The Godfather* – back of the hand pinned to the counter, for starters; drug injections to induce addiction and ensuing psycho-social dysfunction and vulnerability; dead animals – or the limb of a loved one tucked in your bed – next time, maybe? Remember the shock of discovering the slit-up pillow case? These are all typical Mafia terror tactics."

He signed the letter, "Much Love, as always, Roy."

The next day, Cindy turned over to police the last letter her husband had sent to her father, plus another letter and card Roy had sent her. She was extremely upset. Police advised her to get a no-contact restraining order against him.

Makepeace wrote his wife another letter March 23. "Hi Loopy," he wrote, using another term of endearment from years ago. He explained that her London Life insurance bill had been mistakenly sent to his address. He lamented that he had not heard from her. "I never even know for sure whether you even receive the mail that I send to you. However, I guess you have your own strange reasons for such lengthy silence, punctuated by only two brief technical communications in nearly two months, neither of them expressing any sentiment or empathy in what is not only a mutual problem of the greatest gravity, but has become a family-wide problem of great concern to all involved." He signed it simply "Roy."

On March 26, Makepeace wrote Cindy a longer letter, this time telling her he had "new information" that might provide police with a fresh lead.

"A social worker phoned me yesterday afternoon out of the blue," he wrote. "She wanted to know if you had ever come across a fellow (e.g., in the singles bar with Colleen) named 'Trevor' – she cannot be sure of his last name, but we aim to find out during the rest of this week . . . some totally unrelated enquiries of hers yesterday suddenly reminded her of this whole episode, and how there seemed to be some reasonable similarities. . . . The more I heard, the more I agreed, and so I questioned her further this morning. . . .

"The social worker's house now has no tenants and she had been phoning around via certain contacts with a view to acquiring a tenant, when one of these contacts mentioned a nanny whose brother was Trevor. She got cold chills as this name brought back vivid memories of eight or nine years ago, when a blonde pal of hers, in her early forties, was briefly involved with this fellow (Trevor ——) who brought down a reign of terror on her that has many similarities in style (or behavioural pattern) as the perpetrator of your unhappy situation."

He enclosed three pages of notes from his conversation with the social worker. The notes outlined for Cindy that Trevor was in his early-to-late fifties, was good looking, and had been employed as a gardener in the Vancouver area. The social worker described him as "charming on the surface but obviously harbouring a lot of suppressed anger and quite sadistic in his retaliatory methods; e.g., destroying potted plants, snipping her clothing, etc."

The man prefers good-looking blondes, Roy noted, like the social worker's friend, whom Trevor dated eight or nine years ago. He threatened the woman's life several times and also threatened the social worker by phone when she called her blonde friend to warn her of his plans. The social worker feels she saved her friend's life by warning her "and she is still scared as hell to this day that this fellow will cross her path one day" so she did not want her name mentioned.

Trevor, Roy explained, tried to strangle the blonde more than once and would cut up her clothing to emphasize his threats when she would not cooperate. Potted plants were her hobby and Trevor would cut them all down in anger to spite her. He is a "local boy," Roy wrote, with an RCMP background. "Remember that three of your calls were traced to the Kits-Kerrisdale-Richmond longitude line."

Trevor and the blonde lived together for a short period, and after they broke up he was very adept at obtaining her unlisted phone numbers. He would phone and threaten her. When the blonde changed her locks – she was living on West 11th in Vancouver – he climbed in through a window to await her arrival home; the social worker had called the house and he told her he planned to kill her friend. She phoned her friend and warned her not to go home.

The blonde, Roy went on, initiated a court action against Trevor because she was in fear of her life. The social worker agreed to give testimony but was never called to the witness stand because the trial was "quashed by a senior judge (whose name is still very well remembered by the social worker, who won't tell me, not yet, anyway) writing a character reference for this fellow, so all she got for protection was a peace bond being issued for them to stay away from each other!"

Police would eventually try to investigate this information, but since Makepeace refused to talk without his lawyer present, police never interviewed him to get further details.

On March 29 at 1 p.m., Cindy went to take her third polygraph. This time it was conducted by an RCMP officer, Sergeant Cal Hood, who talked with Cindy for close to ten minutes before the test, explaining the procedure, trying to get her to relax and not relive the events of her past. These would upset her and possibly have a negative affect on the test results.

Finally, Hood began to ask his questions.

"On January 30, did you stab yourself in the hand?"

"No."

"Did you tie a stocking around your neck?"

"No."

"Did you make the note?"

"No."

Hood judged Cindy to be telling the truth. Afterwards, Cindy seemed very emotional, yet relieved. Hood talked to her for another 45 minutes. "She responded to me as I would expect a victim who has suffered a traumatic incident," Hood would recall six years later. "She wondered if the assaults would continue and where it would all end."

EIGHT

Chopped Bodies

BEGINNING in May 1984, Kaban started Cindy on a "reporting" system – she would phone his office before leaving the house and call again when she had arrived safely at her office. She repeated the routine when going home and if she was going out in the evening, even to walk the dog. Kaban felt that whoever was after Cindy would seize upon any opportunity to terrorize her.

On May 15, Cindy turned over to police the additional letters she and her father had received from Roy. She also reported she had received eight no-talk calls in the last three weeks. Six days later, Kaban employee Steven Cox found Cindy's telephone lines cut. Cindy's office also began to receive calls that month. A "Brad Clark" called at 2:45 p.m. one day and asked for Cindy. When the call was transferred through, he hung up. Three days later, roughly the same time of day, Cindy picked up the receiver. A male voice told her, "You're dead," then hung up.

Blenheim House secretary Denise Perkins got a call one morning about 9:30 a.m. from a Greg "Lihan or Liner," asking for Cindy. When she transferred the call, the man called Cindy a "fucking cunt, bitch, whore." He ordered: "Get rid of the big pig or we'll take him out too."

"Who is this?" Cindy asked.

"You'll know, fucking cunt, but it'll be too late," replied the hoarse voice. The man laughed before slamming the phone down.

Cindy received another strange call later in May. A man, identifying himself as Sergeant Fisk of the Vancouver police department, said he wanted to see her at 4:30 p.m. at her home. To be on the safe side, Cindy phoned police and learned that "Sgt. Fisk" did not exist. Police staked out Cindy's home but the fictitious Fisk did not show up.

During the first week of June, Cindy discovered some new stereo equipment, still in factory boxes, sitting on top of the compost box in her back yard. Frightened, she phoned police. Constable Hugh Campbell investigated. Cindy showed him the stereo receiver and cassette deck. One of Kaban's employees, Brian Lee, was also there. He explained he had been doing surveillance of Cindy's house and had driven down the lane at 1:15 p.m. but he had not noticed the boxes then. Cindy found them about 2:30.

While police were examining the goods, Roy Makepeace pulled up in his 1979 four-door Caprice. He went into Cindy's garage and began to load boxes into his car. He said he had notified Kaban's company earlier in the day that he was coming over to remove some of his belongings. Cindy had written her final letter to Roy in May, asking him to vacate her garage by the end of June and "not come onto my property at any time except by prior arrangement with Kaban Enterprises to remove your stored belongings." It appeared Roy had abided by her request. Police tried tracing the owner of the stereo equipment, but without success.

Cindy arrived home from work June 18 about 5:30 p.m., had dinner and started to work in the front garden. It was a bright, warm summer evening, with the flowers in bloom and the sun slanting through the branches of the large chestnut trees that stood sentry along the boulevard at the front of her house.

Cindy had left the back basement door open to allow easy access to her gardening tools, and her dog Heidi was trotting behind her as she went to and from the basement to get yet another tool. About 8:30 p.m., Cindy heard Heidi barking in the back yard. Probably just yapping at neighbours, she thought.

About 45 minutes passed when she realized she had not seen Heidi for some time. Cindy called the dog, but still no Heidi. Worried, she went around to the back of the house and saw her basement door was closed. Thinking someone was lying in wait for her inside, she used a neighbour's phone to call Kaban.

When Steven Cox arrived minutes later, Cindy was standing in front of her house. "Heidi's missing!" she told him. She was crying, trembling. Cox told her to get in the car and they would watch the house and wait for Ozzie, who pulled up minutes later. Another Kaban employee arrived simultaneously. Kaban opened the basement door and saw a note on the floor nearby. The jumble of words, cut from magazines and pasted at jarring angles, had become a signature of sorts. In its free-associative style, it read: "Fuck. Last Days. Warning. Run. Death. Happy Birthday. Love."

In a corner of the basement Kaban found Heidi cowering under a chair, soiled by its own feces. The dog was cut, bruised and had a cord around its neck. Although the cord was not tied to anything, it obviously provided a psychological restraint – the dog would not budge from its smelly, captive lair. "The animal seemed to be in some kind of shock," Ozzie recalls. He cut the animal loose and it ran outside into Cindy's arms. Kaban knew Cindy loved her dog like a surrogate child and would never mistreat it. She even took Heidi to Blenheim House and let the children feed her at snack time.

Kaban and his men checked the house and found a Rothman's cigarette butt on the basement floor. It was not Cindy's brand – she smoked Cameo Menthols. Another Rothman's stub was on the windowsill of the front basement bedroom, which offered a clear view of where Cindy had been working in the front garden. Kaban felt someone had been lying in wait for Cindy inside, using Heidi as bait.

A week later, at about 4 a.m. on June 23, Cindy heard a loud bang at the rear of the house. Peering outside she saw the back gate hanging open. She phoned Kaban, who came over in the morning about 11:00 A dead cat with a cord around its neck was discovered in the basement stairwell.

The following night, Cindy went out about 8:00. Returning home at 9:30 she found the two floodlights at the rear of her house had been unscrewed. Again, the back gate was left open.

On June 25, Kaban installed a TV camera in Cindy's garage that viewed the back door and the gate. It was connected to a closed-circuit TV monitor and a video recorder in her bedroom. "I realized she was short of funds," Kaban recalls. "But it's difficult to tell somebody, 'Sorry, you can't pay your bill. Go ahead and die.'" He figured he had been hired to provide her with proper protection and he would work out the bill later. Until then, it would come out of his own pocket.

After the scare with Heidi, police also put a "special attention" designation on Cindy's home, increasing patrols on the afternoon and night shifts. Again, all was quiet during that time. Cindy received two no-talk calls at work, five minutes apart, on June 26. Kaban, who was at Cindy's home that day, also received a no-talk call while Cindy was at work.

The elusiveness of the person behind Cindy's ordeal was becoming more exasperating by the day for Kaban, his employees, police and Cindy, who was losing faith in the authorities' ability to catch her tormentor.

Another week passed without incident. Then on July 1, Cindy was awakened after 3 a.m. by her dog's growling and barking. Five minutes later, the doorbell rang. Cindy flicked on the front porch light. She saw a man's face extremely close to the "peep hole" of her front door.

"Vancouver City," the man called out. "We've had a call of a prowler in the area of your house. We want to talk about it with you."

Cindy said that she had not called police. The man said he could not hear her. At this point, she noticed the back of a second man standing on the porch.

"We're the Vancouver police, could we come in and talk with you?" the man asked, raising his voice slightly.

"I can't see you," Cindy told him, nervously. "Would you go around to the back so I can see who you are?" The man repeated that he could not hear her, so she shouted her request that he go around the back. She went to her bedroom to watch the TV monitor, but no one came in the back yard. Panicking, she tried the telephone. The line was dead. She radioed Kaban for help, and his office called police. Cindy told the investigating officers that the man at the peep hole had dark hair and a moustache. She could not provide a very good description because his face was so close that it was distorted by the "fish eye" effect of the lens. She could only provide the barest description of the second man: he had dark hair.

The telephone company rewired Cindy's lines the next day, relocating them higher on the side of the house so they would not be accessible without a ladder. While at Cindy's house that afternoon, Bowyer-Smyth answered the phone. It was a no-talk call.

On July 9, Cindy's mother Tillie was staying overnight, as she often did to help alleviate her daughter's fear. At 2:30 a.m., Heidi began to bark. Cindy heard a loud bang half an hour later. She checked on her mother in the downstairs bedroom. Looking outside, they saw no one was there. Later they discovered the front window was cracked in concentric circles, indicating it had been struck from the outside, probably from the porch. The phone line to her bedroom had also been cut. A police dog was sent to track the property but no trace was found.

Having had a strict religious upbringing, Cindy now began to question why God was allowing the terror to continue. "I spent a lot of time with her," Tillie Hack recalled. "She would say to me, 'Why is God letting these things happen to me?' And I would just try to say to her, 'Well, I don't think God is involved. . . . Why are there airplane crashes? Why are there starving children?'"

Two days later, on July 11, Heidi began barking about 4 p.m. while Cindy was gardening in the front yard. An overweight man ran north between Cindy's yard and her neighbour's. She failed to get a glimpse of his face, but he had dark hair and was dressed in jogging attire – white running shoes, white shorts, white T-shirt. She passed the information along to police.

Cindy received more hang-up calls two days later. Then, on July 15, Cindy heard a loud bang like a cymbal crash at 1:45 a.m., followed by the sound of footsteps between the houses. About 45 minutes passed, then her doorbell rang. Again, the doorstep was empty, but Cindy saw a silver-grey car parked on the street behind her car. A man walked toward Cindy's car, stopped beside it, looked toward the house, waved, then drove off. He reminded Cindy of the fat man she had seen earlier running alongside the house. She tried to call Kaban but her phone line had been cut.

Each snip of the wire-cutters was snapping another taut strand of Cindy's nerves.

On July 19 she got two silent calls after 1 a.m. At work later that same day, a man telephoned at 1:20. "You're dead, bitch, and it's going to feel good," he said, then hung up.

Clearly, the latest campaign of terror was escalating. Finding it almost impossible to sleep, Cindy was became more distraught and fatigued. She was having trouble pulling herself together to go to work each morning. Then a caller would phone her at work, and she would be anxious for the remainder of the day.

Although Cindy's patience was stretched thin, her friends and colleagues were amazed that she was holding up as well as she was. She was determined not to let the terror get the best of her. One day soon, she kept saying, she would live a normal life.

At 8:30 p.m. on July 23, Cindy phoned Kaban's office to say she was going to take Heidi for a walk. She would be gone about an hour and would call upon her return. When two hours passed without Cindy calling in, Kaban drove by her house and became concerned when he saw that her car was not parked on the street beside her house. He notified his employees that Cindy was missing and immediately called police.

Just after midnight, a Kaban operative heard a call on the police scanner in his car: an ambulance was needed for suspected strangulation at a house on West 33rd. Kaban got there before police, to find ambulance paramedics examining Cindy on the living-room couch.

The couple who lived there, Rosie and Regan Trethewey, thought Kaban was a detective since he barged into their home without knocking or introducing himself. Said Rosie: "I thought [Cindy] was a hooker and she had been assaulted by a bad trick. Her eyes were bugged out from being strangled."

In recounting the incident, Regan Trethewey said he had heard somebody trying to push open his front door, which would not open more than a few centimetres because of a restraining safety chain. Rosie, who had just come home from hospital with their new-born baby, urged her husband not to open the door. "Regan, if it's a drunk don't let him in."

Trethewey looked out the window of the front door to see a blonde woman standing there, trying to say something – she was mouthing words but making no sound, just grabbing at her throat. She appeared dazed, ready to pass out.

Trethewey noticed she had something tied around her neck. He ran to the kitchen, grabbed a knife and went outside to try to cut what was a dark nylon wrapped twice around Cindy's neck and over her blonde hair. It was so tight he couldn't get his fingers under it. Finally, he managed to cut the nylon as Cindy collapsed in the doorway.

He picked her up and carried her to the couch. She seemed incoherent, but then suddenly asked where her dog was. The Tretheweys remembered a little dog had run in the open front door and out again. Eventually, Kaban found Heidi outside, then followed the ambulance to nearby University Hospital, where he asked the attending emergency physician or possibly an ambulance paramedic – he cannot remember whom he spoke with – to check Cindy's arms for needle marks.

"I thought possibly the assailants were using drugs on her when they were doing whatever they were doing to her," Kaban said. He had seen two fresh needle punctures on the inside of Cindy's right arm when she arrived at hospital.

As hospital staff undressed her, they came upon twigs and leaves inside her underpants. Cindy provided no explanation. She remembered nothing other than that, earlier in the evening, she had stopped to talk to two people in a van.

When Dr. John Kent, a resident physician, examined Cindy, she was lying on a stretcher with an oxygen mask covering her mouth. Drowsy, unable to breathe properly, she had puffiness around the edges of the eyes and broken blood vessels on the right side of her neck – a normal effect from strangulation. Cindy found it quite painful to swallow. Kent also noted her right ankle was tender and there was a small clustering of blood in her right nostril. However, he saw none of the mysterious needle marks that Kaban had.

Cindy initially appeared quite calm and talkative, smiling after a few minutes and remembering Dr. Kent's name, even though he was not wearing a name tag. Seven hours later, however, when she was examined again, Kent was surprised to find his patient weepy, highly distressed and reticent. He wondered if she had been drugged. Cindy replied that she had taken an Ativan tranquilizer within the last three days, but she was not taking any other drugs or medication.

Kaban later helped police search Dunbar Park, which has heavily wooded sections, two kilometres west of Cindy's house. A drag mark was found in the dirt about 10 metres from a sidewalk. They also retrieved one of Cindy's shoes and her canister of dog repellent, about 30 metres from the home where she had collapsed. A Kaban employee found Cindy's car in the Dunbar Park Community Centre parking lot.

Hospital tests showed the presence of benzodiazepine, a Valium-type prescription sedative, in Cindy's blood. Ativan is a type of benzodiazapine. The tests, however, were only qualitative, not quantitative, so it was not determined how much of the drug was in her system.

After the attack, Kaban wrote a letter to Bowyer-Smyth, telling him that drugs had been injected in Cindy's right arm and that drugs may have been involved in the January 30 attack.

Noting that benzodiazepine had been found in her system after the July 23 episode, Kaban suggested that if it had been injected, it would have caused "general confusion and impairment of the memory . . . it is very quick-acting." He urged police to take a very serious look at the possibility of an injection being made with a prescription or restricted drug. "And who would have access to such medication?" Kaban asked.

On July 24, Bowyer-Smyth interviewed Cindy as she lay in her hospital bed. She reiterated how she had called Kaban's firm the night of the attack. She parked at Dunbar Community Centre a few minutes after 8:30 and, since it was a warm summer evening, the park was busy. She stopped to watch people play tennis, then continued past the bowling greens. She remembered looking at her watch as she walked west on West 33rd. It was 9:05. "I was thinking I had half an hour to arrive home."

She was more than halfway down the length of the park when a dark-green van pulled alongside on West 33rd. The van had a dark, smoked-glass window on the passenger-side door, which was closest to Cindy. "The driver spoke to me through the open passenger window," she told Bowyer-Smyth. "He leaned across and said, 'Excuse me, m'am, do you know where Churchill Street is?' I started to reply. . . . The next thing I remember is talking with Dr. Kent."

The driver of the van, she said, had long dark hair, a "longish" bushy beard, and was wearing dark, squarish horn-rimmed glasses. A woman with blonde hair was beside the driver, but Cindy didn't clearly see her face because she was leaning back to permit the driver to talk out the passenger window.

Later on July 24, hospital clerk Lisa Lattimore reported she had taken a strange phone call. Calling in on one of the few numbers that could be dialled directly, without going through the hospital switchboard, a man asked, "Do you have hospital security?"

"Who would like to know?" asked a suspicious Lattimore.

The man hesitated. "Well, do you have security guards? Do you have security staff?"

Lattimore said she was sorry, but that information could not be given out.

"What time does Emergency close?" the man queried.

"It doesn't close," Lattimore replied.

"How many floors does the hospital have?"

Concerned by these questions, Lattimore told the caller that she could connect him with her supervisor.

"No," he said, and abruptly hung up.

When Lattimore was interviewed by Bowyer-Smyth, she said the caller sounded like he had a New Zealand accent, although Lattimore had no expertise in speech patterns. "His voice seemed hurried. He seemed impatient. I might recognize his voice if I heard it again," the unit clerk said.

The detective then played a tape-recording of Roy Makepeace's voice for her. "The accent is the same," Lattimore noted, in effect making no distinction between a New Zealand and South African accent. The clerk also felt the timbre of the voice seemed similar, although "the voice on the tape is more agitated than the voice I heard on the phone. The voice on the tape seems to accentuate or stress similar words."

Bowyer-Smyth's interview with Lattimore was his final involvement in the case. With the incidents escalating in number and seriousness, the Cindy Makepeace file was transferred to the major crime section, which, as the name implies, handles the major crimes in the city – sex offences, robbery, attempted murder, suspicious deaths, and the ultimate crime, murder. Cindy's case was assigned to a young, ambitious, bright detective, Sgt. Kris Bjornerud.

For his part, Makepeace said he knew nothing of the attack until he spotted a small item in the July 26 edition of the *West Ender*, a weekly paper serving the city's downtown and west side. The one-paragraph story stated: "A leisurely stroll around the park turned into a nightmare for Cynthia Makepiece [*sic*] Tuesday evening . . . when she was attacked from behind and strangled with a pair of pantyhose. The incident took place about 12:08. Police have no suspect in custody but are treating the attack as attempted murder. Makepiece is in stable condition in UBC Hospital."

Roy thought it ridiculous that the newspaper reported where Cindy was recuperating. "It was like saying to her attackers, 'Come and get her, finish her off.'"

Earlier he had received a letter from his daughter Gwen, telling him that Interpol had contacted South African police to interview her and Roy's first wife, Lois. "Are they really going for you?" Gwen wrote. "Please keep in touch. If they arrest you, I want your phone number wherever they take you. I tried to phone your work all night after Mom said they questioned her, but your work said you're on your yacht. I hope you are. I would love to think you're having two weeks tranquil away-from-it-all sailing amongst the islands. . . . Please write as soon as you get this and tell me everything, even if you drop me one page. And if anything develops, please let me know straight away. I'll even come to Canada if it would be of any help."

Makepeace wrote a letter to his lawyer complaining of what he felt was harassment. "My first wife informed me that they had been interrogated by South African police at the request of Interpol regarding violence during our 16-year marriage. My wife's reply to them, and I quote her spontaneous words to me, was, 'They got bugger-all out of us because there's bugger-all to get.' "

Commenting on his ex-wife's language, Makepeace explained to his lawyer, "We South Africans tend to be very direct and a trifle crude in our verbal expression, and utilize hyperbole with violent overtones . . . the cultural difference is not understood here, but is easily taken as an indication of potentially violent behaviour."

In the meantime, frustrated by Cindy's poor recall of the July attack, Kaban asked his client to try hypnosis to enhance her memory of the van and the two people inside. She resisted the idea at first but finally agreed to give it a try.

The first two sessions with hypnotherapist Hal Booker, on August 8 and 28, 1984, provided some new information. Cindy recalled that it was a metallic-green Vandura van. It had chrome mirrors, a rubber pad on the bumper and a smokey-coloured air vent on top that ran three-quarters of the way down the van.

She also recalled being dragged into the van, which had carpeting in the back and several people inside. One had a mask on and removed a wig. She recalled feeling a "prick" on her arm like a needle, and she remembered hearing voices.

"Hombagosh," she heard one man say. It was, she said, a South African phrase, which roughly translated, means: "Be warned. Do as I say."

Also, during the August 8 session, Cindy recalled more details of the January 1983 attack. Booker and Kaban, however, were not prepared for the startling new material that Cindy came out with during the third session, held on October 2, 1984.

In her hypnotized state, Cindy recalled the July 1981 boating trip. She and her husband were aboard their boat, *Peacemaker*, heading toward Thormanby Island, staying the first night at Buccaneer Bay. The next day, Cindy and Roy stayed at a friend's A-frame cabin.

Cindy and Roy took the boat to go fishing the following day, she said. Her husband moored the boat on an island somewhere; she could not say where exactly because she had fallen asleep below deck for a while. She recalled Roy docking at a log boom and saying he was going to look at some property that was for sale. For an hour, Cindy stayed aboard to read a book while sunning herself on deck. Then she heard yelling. Roy's calling, she thought. She shouted back but there was no reply. Concerned, she put on her shoes and slacks and set out to find him.

Cindy said she walked up a trail to the top of a hill and came upon a little log cabin. There was a stack of firewood outside. A little roof sheltered the front porch. Knocking at the door. she received no answer. She opened the door.

"See blood," the hypnotized Cindy said. "Two people. Woman and a man. See Roy. Looks frightened."

"What the hell are you doing here?" Roy shouted.

At this point in the trance, Cindy became horrified, and was too upset to continue. "It's not safe to remember," she said.

Before bringing Cindy out of hypnosis, Booker gave her a post-hypnotic suggestion, telling her she would feel better after the session.

"When this came out it was a little overwhelming," Kaban recalls of Cindy's hypnotic experience. "I didn't know what I was getting myself into." Later, he took Cindy with him in his own airplane as he flew over the

Gulf Islands trying to pinpoint where the alleged incident had occurred. They had no luck. Cindy could not recognize the spot from the air.

At the same time, Kaban wanted police to hear Cindy repeat her story under hypnosis. A fourth session took place on January 29, 1985, at Booker's Richmond office. Bjornerud and another major-crime detective attended. Once hypnotized, Cindy was led by Booker back to the 1981 boating trip. The officers sat in silence as the hypnotized Cindy again recounted the story of the two mutilated bodies in the cabin.

This time she provided more details than before, but the essential story was the same: under hypnosis, Cindy Makepeace alleged that her husband had killed a man and a woman with an axe or a knife, then placed their dismembered remains in bags for disposal in the ocean.

The dead man in Cindy's trance appeared to be about 35 years old. He had a burn scar above the elbow, bare feet, no shirt, hair over his ears and hairy arms. The woman was about 30. She had brown hair and bare feet.

Cindy also described the cabin interior and furnishings. The room had a rough wooden floor, metal-frame beds, two white pillows, a grey blanket, a wooden cupboard stacked with paperback books, two wooden chairs, a rickety old table, writing paper, unfinished walls, a wood stove vented through the ceiling and maps on the wall.

The hypnotherapist believed that Cindy was in a true hypnotic spell. "It was very real to her. These were very, very difficult sessions for her." Booker admitted that fantasies, delusional experiences, can come out during hypnosis, but usually without the kind of emotion Cindy displayed.

Police treated Cindy's experience under hypnosis seriously, and began to check missing person files throughout B.C. to see if a man and woman, possibly a couple, had been reported missing around the time of the alleged incident. None of the people reported missing matched Cindy's descriptions.

Detective Bjornerud was skeptical of the hypnosis sessions. "I came out thinking, this may have happened." At the same time, he did not interview Makepeace about the allegations because "I wanted something more concrete." (Later, under oath, Makepeace would vigorously deny Cindy's wild allegation. Police investigations confirmed his denial.)

On April 19, Bjornerud accompanied Cindy aboard an RCMP boat for a full-day cruise of the small islands surrounding Thormanby Island. Nothing was revealed. Things had changed in the area during the four intervening years, she said. There were more houses. The spring vegetation was different than she remembered it.

Cindy's case became more bizarre by the day. On December 22, 1984, her telephone lines were cut, and large, fresh footprints were found glistening in the snow. Her lines were cut again five days later. This time there were no tracks. Meanwhile, the threatening phone calls and letters continued.

By now police were visiting Blenheim House regularly. Staff were beginning to feel the tension creep into their work environment. Women staff, especially, began to worry about their safety. A few of Cindy's colleagues talked to her about their concerns, and she tried to assure them she was the only one in danger.

Not knowing who was behind the events, however, fueled speculation at Blenheim House. Maybe, some thought, it was a deranged parent of one of the children.

Speech therapist Sue Fisk noticed Cindy had become more rigid in her therapy with her group of children, while staff began questioning Cindy's decision-making ability. Cindy's nerves were obviously frayed. She was sleeping poorly, eating improperly and smoking too much, at least a pack and a half a day. Looking haggard, her complexion was sallow, her eyes cowered in their sockets. Her terrorized expression was underlined by dark bags under her eyes.

On June 21, 1985, Kaban got a phone call from Dr. Allan Connolly, Cindy's physician, who told the detective that his client was suicidal. "I cannot go on anymore," she had said. "Suicide is the only alternative." Connolly had been prescribing Cindy sedatives and sleeping pills since 1983. He had also taught her "relaxation therapy" techniques.

Later, Connolly met Kaban at Cindy's home and they agreed she needed to go to hospital for a rest. Connolly was leaving the country on a month-long holiday and wanted to make sure she received proper attention while he was gone.

Connolly and Kaban convinced her to go to Lions Gate Hospital in nearby North Vancouver, where Dr. Paul Termansen could keep an eye on her. She was admitted to the psychiatric ward under an assumed name, Cindy Jacobs. Termansen and another psychiatrist concluded that she was severely depressed, an extreme suicide risk, in fact. Cindy admitted she had a plan to harm herself. With this in mind, the doctors committed her under the Mental Health Act, meaning she could not voluntarily leave the hospital.

Feeling betrayed, Cindy phoned her brother Doug and asked him to help her get out. She had only come for a rest, she tearfully explained, and now she was being held prisoner.

Doug took the ferry from Saltspring Island. He tried to explain to medical staff the kind of hell his sister had been going through. The cut phone lines. The dead cats. The strange notes and threatening phone calls. Cindy needs a rest, he told them, not a committal to a psych ward.

Medical staff, however, still refused to release her. Doug did manage to get Cindy a day pass and took her out for Chinese food. The following night Doug tried again to have Cindy released, but Termansen still felt she should stay for treatment.

On June 26, Doug promised that, if Cindy was released, he would spend 24 hours a day with his sister for four days. He would even bring her back if she would not eat. Psychiatrist Dr. Mark Blunderfield agreed to release Cindy to Hack's care, but she would be his entire responsibility if anything happened. Doug agreed to the terms, signed a form that stated she was being released against medical advice and took Cindy home at 6:30 p.m. Two days later, the phone lines of her home were cut.

Shortly after her hospital stay, Bjornerud met with Cindy to discuss a plan to have her phone her husband to confront him with her experiences under hypnosis. Police would tape the call.

Cindy agreed, and on July 2, 1985, she dialled Roy's number. She got his answering machine. She tried again after 10 p.m.

"Hello," Roy answered. He was watching the TV news.

"Hello, Roy," Cindy replied. Roy didn't recognize her voice at first. It had been more than a year since he had talked to her. The call took him by surprise.

"It's Cindy calling . . . um . . . because I wanted to talk to you about what's been happening over the last couple of years and, um, I've been getting, um, some psychiatric help and, um, with the help of hypnosis I've been able to remember a lot of why things are happening and . . . what happened four years ago. . . . We've been out on a police boat looking over the area and, uh, I wanted to talk to you, um, before letting police know that I now remember everything."

"Yeah?" said Roy. He sounded flustered, perplexed. Later he said he initially thought Cindy was calling to discuss the subject of divorce. "Well, um, um. It puts me in a pretty difficult spot," he told her, "just out of the blue like that. . . . Where do you propose to talk to me?"

"I'm proposing to talk right now," Cindy replied calmly.

"Oh, I see. Okay. You mean on the phone. Yeah, okay. Fair enough," said Roy as he pulled up a hassock to sit on. "You know, I don't know if you perhaps realize where I stand in all this. . . . Maybe, you know, you can only see things from your perspective, but I feel pretty badly used by the police. . . . My lawyer, uh, advises me that it would be inappropriate for me to discuss anything about this case with anybody but himself. . . . I'm just trying to explain why I feel somewhat taken broadside. . . . I really don't know what to do. I'm prepared to listen to anything because I'm certainly very, very curious about what the hell has been going on, you know, because it has affected me badly and damn nearly cost me my job. . . . It's cost me a fair amount of money with lawyer's fees, etc., and quite apart from that, let's just say I feel somewhat abused. Now I know that none of that parallels what you've been through. I'm not trying to draw comparisons or allot blame or anything else. I have got a lot of curiosity about this [but] I am also warned by what seems to me the only person who can protect me from being drawn into a lot of damage. So I will listen, by all means, uh, but . . . I don't think I have a lot to say. I will certainly listen."

"I understand that," Cindy replied, hesitating, "what I walked in on four years ago, I may have misunderstood, um, and I would like to give you the opportunity to [sigh] explain to me what happened . . . [sigh] I may have misunderstood exactly what happened . . . I guess what I can't understand is what you've been doing to me for the last couple of years."

"What I've been doing to *you* for the last couple of years?" Roy said, surprised.

"That's right."

"Like what? . . . Here I am, sitting trying to understand what *you've* been doing to *me* for the last couple of years. . . . I would like you to state what you mean by that statement."

"I think you know very well what I mean, Roy . . . " Cindy chided.

An impatient Roy cut in: "No, I don't know what you mean, and for the past year, out of those two years, I've had absolutely no contact with you at all. In fact more than

a year, probably a year and a half out of those two years.
. . . You might as well make a statement you want an
explanation [of] what I've been doing to the Queen of
England. Frankly, I've had nothing to do with her whatsoever for the past 18 months, nor you. So now, would you
explain to me what you mean by an explanation of what I
have been doing to you? . . . I mean, you know, you must
surely be able to explain that statement."

"Roy, you must know that this cannot go on indefinitely.
I don't understand . . . "

"What cannot go on? What?"

"Harassment, for one," replied Cindy, her voice rising.

"Are you attributing that to me?"

"Are you denying it?"

"My God!" he said. "I think you ought to have anything
you have to say [said] in front of my lawyer. I am certainly
denying it. I have always denied it. I have absolutely nothing whatever to do with it . . . I positively resent, uh . . . if
people go on harassing me and trying to dump this on me,
they may well end up in court because I will have to sue
for damages . . . So if I were you . . . "

"Roy, what is the point of all this?" Cindy interjected.

"Exactly, what is the point of you trying to dump this on
me? I mean, really. . . . What are you trying to do? What
do you want to achieve? What is this all about? . . . "

"I'm trying to get you to stop. And I'm trying to . . . "

"I have never done anything," Roy said. "There is nothing to stop. I am trying to get *you* to stop. . . . I warn you
that you had better stop because if you keep harassing me
by getting your family to ostracize me, by interfering with
my complete socioplasm . . . by telling lies about me to
your work people . . . and making accusations . . . then I
warn you, you have to take the consequences because it is
all entirely unfounded. It cannot be substantiated because
I have nothing to do with it, and I think you are not only
treading a very dangerous path, but you are siccing the
police on me, which means you are distracting them from
where the real source of your problem is emanating, and I

can only imagine that that could be one of two or three purposes. One, either you're insane or (b) you've got something to hide and you are siccing them on me . . . so they can't spend any time on the real trail, or thirdly, you have some fantasy for which . . . you want to extract some enormous kind of revenge."

"Roy, that isn't going to work any more," Cindy taunted. "I'm not insane. . . . It's just not going to work any more."

"My God, boy, you make that statement in public and I'll have you in court. And I am going to have to, I'm afraid, report this conversation to my lawyer, which again, is going to cost me money and I, uh . . . Could you give me any reason why you would make that accusation? Any reason whatsoever?"

"Why don't you give me the reason?"

"I have already told you. I have absolutely nothing whatever to do with it. I did everything I could to try to assist you with this problem, which you brought on yourself. God knows how or why. And I got nothing but backlash from it, which has cost me in every way and, uh. . . . "

"Roy, I'm not going to listen to that garbage any more."

"Oh, okay. Oh well."

"Bye," Cindy said.

"Bye," Roy replied.

Roy did not realize it, but this would be the last time he would ever speak to his wife.

The moment Roy returned the receiver to its cradle, police began 24-hour surveillance of his apartment and Cindy's home. Up to 14 officers were used in the round-the-clock operation. But after seven days, with nothing extraordinary reported about the routines of Cindy and her ex-husband, surveillance was discontinued. It had already cost $75,000 in manpower. A full month would have run the tab to $243,000.

There was only one odd event during surveillance: on July 7 at 3:03 p.m., Cindy dialled her own number, which was being tape-recorded by police, from home. "Hello?" she said three times. She hung up and dialled again, this time phoning Rena O'Donnell.

The next day, Cindy told Kaban she had received a strange call. "I tried to call," she explained, "and couldn't because the, um, it wouldn't ring after I dialled. It just kept clicking. So I hung up. And after I hung up, then the phone rang. I picked it up, I think after three rings. Then just nothing. Nobody said anything. So I hung up." Kaban assured her that he would pass along the information to police.

Bjornerud thought Cindy's flub was probably an honest mistake. She was uptight, nervous. She had just been released from hospital. She could have dialled her own number thinking she was calling a friend. People get absent-minded and do that. And when Cindy told Kaban about the no-talk call, her recollection of what took place was consistent with the tape-recording of the call. She did not try to make it into something more than it was.

Four days after surveillance was terminated, a package arrived in Cindy's mail. Inside was a book titled *You Can Heal Your Life*. A black nylon stocking was used to mark a page where the phrase "Blood flowing freely" was heavily underlined. The only fingerprints police found were Cindy's. Bjornerud traced the book to a New Age bookstore. Staff there did not recognize photos of either Roy or Cindy. Bjornerud did find that the envelope used to send the book was identical to those used by B.C. Hydro.

Another package arrived in Cindy's mail two weeks later, after Cindy returned from a holiday. The outside of the package bore a stick-on address label and six uncancelled 25-cent stamps. Kaban delivered it to Bjornerud at his office downtown.

Unwrapping the paper, Bjornerud found a black plastic cosmetic bag, containing rotten meat of some kind. As he examined it, the other detectives started to complain about the stench, forcing Bjornerud to take it to the roof of the station. The meat appeared to be an animal organ. Maybe heart. The lab tried analyzing it further, but it had decomposed too much.

For Bjornerud, it was just one more investigative cul-de-sac.

NINE

The Lost Afternoon

B Y JULY 1985, it seemed as if every officer in the Vancouver police department had heard of Cindy's case. And each one of them had a different theory. Some thought Cindy was manufacturing the whole thing. Detective Bjornerud, for his part, had some hunches, but he was keeping an open mind. He didn't want to jump to conclusions. The puzzling events of August 21, 1985, however, would trouble him for months to come.

Early that morning, around 4 a.m., someone forced open a basement window at Cindy's home and set fire to her downstairs bathroom. Kaban had installed an extensive burglar alarm system that would trigger a high-pitched alarm if exterior doors or windows were opened while the system was on. The alarm didn't go off that night, as the bathroom window was one of the few not wired to the system. It was the same window that had been forced open two weeks earlier, which police had investigated but found no fingerprints. Kaban had also installed a motion detector in the basement that would pick up any movement three metres outside the bathroom. And it obviously hadn't picked up anything.

Cindy told police she had heard a crackling sound and could smell smoke before calling the fire department. Police found no signs of forced entry on the window, although Kaban said he observed pry marks on the outside. The dust and cobwebs were undisturbed on the window sill. There were no fingerprints, just an odd mark that looked like a footprint, running horizontally in the middle of the glass. And dead-centre of it was what appeared to be a tiny X. Kaban told Bjornerud it was not *his* X. So who did it? The elusive Mr. X?

Bjornerud visited Cindy's home on West 14th about 11 a.m. that day for a follow-up investigation. He carefully examined the window from inside and out. It was hinged at the bottom and opened downward, not fully, only three-quarters of the way. It would be a tricky manoeuvre for a person to climb in without putting weight on the window and breaking the glass. He decided to try it himself.

Climbing from the outside, he found it extremely awkward to get a foothold. He had to grab onto the dust-covered sill to support himself. By the time he was inside, his fingerprints were all over the sill. The plainclothes investigator also had grimy smudges all over his suit; when he got home from work that day, his wife got angry at her husband for getting his clothes so filthy.

It was possible, Bjornerud thought, that a suspect could have lit paper outside and thrown it into the bathroom to ignite the fire. But the theory was contrary to the findings of arson investigators, who determined the fire was started in six separate places. The toilet paper had been completely unravelled from its roll and, it appeared, was used to set the fire. A charred *Reader's Digest* magazine also appeared to have been used to ignite a towel hanging on the rack.

Most puzzling was a large, sooty smudge on a wall farther than an arm's length from the window; investigators believed it was evidence that someone put a lit match or lighter to the wall for several minutes in a failed attempt to ignite the wallpaper.

Constable Brian Westad, the patrol officer who investigated the scene shortly after firefighters had extinguished the blaze, overheard Cindy and Kaban having a heated discussion. She told Kaban she had been out walking her dog and did not smell smoke when she returned around

3:15 a.m.; Kaban chastised Cindy for going out alone at that time of night.

Westad did not mention the heated exchange to Bjornerud. At the time, he didn't think it was important.

A month later, someone called Cindy to say "On fire!" then hung up. The called was traced to the Richmond exchange.

On August 13, Detective Gary Foster of the city's north detectives unit and Detective Bob Young of the Vancouver Integrated Intelligence Unit met to review Cindy's file.

Foster, who wrote the summary report, noted that more than 95 incidents had been reported by Cindy since October 1982, including three serious physical attacks.

"Prior to each attack there is a definite escalation of events," he wrote. "Throughout the police investigation there has been a lack of physical evidence to conclude the case. . . . A schizophrenic mental disorder has been suggested . . . but has been emphatically discounted by psychiatrists who are close to the victim and husband."

Foster stated he believed the latest events were part of another escalating pattern that would likely culminate in a fourth attack if police action was not taken. He offered three options.

The first was to write off Cindy as a "crank" who was instigating the incidents. Foster cautioned that there was a lack of evidence to come to that conclusion. In addition, psychiatrist friends of the victim contacted by police believed Cindy was truthful and showed no signs of schizophrenia. And Cindy's father had contacted the major crime squad and offered to formally request the assistance of "his personal friend, the Attorney-General" of B.C. if increased police manpower was needed to conclude the case. With that in mind, Foster noted, "Should anything happen to the victim after police have made the decision to shelve the file, it is obvious that the media would be able to criticize the [police] Department in a rather unhealthy political forum."

The second option was for the department to continue on the same course it had taken for three years, investigating events as they arose. "This course is a totally reactionary one where the police investigators are always in a follow-up mode," Foster pointed out. "This option, like the first, will leave the department in a bad political position should the inevitable future physical attacks result in the death or serious injury to the victim. . . . Can the police Department ignore this possibility?"

The third "and only viable option," Foster wrote, was to take "affirmative action" – to use surveillance to solve the case. Foster recommended 24-hour surveillance on the victim's residence "in such a manner as to ensure that the victim never discovers the police activity." The reasoning was that Cindy expressed distrust of the police and that, during past surveillance of which the victim was aware, nothing happened. Foster noted that 90 per cent of the incidents had occurred at Cindy's home.

The detective said if surveillance was approved, "voice privacy radio transmission" would be required by police to avoid detection by Kaban's sophisticated electronic monitoring capabilities.

Still, the detective allowed that all past incidents "have been carried out by the victim's husband and/or persons unknown. This would mean that the perpetrator is highly organized and is operating some counter-surveillance techniques that would make him aware of all past security activity. Any surveillance by police must consider this possibility and again take highly controlled steps to avoid detection."

Foster detailed a number of surveillance proposals, including combined stationary and mobile observation posts, which would require 16 officers on each 12-hour shift or 24 officers working eight-hour shifts.

The inspector of the major crime section, John Lucy, passed along Foster's report to Corporal Rob Kuse of RCMP Special Intelligence for a feasibility study. He concluded that closed-circuit TV cameras could be used to monitor Cindy's home.

During this time, however, Cindy's life passed uneventfully, and after 25 incident-free days, police decided Foster's surveillance plan was unnecessary.

Cindy and Kaban met with Bjornerud and Inspector Lucy on October 7, 1985. Police stated that the investigation was at a standstill.

Unhappy, Cindy decided on an affirmative action plan of her own. She put her house up for sale and found a duplex for rent at 5400 Blundell in Richmond. She then took down the for sale sign on her house, having decided to rent her home to her friend Dorene Sutton.

Cindy moved December 1, hoping to elude her tormentor. Kaban phoned Richmond RCMP to brief commanding officers of Cindy's long history of problems and possible suspects.

Cindy's hope for a reprieve was short-lived. On December 11, 1985, a passing cyclist discovered Cindy Makepeace in a ditch beside 16th Avenue at the edge of the University Endowment Lands, a large wooded park surrounding the sprawling University of British Columbia campus in Vancouver.

It was very dark and cold as 21-year-old UBC student Desirie Elsaesser pedalled along the broad, wooded boulevard. Not having a light on her bicycle, and wearing dark clothing, she hugged tight to the paved shoulder, out of the path of passing cars. She was within six blocks of her rented basement suite when she noticed a blonde stumbling westbound in the ditch.

"My first thought was this was a student who had just finished exams and was drunk and disoriented," Elsaesser recalled.

She got off her bike to investigate. Standing at the top of the ditch, she looked down and realized it was a woman.

"I couldn't tell before because she was walking with her head down."

"Are you okay?" Elsaesser asked. There was no response. She repeated the question three times. Cindy looked at her briefly.

"She had a frenzied expression on her face so I decided not to go down and help her, thinking about my own safety. I told her twice I was going to get help. At this point she was hunched over, with her back towards me, making quiet sounds."

Elsaesser flagged down two passing cyclists, a young man and woman. "Watch this woman while I call an ambulance," she said. The area was surrounded by forest, but there were houses a block east.

UBC student Michele Desjardins, 22, went down in the ditch, careful not to slip on the frost-covered bank. She squatted beside Cindy, who was lying thigh deep in icy water. She noticed Cindy's left shoe was missing. On her right foot was a man's brown leather boot. Cindy also had a black rubber glove on her right hand. The glove's mate and a black woollen toque were later recovered by police in the ditch.

"I immediately thought about sexual assault and told Michel [her male friend] to stand away from her," said Desjardins. "I told her, gently, help was coming."

Afraid of moving her in case a bone was fractured, the young student massaged the victim's shoulders. At this point, she realized something was wrapped around the woman's neck.

"It was a piece of black nylon, wrapped three times around and tied at the back. I called Michel and we tried to undo the knot but could not. And we had no knife. So I managed to rip the nylon with my fingers, to let the girl breathe freely."

"Cold," Cindy whispered.

"Are you hurt?" Desjardins gently asked.

"Leg," Cindy moaned.

Elsaesser returned and rubbed Cindy's bare, freezing hands until ambulance paramedics arrived at 6:28 p.m. They found the victim soaked, chilled to the bone. Cindy was dressed lightly in an unlined, blue nylon jacket, blue blouse and jeans. Her pulse rate was regular but weak. Hypothermia was setting in. Her blood pressure was above normal, her breathing noisy. The paramedics noted a clean, eight-centimetre cut over her left eye, apparent fingernail scratches over the left breast, and bruises on her arms and face. She was not wearing a bra or underpants. The crew wrapped her in blankets and put her in the ambulance. During the ride to University Hospital, Cindy was conscious and started to talk, but didn't make sense. An oxygen mask covered her face.

Once in the emergency ward, medical staff examined her pupil response – it was slow, indicating either hypothermia or the influence of alcohol or drugs. Emergency physician Dr. Harold Schubert noted Cindy was pale, cold and drowsy, but answered questions intelligently. She knew who she was, where she was and the approximate time and date. She told the doctor she had a three-year history with the Vancouver police department and claimed "someone was trying to kill me," but police were never able to find enough evidence to catch a suspect.

Schubert examined the swelling on her neck from the nylon, swelling on her left cheek and cuts on her forehead and right hand. He also noticed a vein puncture in her right arm. It was fresh; the blood was not yet dry. Probably less than an hour old. Possibly an injection site, the doctor thought.

Cindy explained she had taken an Ativan tablet, a mild tranquilizer, earlier in the day, but the doctor felt this would not cause the symptoms she was presenting. She was slurring her words and her eyelids were drooping.

"I was puzzled," Schubert recalled.

As a precaution, he gave the patient an "antagonist" to counteract any morphine or heroin overdose. A blood test was ordered to check for drugs. The results later showed the presence of lorazepam, a sedative, but an absence of alcohol or opiates.

Cindy was referred to neurologist Dr. Joel Oger, who checked for signs of serious head injury, possibly a skull fracture that would cause a blood vessel to bleed inside the skull, which would, in turn, compress the brain and cause odd behaviour or loss of consciousness.

Oger found nothing, neurologically, that would explain her groggy condition. The patient had absolutely no memory of the events preceding the attack. He knew strangulation could starve the brain of oxygen and cause unconsciousness and even memory loss, but not the kind of memory deficit pre-dating the incident that Cindy was experiencing. Severe psychological stress can produce "retrograde amnesia," which might account for Cindy's condition, and an abduction and strangulation by a stranger would be extremely stressful. Oger also considered the possibility that the patient's injuries were the result of a suicide attempt. Still, he had no firm idea what had wiped out Cindy's memory. To be on the safe side, she was put in intensive care for observation.

Dr. Don Cameron, who was doing his residency in neurology at the time, also examined Cindy. He noticed "nystagmus," an abnormal eye movement where a person slowly loses focus of, say, a doctor's upright finger when held in front of the patient's face. It's a sign of disrupted connections between the brain and the eye nerves, which could be caused by a blow to the head.

Cameron tried not to pass judgment on Cindy even though, as he and other hospital staff knew, medical records showed she had previously suffered from depression and been admitted to a psychiatric ward. Sometimes, he knew, information gets passed from one medical person to another until a doctor who has never seen the patient before already has a bias.

In the meantime, police continued the investigation that had begun once Cindy was reported missing after she had failed to show up for a 2 p.m. appointment with a pre-school client who lived in southeast Vancouver. When first admitted to hospital, Cindy recalled leaving Blenheim House about noon and picking up a prescription at a nearby drugstore. That was her last memory before arriving in hospital. She had lost an afternoon, a six-hour chunk of her life had mysteriously vapourized.

Police knocked on the doors of homes near the area where Cindy was found. They were asked if anyone saw or heard anything unusual on December 11. No one did.

Detective Caroline Halliday was now in charge of Cindy's file, having taken over earlier in December when Bjornerud was promoted to Staff-Sergeant and transferred out of the major crime squad. Earlier in the year, after Cindy's basement window had been forced open before the basement fire, Bjornerud had requested that Halliday read Cindy's file and offer an opinion. Halliday told him she believed it was an inside job and Cindy was responsible.

Although not a large woman, Halliday had a no-nonsense demeanour. She had presence. And an attitude. She didn't flinch when investigating messy murder scenes or mince words when it came to interrogating suspects. Just the kind of cop major crime wanted.

Halliday was sceptical but tried to keep on open mind as she arrived to interview Cindy in her hospital bed at 9:30 p.m. on December 11. Cindy didn't respond well to Halliday's initial questions. She was groggy, her answers fading into a dazed silence. The detective stayed only a few minutes. She thought she would return later in the evening.

Prior to Cindy being admitted to hospital, Halliday checked the contents of Cindy's locked car, which had been found a few blocks from Blenheim House. The victim's keys were located underneath the car on the driver's side. Her purse contained $19.50 cash, an address book, cheque book, two packs of cigarettes and an unopened prescription – nine one-milligram Ativan tablets – dated the day of the attack. Halliday interviewed the drugstore clerk, who said Cindy picked it up around lunch time; she paid for it by cheque.

Also in Cindy's purse was a note about a threatening phone call December 5, 1985, six days before the attack. Cindy had picked up the receiver and a man whispered in a low, deep voice: "You're a dead bitch and it's going to hurt real bad."

The day after this episode, Ozzie Kaban had phoned Halliday to tell her Cindy had served divorce papers on Dr. Makepeace. He was of the opinion that his client would either commit suicide or be murdered. In jest, Kaban asked if the major crime squad wanted to take out some insurance on her.

Returning to visit Cindy at 10:40 p.m. the night of the attack, Halliday found her more alert. At the same time, her memory of events leading to the possible abduction were still virtually non-existent. She remembered leaving work about 1:30 p.m., but that was it.

"What did you do after you picked up your prescription?" Halliday asked.

"I don't know," Cindy replied. She began to slur her words. "I feel like today's Tuesday."

Halliday asked Cindy about her regular routine. Cindy said she gets up every morning about 6:30 and washes her hair, makes her bed and leaves for work by 7:30.

Cindy recalled wearing blue jeans Wednesday morning. She said she usually wears blue socks with blue jeans, but couldn't recall what socks she was wearing before the attack. She said she was also wearing underpants, bra and grey boots. She had no recollection of what else she was wearing that day.

Her memory of what she did Tuesday, the day before the attack, was clear. She had phoned her friend Dorene about 7:30 p.m. and planned a Christmas get-together. She had chicken for dinner, watched TV, and went to bed about 10:30.

Halliday tried to return to the events of Wednesday but

again Cindy began to slur her words and her eyes started to roll.

The detective ended the interview shortly after 11:00 but returned to the hospital at 1:20 a.m. Cindy was now in a private room and sitting up in bed. She seemed back to normal.

"I'm not going to be able to help you – I can't remember anything," Cindy said.

"Police can't do anything with nothing to work on. What do you expect us to do?" the detective asked.

"Nothing . . . There's nothing you can do."

Halliday asked if she was willing to see a psychiatrist "of our own choosing . . . to help us make sure you're not imagining things." Cindy didn't like the idea, but she agreed on the condition that her own physician, Dr. Allan Connolly, could be present. The detective mentioned she wanted Dr. Tony Marcus to examine her.

"No way," Cindy said. "He used to work with my husband."

Marcus was a forensic psychiatrist with 25 years expertise who practised at University Hospital and taught at UBC. He had been head of the forensic psychiatry department at the university in the 1970s, the same time as Cindy's ex-husband was head of social psychiatry. "I would use the term colleague in a more distant manner," Marcus would later say. "We were never that close." The only times he and Makepeace socialized was at departmental functions.

For years, Marcus had worked for police as an occasional consultant. He was often provided with police files and asked to give a psychiatric profile of, say, the perpetrator of a gruesome unsolved murder. Detective Bjornerud had contacted Marcus in the fall of 1985, asking him to look at the confidential police files in the Cindy Makepeace case and to provide a thumb-nail psychiatric sketch of who might be a suspect. Marcus offered a verbal opinion that Cindy was the author of her own misfortune. Still, he told police, it was possible that police were

Cindy James, far right, shares a happy moment with her sisters, Marlene Weintrager, left, and Melanie Cassidy.

Cindy, at right, with her family: left to right, back row, brothers Roger and Ken Hack, father Otto Hack, brother Doug Hack; front row, Melanie Cassidy, mother Tillie Hack, Marlene Weintrager.

Cindy graduated as a nurse from Vancouver General Hospital in 1966. This photo was her first gift to Dr. Roy Makepeace, whom she would marry in December. *(Courtesy Roy Makepeace)*

Conjugal bliss aboard *Peacemaker*, Cindy and Roy's nine-metre boat. *(Courtesy Roy Makepeace)*

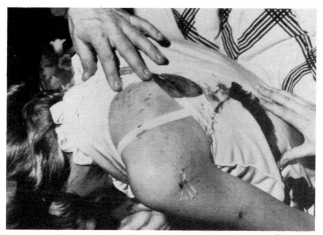

Cindy received these wounds to her back during the first attack, January 27, 1983. She claimed to have been assailed by two men in her garage.

April 16, 1986: fire inspectors determined that the blaze that destroyed the basement den of Cindy's rented home began at a bookshelf containing her personal memorabilia.

Three examples of threatening notes Cindy received. The note reading "SOON CINDY" was found on her car April 8, 1989, six weeks before she disappeared.

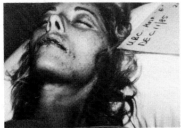

Cindy in University Hospital after the fourth attack, December 11, 1985.

The abandoned Richmond house, used as a "party house" by local teenagers, where Cindy's body was found, June 8, 1989.

The blue van where a squatter had been living for three weeks before Cindy's body was found. He said he noticed nothing suspicious, even though he cooked his meals five metres from where the corpse lay.

Cindy's body was found with her arms and legs bound behind her back with a black nylon stocking, and a second nylon tied around her neck. This sketch is based on police photographs that were banned from publication by order of the coroner. *(Jackie Haliburton)*

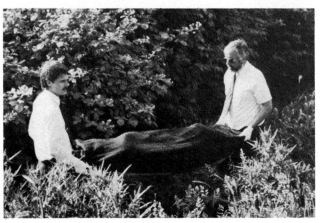

Cindy's remains being removed from the death scene by Pacific Body Removal. *(The Province/Vancouver)*

Front-row seats for Cindy James's family at the opening day of the coroner's inquest, February 26, 1990. *(The Vancouver Sun)*

Ontario knot expert Robert Chisnall holding the stocking used to bind Cindy's arms and legs. Chisnall concluded that Cindy could easily have tied herself in this fashion, which he demonstrated on himself in court.

Richmond RCMP Constable Jerry Anderson, the chief investigator of Cindy's case from the fifth attack, October 26, 1988. *(The Vancouver Sun)*

Gerald Tilley, presiding coroner at the Cindy James inquest. *(Blake Williams)*

Private investigator Ozzie Kaban, hired by Cindy in November 1983, after the first attack. *(Courtesy Ozzie Kaban)*

The police composite sketch of Cindy's attacker, based on information she provided about the second attack, January 30, 1984.

dealing with a very sophisticated assailant who was perhaps aware of police investigative procedures and doing counter-surveillance.

Marcus usually never met the people he wrote about for police. Two days after the attack, however, he visited Cindy briefly. She was lying in her hospital bed, distressed and exhausted. Marcus sat beside the bed and spoke in a soothing, avuncular tone.

He discussed with her only the events of the day previous to the attack. Cindy told him of her routine – work until 4:30 p.m. and then usually shopping for groceries. She generally swallowed a two-milligram Ativan tablet at night and a one-milligram pill during the day, around noon, to calm her nerves.

When Marcus shifted the conversation to the day of the attack, he noticed her voice alter and her eyes change.

"It's a total blank," she said, beginning to cry. "Why can't I remember? . . . I guess it's part of what's going on. I don't know for sure."

He tried shifting the conversation back to ordinary, non-threatening memories and Cindy was back on track. She told him she was getting a divorce after a 3½-year separation.

Again, Marcus tried gently to nudge Cindy back to the day of the attack and once again her eyelids drooped. She paused. "I don't know anything," she said.

After 30 minutes of questioning, Marcus felt she had had enough. "While you're here you'll be protected and you'll be safe," he told her before leaving.

Three days into her hospital stay, Cindy complained of vaginal discomfort, a burning sensation when urinating. Concerned about a possible sexual assault during the attack, Cindy was examined by gynecologist Dr. George Mitchell, who found no signs that would suggest forced sexual assault. He did find Cindy had mild vaginitis, a common yeast infection. The only other abnormalities were two faint bruises about two centimetres in diameter on each thigh and two ulcerated areas on the left labia minora, which Mitchell thought might be herpes lesions. Swabs were taken and cultured in the lab, but the results proved negative. Cindy would later say the sores were caused by cigarette burns inflicted by her sadistic assailant.

On December 15, the day before Cindy was released from hospital, Halliday met with Otto and Doug Hack. She pointed out that police had interviewed Roy Makepeace many times, but now Makepeace's lawyer was advising police not to approach the doctor directly. Furthermore, the supervising officers in major crime had told detectives to "lay off" Makepeace.

Marcus arranged a second meeting with Cindy on January 18, 1986, at his office in the psychiatric unit beside University Hospital. He gently tried to probe her family background. Cindy provided some general comments about her brothers and sisters, and her parents. When she spoke of her ex-husband, she became visibly upset.

"His goal was to have an inaccessible fortress with walls and booby traps to keep others out," she confided. "He was always complaining others had unfair advantages. . . . He was concerned about his salary and he had rages."

Marcus recalled that Cindy felt very alone and believed she wasn't a good wife, that she had let her husband down by not going sailing with him.

He asked her where she would feel safe. Not in the psychiatric unit, Cindy said. She thought she could stay with her parents. She did not want to stay with her brother Doug, she said, because he had three kids and she didn't want to upset the children.

In his report to police, Marcus wrote that he could not exclude the possibility that a suspect may have cleverly eluded police detection. But it was his opinion that the events Cindy reported to police were "self-initiated," not a perpetrated campaign. He believed that Cindy was casting herself centre-stage in a fantastic plot of her own making to embarrass, or to bring criminal charges against the person whom she felt had rejected and abandoned her.

Marcus believed the case was more complex, psychologically, than Cindy simply "faking" incidents. He later suggested she may have gone into a "psychogenic fugue," a state of altered consciousness whereby she might not remember doing things to herself. And her deep-seated psychiatric problem likely stemmed from her childhood, when she may have been sexually abused.

"This woman suffered very, very deeply. . . . She was under siege from whatever source, from within or without," Marcus recalled. "She was in a living nightmare."

TEN

Hitting Bottom

ON DECEMBER 22, 1985, four days after her release from hospital, Cindy began a three-week Christmas holiday with her brother Roger, stationed in Germany with the Canadian High Commissioner's Office. Away from home, Cindy was free of always having to look over her shoulder. She was relaxed, even upbeat at times, just like the old Cindy.

On her return, all was was quiet. Months went by without a threatening letter or phone call.

Cindy Makepeace's divorce hearing was held March 12. Her husband did not oppose the proceeding – he did not even attend. "There have been no efforts to effect reconciliation," the divorce papers stated. Cindy listed her gross monthly income on the divorce papers as $2,586 and Roy's estimated annual income as $60,000.

Cindy did not realize it, having had no contact with Roy for two years, but her ex-husband had lost his job when B.C. Hydro disbanded its occupational health services department on November 1, 1985. However, with a $1,200-a-month mortgage payment on his Kitsilano condo, Makepeace could not afford to retire. He was being forced to start over at 59, an age he felt was too old to set up a private practice. The future seemed bleak.

Makepeace had become extremely cautious by this time. Knowing he was the prime suspect in Cindy's troubles, he had begun to document his every move, sometimes down to the number of minutes he spent on his morning ablutions. He made extensive notations on his home calendar – a habit he acquired from Cindy. The calendar became a diary of sorts, with entries each day about who phoned, who his companions were aboard his sailboat, who he went to dinner with, where he went, what time he got home, what time he got to bed, what he had done on his days off.

A series of crank calls were made to his home beginning March 31, 1985, when someone phoned about 9:35 p.m. "Is Roy there?" the caller asked in a hoarse voice. Then Makepeace thought he heard the person use a Zulu phrase, "Hamba Goshle Wena." When he heard it repeated, Makepeace called out the phrase to see if his suspicion was correct. The line went dead.

As the strange phone calls became more frequent, Makepeace refused to answer his phone. He spent $292 on a sophisticated answering machine to screen calls and record conversations. He would sit listening to the caller's voice on the machine, lifting the receiver to talk only when he was certain who the caller was.

Paranoia, meanwhile, was beginning to creep into Cindy's life. She would often ask friends and relatives to stay overnight at her home, so great was her fear of being alone.

Tom and Agnes Woodcock were staying at Cindy's rented duplex on Blundell Road in Richmond the night of April 2, 1986, when the burglar alarm sounded at 2:52 a.m.

Agnes remembers that she, Tom and Cindy were playing cards at the time – they often played until 3:00 in the morning on weekends because Cindy had trouble sleeping. "She was sitting right at the table when the alarm went off," Agnes recalled. "She had never left the room." When they checked the house they found the glass window of the rear basement door had been completely removed.

Fearing for Cindy's life, the Woodcocks stayed with their friend every night beginning April 7. Almost two weeks later, Tom was awakened at 2:30 a.m. by a loud thump. He was just putting on his pants to investigate when Cindy knocked at his bedroom door, across the hallway from her bedroom.

"Tom? I heard a thump downstairs, did you hear it?"

As he opened the bedroom door to step into the hallway, Woodcock smelled smoke. Agnes came into the corridor. Cindy tried to call 911 on her bedroom phone, but the line was dead. She noticed a red glow outside the living room window. Peering outside, Tom and Cindy could see yellow and blue flames shooting from downstairs, and red embers dancing in a column of heat rising into the night sky.

Tom Woodcock went out the front door to get a better look at the fire. He was surprised to find a tall man, wearing a denim suit, standing in front of the house. "Go get help!" Woodcock shouted. The man ran down a side street, never to be seen again.

Wearing only her pajama top and bottom, Cindy went outside and pounded on the door of her duplex neighbour. Muriel McDonald stuck her head out a window. "There's a fire!" Cindy shouted. "Phone the fire department!"

Cindy suddenly realized she had left Heidi inside the house. She went to the back door and shouted Heidi's name, but there was no response. She could hear the dog but was unable to see through the thick, choking smoke. Cindy and the Woodcocks formed a human chain to find the dog, but they were blinded by the smoke. Letting go of Agnes's hand, Cindy crawled on the floor and found Heidi by the kitchen counter. Clutching Heidi outside, Cindy gave Tom her car keys so he could move her car. It was parked in the driveway only metres from the flames that were licking the front of the house. In fact, the car paint was beginning to smoke from the heat.

Firefighters arrived within minutes and quickly doused the blaze through the window of the basement den.

Checking the upper floor of the house after the fire was doused, firefighter Grant Cleise noticed something odd. The top sheet of Cindy's bed was drawn back but the bed sheets were neat and crisp, not rumpled. It appeared the bed had not been slept in. Either that, or Cindy was an extremely neat and tidy sleeper.

Examining the rubble in the darkness, fire investigator Gordon Gill's first impression was that the fire was arson, probably started from a firebomb thrown through the window of the basement den.

But on his return in daylight for a closer examination, Gill noticed all the glass from the front window had fallen outward, indicating it was blown out by the heat explosion inside the room. If a Molotov cocktail had been thrown inside, he would have expected to find glass in the den from the window and the glass container.

Gill also found no signs of forced entry on the window, and the room itself had been locked when firefighters arrived. He considered the possibility that someone could have used a glass cutter and a suction cup to remove a section of the window, then thrown a flammable liquid inside.

After removing ash from the carpet in the room, Gill saw an uneven "puddle burn" pattern on the rug, which indicated a liquid accelerant such as gasoline had been used to start the fire. A carpet sample was sent to the RCMP lab for confirmation, but the lab could only determine that neither gasoline nor any other hydrocarbon-based accelerant had been used.

Gill also noticed the charring of the wooden ceiling joists was heaviest in the northwest corner of the room, where, he concluded, the fire began. Examining a bookshelf that had fallen over during the fire, he observed that the undersides of the bookcase shelves were heavily charred, indicating the fire started at floor level.

"One possibility I considered is that liquid [accelerant] had been poured on the shelf and floor . . . and either ignited on the floor or the shelf," Gill said. The other possibility was that a candle had been used. After burning down for several hours, it could have ignited the accelerant.

An iron bar normally used to secure the back basement door from inside the house was found leaning against the wall in the downstairs hallway. Usually it was fitted in brackets to keep an intruder from forcing the door open. Tom Woodcock had installed the bar and remembers ensuring it was in place before going to bed the night of the fire.

Gill eventually ruled out an accidental fire start. "It was a quick, hot fire, not a slow, smouldering fire like a cigarette or electrical fire." The blaze had caused two of the electrical circuit breakers to trip and had melted the telephone electrical system. This would explain why the phone failed to work.

With no signs of forced entry, Gill felt the incident was an arson set by someone in the home. He later passed his conclusion to police and Cindy's insurance company.

Seven hours after the fire, Cindy was met at the Richmond RCMP building by Constable Brian Andrews, who led her to a small room for an interview. Cindy was naturally tense and upset. Someone had fire-bombed her home. Someone was trying to kill her.

She began by telling Andrews what happened that night, explaining she had been awakened by Heidi barking or crackling noises, she was not sure which. "I keep thinking if I'd been in there alone I wouldn't have got out of my room." She started to cry.

"Everybody escaped," Andrews assured her. "So there's no use worrying about what might have happened. All that does is just work you into a frenzy for no reason at all. You could have been killed walking across the road yesterday, but you weren't. Okay?"

He suggested she step back from her memory of the fire and look at it. "It's like watching a horror movie on TV. It's not gonna hurt you. It might scare you to look at, but it's not gonna hurt you."

Step by step, he slowly led her through the progression of events. Cindy did not recall her burglar alarm going off. She had already phoned Ozzie Kaban's company to tell him it did not go off. She could not remember leaving the house with her car keys, but she recalled Tom moving her car to prevent it being consumed by flames.

Once he got the facts established, Andrew turned to another line of questioning. Who might be responsible for setting the fire? "What I'm trying to establish is someone who would have a motive to do this," he said.

"Well," Cindy explained, "the Vancouver police said that there's one of three possibilities. It's either [a relative or ex-relation] or it's myself with the help of Ozzie and his people, or it's some kook."

"Okay, . . . some kook I can understand, but I don't understand the part about yourself with the help of Ozzie."

"I don't either," Cindy said.

"What do they mean by that?"

"Uh, to quote my brother . . . they have to look at the possibility that I'm orchestrating the whole thing and getting somebody to do the whole bit."

"And are you?"

"Huh? No. Why would I?"

"I don't know. As I say, I don't know very much about you."

Andrews tried to probe the reason for Cindy's most recent hospitalization in December. As he understood it, he said, she had been attacked in Vancouver. Was she now under a doctor's care? Cindy said she was seeing a Dr. Allan Connolly. "If I'm feeling really stressed, uh, I call him, you know, and he comes over for a while and tells me if I'm coping."

"Okay. Have you not been under psychiatric care?" Andrews asked. Cindy said a Dr. "Martin," but probably meant Marcus, had been to see her at the request of Vancouver police. "But I only saw him once and I told him that I didn't want to come back again. . . . He told me it was my subconscious that, um . . . . He tried to explain that [at] night my subconscious or something was doing it and I guess . . . that could be possible. . . . I asked him if that meant my subconscious was, wasn't communicating."

Asked about her relationship with Ozzie Kaban, Cindy said: "I just think he's a very, very incredible man who cares about people and wants to help them and really . . . " She broke into tears. "It's, it's funny, it always makes me angrier and hurts more that, that, that Ozzie's integrity could, could. . . . " Again tears interrupted her. "That this kind of thing could be said about the way he arranged . . . trying to help."

A long pause ensued, then Cindy sat straight in her chair and, in a firm voice, told Andrews, "I am not crazy. I am not doing it. I am not hiring . . . anybody else to do anything. . . . "

"You haven't heard me say you are," Andrews hastened to remark. "I'm not accusing you of doing anything." He told her he sensed she was giving up, that she was not expecting her tormentor to be caught. Cindy agreed.

"You're running away," Andrews admonished.

"Yes . . . you're absolutely right," Cindy confirmed. She said she wanted to move out of the country.

"So, in other words," Andrews groped for clarification, "it wouldn't be safe enough to just move out of the Lower Mainland? You wouldn't be safe enough to move to another western province? It wouldn't be safe to move to Eastern Canada?"

"I don't know," Cindy said, wiping her tears.

"But it's safe enough to leave the country?"

"It feels like the only option is that you-you-you've gotta run," Cindy said. "There's no other option."

"Yes there is," Andrews insisted. "There is an option. You've been saying 'The buck stops here.' So your options are really quite clear. You either stop, make a stand here right now, or you run. . . . You get a job in Alabama and things go fine for six months or a year and the next thing you know, the notes start all over again. So you up and run and move to Brazil. Things would be fine for a year and the notes start, and it's [happening] all over again."

Cindy burst into tears at this horrid thought.

"Cindy, all I'm saying is, all you're doing is . . . fooling yourself. That's all you're doing. This is pretty serious stuff we're talking about, okay? We're talking about your life, all right?"

"I don't have a life any more," Cindy said.

"Oh, yes you do. . . . You've got a lotta living to do yet. Come on now! Don't give me that garbage about having no life any more. Oh, yes you do! The only problem is, you've got somebody standing over you with a whip and chair, and they're making you jump. . . . And you're jumping and jumping. Okay, now what you've gotta do, if you want to do it, is let us help – maybe we can cut the whip and throw away the chair. And maybe we can let Cindy get on with her life, become a human being again, instead of a caged animal who jumps and runs, jumps and runs some more. Because I'm quite sure, when you go out the door you look behind your back."

"Yes, I've become quite paranoid."

"When you're going down the aisles in the supermarket, you look behind you?"

"I never go alone any more. I don't go anywhere alone any more."

"And when you're driving to work I bet your rear-view mirror is almost worn out."

"Either that or I just totally make myself go blank – don't think! Don't let yourself think!"

Cindy said there was nothing Andrews could do for her. She cried again for a few moments. "I have to honestly say," she added, "that there have been some people who have, I think, gone way beyond the call of duty in trying to help. I-I-I really believe that, and I'm, I'm very grateful for that. But there have also been promises made that weren't kept. . . . "

She broke down again, and Andrews ended the interview exactly two hours after it began.

Richmond RCMP Constable Janet Fisher was the plainclothes officer assigned to investigate the arson at Cindy's home. She interviewed Cindy's next-door neighbours in the rented duplex a few days after the event. Muriel McDonald told Fisher that her husband heard a "tinkling" sound like glass breaking. Then the doorbell rang. "My husband called out not to open the door unless I looked to see who's there at 3:00 in the morning. So I looked out the upstairs bedroom window and I see flames shooting out of the downstairs window."

She saw Cindy and let her in, then called the fire department. She recalled Cindy saying about 6 a.m., "I sure hope I didn't leave a cigarette burning."

Fisher had briefly talked to Cindy when she returned to her home the morning of the fire, to retrieve some clothes and her insurance papers. She told Fisher she moved into the duplex the previous December because of threatening phone calls and an arson at her previous residence, which caused $7,500 damage. Cindy mentioned to Fisher that she had gone into the den – her sewing room – about 8:30 p.m. prior to the fire "to see if I had a sympathy card." She was not smoking at the time.

The morning after the fire, police noticed a young man on the property. He was standing on a planter, using a screwdriver to fiddle with Cindy's phone lines. An officer told him to "get the fuck out" of there. The young man turned out to be Ozzie Kaban's son, Alan, who was checking to see if the line had been cut.

When Fisher interviewed the Woodcocks, they described what had been in the basement room. A sewing machine was in front of the window, flanked by potted plants. There were a chair and writing desk, Cindy's exercise bike, and a bookshelf containing books and all Cindy's memorabilia – old photographs, postcards, letters, personal keepsakes. The Woodcocks also mentioned a large sand-cast candle had been on top of the bookshelf. No trace of a candle had been found by the fire investigator; it had been consumed by the extreme heat. Fisher then made a sketch of the position of objects in the room before the fire broke out.

Following the fire, Cindy stayed at a Granada Inn in Richmond. She expected her insurance company would pay the bill until she could return home.

On April 21, however, Cindy's landlady gave notice of eviction. Mrs. Walter Burki wrote: "We regret very much that the police cannot find this horrible person who is causing you so much trouble. . . . This sick individual being at large is a sure guarantee that more nastiness and perhaps tragedy will occur. This duplex has far too many escape routes to be safe for you. . . . We cannot take a chance on a repeat performance, as I am sure you agree." Cindy was given until the last day of May to move out her furniture and remaining possessions.

On April 22, Fisher talked to Gill about his fire investigation. Three firefighters at the scene, Gill said, had noted Cindy was "calm, cool and collected" until police arrived, then she became hysterical. Fisher also thought Cindy's dress at the scene – barefoot, wearing only her pajamas, even though Tom and Agnes were fully dressed – was "dramatic." The arson, she had decided, was an "inside job" and Cindy was responsible.

Fisher told the Woodcocks her suspicion, but they refused to entertain the notion. "They were very protective of her," Fisher recalled.

While staying at the hotel, Cindy learned of Fisher's suspicion and vowed: "I'll kill myself if people don't believe me." Fisher subsequently wrote a memo to all watches of Richmond RCMP, stating Cindy "is mistrustful of police and she is capable of discrediting police at any cost."

During Cindy's hotel stay, her sister Melanie visited her room one night, but for the most part slept in her van in the hotel parking lot. She tried to get Cindy to eat pea soup – her favourite – and salad, but Cindy only poked at it, eating a tiny amount once a day.

After a week, hotel management told Cindy it needed her room for a convention so she went to stay at the Woodcocks' two-bedroom apartment in Vancouver. She was extremely depressed, refused to eat and chain-smoked two packs of cigarettes a day. She had lost nine kilograms since the fire and was looking emaciated and haggard. She began to declare it was an individual's right to end her life if she chose to. This, naturally, alarmed the Woodcocks. "She had sort of given up," Agnes recalled. "She felt police wouldn't believe her."

Cindy had told her sister Marlene: "Now he is coming after my friends. I may as well give up. If he starts going after my friends and family, then I've lost."

Cindy's friend Dorene Sutton phoned Doug Hack to tell him Cindy was suicidal. Doug took the ferry over and talked with Agnes Woodcock in the hallway outside her apartment. "He didn't want Cindy to know he was there," Woodcock explained. "I said, 'It's up to you. You're her family.' Cindy asked me and asked me not to let them take her to the hospital. She just wanted to rest. It was out of my hands because they were her family. Melanie and Doug decided she should go in the hospital."

Cindy's physician, Dr. Allan Connolly, was next on the scene. Cindy told everyone Connolly was her psychiatrist, even though he was, in fact, a general practitioner not certified in psychiatry. Still, she trusted him fully. Over the phone, Cindy told Connolly she planned to overdose on sleeping pills. The fire was the final straw, she said, and she had no desire to continue living. Connolly told her to stay where she was. He arrived at the Woodcocks' apartment, met with Doug on the roof to discuss her problem, and decided to call an emergency mental-health doctor. A suicide note later was found in which Cindy bid farewell to her friends and to Connolly.

By the time she was admitted May 3 to the psychiatric unit of St. Paul's Hospital in downtown Vancouver, Cindy was sobbing uncontrollably. Her shoes were taken away to make it difficult for her to leave the hospital. During her first 48 hours in hospital, she remained mute, refusing food and water. On her second night, she bolted from the ward and ran on to the street, where she was grabbed by hospital staff.

On May 5, Cindy was transferred to Riverview Hospital, a more secure psychiatric facility that kept patients, including the chronic mentally ill, in locked wards.

At Riverview, Cindy learned the true "meaning" of depression. Here she was surrounded by patients who were either catatonic or laughing hysterically. "It is horrible here. The patients are all like zombies!" she told nursing staff.

Dr. Alan Cashmore, a psychiatrist at Blenheim House, visited Cindy during her stay at Riverview. "She really didn't want to talk," he observed. Cindy had previously stayed with the Cashmore family shortly after her 1982 separation. During that visit, Cindy would often awake in the night screaming, rousing everyone in the house. "She had frightening dreams of men attacking her," Cashmore said. "I felt she was reacting to the stress from all these incidents that terrorized her. . . . I was amazed she stayed intact for so long."

Cindy's parents were in Australia when their daughter Melanie phoned to tell them Cindy had been hospitalized. "We tried to come back," Tillie Hack said later, "but it's pretty difficult when you're in Australia to get on an aircraft just like that. So we still had to wait a week longer before we could come back."

By the time they returned, their daughter was in Riverview, still refusing to eat. She spent most of her time staring out the window. At most, she would give one-word answers to questions from medical staff, talking in a soft, low voice. She was often tearful and refused to make eye contact. She weighed only 45 kilograms and, without any solid-food intake for almost three weeks, was naturally weak and unsteady on her feet. Nursing staff paid constant attention to Cindy as she had been classified a "severe suicide risk."

The Hacks – Otto, Tillie, Doug – met with Riverview psychiatrist Dr. Soon Mo Choi on their first visit May 6. Cindy had told Choi about the history of harassment and terror in her life. She told him she could not continue. She wanted to die.

The Hacks tried to explain to Choi some of the reasons why Cindy was in hospital but, said Tillie, "it sort of felt like he wasn't interested in what we were trying to tell him. Finally I just said . . . 'why don't you listen to what we have to say to you?' "

"Mom, "Doug interjected, "take it easy."

"Well, you will admit she needs help," Choi stated.

"Of course she needs help," Mrs. Hack agreed.

Choi then told them that, in the next few minutes, hospital staff would begin to force-feed Cindy.

"You're not going to touch her until I see her first," Cindy's mother insisted.

Choi agreed to this. Tillie Hack found her daughter sitting on a chair in a corner of her ward. Other patients were laughing and talking hysterically. Kneeling in front of her daughter, she took her hands and asked, "How are you?"

"Mother, I am just absolutely and utterly mortified. I am a psychiatric nurse. I look after people like this. How do you think I feel? It's very devastating."

"Cindy, they're going to force-feed you."

"Mom, how can they?"

"Well, Cindy, they are. You are dehydrating and they feel that you should have some liquid at least. Please try."

At one point, Mrs. Hack told her, "Damn it, Cindy, damn it! Don't give up! Fight, girl! Fight, damn it!"

Before their conversation was over, staff came with the paraphernalia to begin the force-feeding. Tillie was sent out of the room. By the time she returned, Cindy was in pain from the attempt to insert a tube down her throat. "She said it was terribly, terribly painful." So painful, in fact, that staff removed the tube. "That's when she had her first drink of something."

The next day, Cindy told a nurse that she was considering moving to Europe or Texas to find a job and to get away from the person harassing her. She woke up that night shouting, "No, no stop!" tossing back and forth in bed. She told a nurse she had a horrible nightmare but would not elaborate. She curled into a fetal position and cried. When a nurse offered a sedative in apple juice, Cindy drank it willingly. The sedative was effective; she slept for several hours. When she awoke in the morning, she asked how she could legally get out of hospital. For the rest of the day she sat silently in a chair, smoking and staring out the window. She answered initial questions from nurses in a quiet, whispering voice, then stated she did not wish to talk any more, wearily explaining, "I'm all talked out."

By the middle of her second day at Riverview, Cindy seemed to change. She ate soup at lunch, then the main course and drank her tea and milk. Choi felt the anti-depressant and anti-psychotic drugs he had prescribed were finally beginning to take effect.

The next day, she ate one piece of toast and three slices of bacon. She drank her milk and coffee, then lay on her bed, staring at the ceiling as if in deep thought. The nursing entry at 10:25 a.m. noted: "Over the last 25 minutes, Cindy several times screwed up her face and made sounds as if crying. There were no tears. However, she was observed by another nurse earlier to be crying and tears were present. Cindy did not answer when asked if she felt like discussing her feelings. She had earlier stated she felt the noise and turmoil on the ward was too much for her."

She broke into tears at lunch that day, saying she felt overwhelmed by the amount of food she was being served. She ate half a grilled cheese sandwich, a small peach and drank her coffee, but she refused to touch her raspberry juice, soup or green beans. Weighed later that day, Cindy had gained 1.5 kilograms since admission.

On her third day, Cindy began a battery of psychological tests administered by Ken Dercole, a consulting psychologist. Cindy breezed through the Wechsler Adult Intelligence Scale, which placed her verbal skills and intelligence "in the superior range."

Little alarm bells rang in Dercole's mind during other tests. Cindy initially was very resistant to his testing and would answer only in one-word responses, without making eye contact. By the second day she was more relaxed and willing to talk. "She made good eye contact except when discussing the terrorizing incidents; she would then look down or cover her eyes and speak haltingly," Dercole noted, adding that Cindy became upset and "cried a great deal when relating these incidents."

During tests in which she would turn over cards or Dercole would ask what she saw in ink blots or picture cards, Cindy would often break into tears and refuse to answer.

Several times she asked if her responses were crazy. When Dercole asked what *she* thought, Cindy admitted, "A number of times in the past three years I have seriously wondered if my thoughts are crazy."

During the Rorschach ink-blot tests, Cindy's responses were emotionally charged and bizarre, full of aggressive interpretations. She saw two birds pulling each other apart. She also mentioned dismembered bodies in the hold of a boat. In a red-picture card test, Cindy saw the piece of paper being "consumed by fire and firemen's hoses spurting blood." Dercole felt she was misinterpreting reality, seeing things that were not there.

During the Minnesota Multiphasic Personality Inventory testing, Dercole noted that Cindy lacked insight and was self-centred, demanding attention and affection. There were also signs of paranoia, suspicion, resentment, hypersensitivity, rigidity, pessimism, over-control and

irritability. She was critical and demanding, somewhat im-
mature and manipulative.

"This configuration would suggest a primary classification of paranoid psychosis with psychopathic personality," Dercole wrote in his report.

The results of Cindy's second personality inventory test,
her examiner noted, suggested "a basic personality style
of passive-aggressive with compulsive tendencies. This
type of individual is characterized as negativistic and
conforming. They have unpredictable moods, pessimism,
sullenness, vacillating with social agreement and friendli-
ness. They tend to anticipate and precipitate disappoint-
ments through their obstructive and negative behaviour.
The compulsive tendencies add rigidity, emotional over-
control, a need for order and organization.

"Behind this conforming, organized front is a set of
contrary feelings which occasionally break through in
angry outbursts."

Dercole wrote that Cindy's overall profile indicated
"this patient suffers from periods of futility, dejection and
self-deprecation, interspersed with 'normal' spans. This
type of person tends to be vulnerable to fears of separation. The periods of cheerfulness often prove to be temporary cover-ups to counter deeper fears of insecurity and
abandonment."

Passive-aggressive personalities have trouble expressing their anger. Instead of confronting it head-on, they do
things like refusing to talk, which fit Cindy's behaviour,
Dercole thought. And compulsive personalities become
upset when things are not done according to their own
particular way. They have a meticulous sense of order and
are sometimes referred to as "neat freaks."

Dercole's summary report concluded: "This 41-year-
old woman's assessment produced extreme scores on all
test profiles, providing a picture of a paranoid schizophrenic patient with high levels of anxiety and depression
overlaid on a passive-aggressive compulsive personality.
. . . The themes of abandonment and rejection seem

important in light of the psychotic symptoms first occur ring at the time of her marriage breakdown."

On Cindy's tenth day in Riverview, a nurse caught her concealing a lorazepam pill in an attempt to save pills for future use. "I just thought I wanted an option," she told the nurse, who, upon questioning Cindy further, found she was referring to suicide. Cindy was switched to liquid medication so she could not hoard pills and attempt an overdose.

As Cindy's condition improved, she talked to Dercole about her future plans. She told him she thought she would change her name, change her job, try something new. She began to smile and laugh with nursing staff, her friends and family. She was also allowed to go out on the grounds, accompanied by a nurse, to see her dog Heidi, who had been brought to hospital by Agnes Woodcock to cheer her.

By May 20, 1986, she was no longer considered a suicide risk, although she was still anxious and tense. She was transferred that day back to St. Paul's. In his transfer notes, Dr. Choi noted Cindy felt "extremely angry and hateful toward her ex-husband, God and the police." She was unable to give any motivation for the history of harassment that led her to hospital, he said, stating that "until five years ago she was quite alive, happy, very competent and strong."

Choi's discharge diagnosis was "Paranoid State, Simple, however I was unable to exclude the possibility of underlying Paranoid Schizophrenia or Affective Psychosis."

Although Choi was unable to determine if Cindy's history of harassment was real or imagined, "my assumption is that most likely her personal experience of harassment might be part of her underlying psychopathology. I understand her parents are heavily involved and they may need some guidance in accepting Cindy's psychiatric problem."

When readmitted to St. Paul's, Cindy was assigned to Dr. Wesley Friesen, a young, handsome psychiatrist who had just completed his residency. He would later recall that Cindy was seen by the hospital's "older psychiatrists" as a difficult case and that they were reluctant to take her on. During his first meeting with Cindy, he found her agitated and convinced she was being harassed and, Friesen thought, she was aware "I may not believe her."

He continued to provide the anti-psychotic and anti-depressant drugs Choi had initiated, but he also wanted to probe more deeply into her apparent problems. He asked her to complete a comprehensive autobiography form, which began with questions about her family background, then progressed to questions about her medical history and the problems leading to her current hospitalization.

Cindy wrote that she was of German, Russian and Scandinavian stock and was a non-practising Lutheran from a middle-class family.

Asked to describe her personality when functioning at her very best, she wrote: "Warm, friendly, loyal to friends; reserved, quiet, calm, cool and collected around people I don't know too well."

She went on to say she enjoyed being with friends and doing "active things like gardening, racquetball, jazzercize, ballroom dancing and long walks on the beach." Her faults she listed as "probably too trusting, somewhat naive and stubborn."

Her most immediate concern, she said, was to arrange for something to be done with her furniture and belongings in her home after the fire, and to have a final meeting with police concerning the fire. "Until this is done, the insurance company will not pay me for the damage or the cost of cleaning everything that was smoke damaged."

She stated she had been unable to work since the fire and was currently on sick leave, although she felt her condition was improving. She did not abuse alcohol or drugs, she stated.

Asked if she had any suicidal feelings, she wrote, "Yes. But not while I'm in hospital. I still feel suicide is my best option in an unbearable situation. As soon as I get out of here I will carry out my plan. I truly believe a person should have the right to make that choice for themselves, if they have really carefully thought about it and all the alternatives."

Asked for details of her family history, Cindy described how her father was "definitely the head of the family" and quite strict. Her mother served as family mediator.

Her brother Doug was described as very laid-back, generous and a good listener who related easily to everyone. She also said Doug was an excellent father who shared equally with his wife the responsibility of bringing up the children. "I am close to all my siblings but if I had to choose one with whom I am closest, it would be Doug," Cindy wrote.

Sister Marlene, Cindy noted, was "treated 10 years ago for reactive depression following the death of her first husband in a plane crash." She described Marlene as physically attractive, a bit overweight, a good mother who was patient, fair and loving.

Her brother Roger was "very diplomatic," which made him perfect for his job with Canada's External Affairs Department.

As for her brother Ken, then working as a cook/manager at a ski resort in Fernie, B.C., and married with four children, including two from his wife's first marriage, Cindy wrote that he "tends to be very strict as a father, sets high standards for himself and others. Wants to join the RCMP and enjoys power and responsibility. At the same time, he is a warm generous family member."

Melanie, the youngest sister, was described as "very bright, a high achiever; somewhat obsessional and sometimes sets impossible goals for herself and feels a failure when she can't meet those goals; a warm, bubbly personality."

"As an adult," Cindy wrote, "I feel much closer to my father. My brother-in-law was killed in a plane crash 10 years ago. That was the first time I ever saw my father cry and . . . we spent a lot of time together during this period. For the first time I saw my father as a vulnerable, caring person and we were able to talk to each other as we never had before. I feel this episode made a significant change in our relationship and I now feel much closer to him and able to talk to him as an equal. I now realize he is, in fact, a very generous, caring person who has a lot of difficulty allowing others to see his vulnerabilities." At the same time, Cindy acknowledged that, as a child, she had been spanked with a leather strap.

She listed Dorene Sutton as her closest friend, "someone in whom I can confide about everything. A wonderful, warm person and a loyal friend." Among her list of "very good friends," curiously, she did not mention Tom and Agnes Woodcock.

Her most recent personal relationship she listed as "Pat [McBride], a man I dated a few months after my separation. This relationship was sexual as well as emotional. Pat wanted marriage and I didn't feel ready to make that kind of commitment to anyone. The relationship lasted a year and ended because I was unwilling to make a long-term commitment."

Cindy turned 42 on June 12 in St. Paul's and gradually began let go of her suicidal urges, but she was to remain in hospital for another month.

RCMP Const. Fisher, meanwhile, tried to obtain Cindy's medical records. Cindy, however, refused to give her permission. Fisher then contacted Dr. Tony Marcus on June 19, since she had been briefed on his consulting report in Cindy's Vancouver police file. Marcus told Fisher that he was 99.9 per cent sure Cindy instigated the incidents.

"I felt she was on a self-destruct course," Fisher recalled thinking at the time. "In my opinion . . . she hated her husband so intensely that she would set up the perfect suicide that may appear to be a murder and her husband would be the suspect." The officer's further discussions with Dr. Connolly and her treating psychiatrist, Dr. Friesen, only confirmed her hunch.

When Fisher told Connolly that she suspected Cindy

was responsible for the recent arson in her home, he was surprised. "If she did, she is deeply disturbed in a psychiatric way," said Connolly, who had been unsure whether Cindy's harassment was real.

Friesen told Fisher that Cindy had a paranoid psychotic personality with features of a histrionic disorder. He felt she was trying to destroy her identity in the fire by burning the keepsakes from her past. Friesen also said that he felt someone was trying to sabotage his treatment of her. He explained that after Cindy's father and an unidentified visitor – Hack's brother from Las Vegas, it was later learned – came to see Cindy, she regressed "back to square one." And he told Fisher that Cindy had agreed to pay Ozzie Kaban $30,000 if her ex-husband ever was charged.

As well, Fisher noted, Friesen felt that if Cindy admitted to setting the fire and faced charges, it could jeopardize his treatment of her. With this, Fisher decided not to charge Cindy with arson. Instead, she put a secret C-237 entry in Cindy's RCMP file, which said she was responsible for the arson. The secret entry, with access only on the approval of a commanding officer, contained the confidential psychiatric information Fisher had obtained.

Fisher also talked with Bonnie Gallagher, the RCMP's psychological counsellor. Gallagher suggested that Cindy's destruction of personal effects in the fire showed she was getting ready to die. Gallagher also thought it possible that Cindy had a multiple personality disorder (MPD), as she had experienced bouts of amnesia, one of the symptoms of MPD.

In Fisher's mind, her initial hunch was gelling in a theory supported by professional medical opinions.

On July 14, 1986, Cindy's father met with Richmond RCMP Sergeant Ken Holmberg, who discussed the April 16 fire. "We believe Cindy set the fire," Hack was told, although the physical evidence from the fire was inconclusive. Hack was skeptical.

On July 15, after almost three months in psychiatric care, Cindy was released from St. Paul's. To clear her head, she decided to take a month-long trip to Germany to visit her brother. Returning August 25, Cindy moved back, temporarily, to her house at 14th and Blenheim while continuing to look for a new house.

On September 3, her offer on a home at 8220 Claysmith Road in Richmond was accepted. The house had a nice garden, a fenced yard for Heidi and no lane that could provide an easy escape route for an assailant.

After selling her house, Cindy legally changed her married name to Cindy James from Cindy Makepeace. She chose the male appellation "James" because, she said, it was short and easy to remember. She wanted a new name, a new identity. By becoming another Cindy she hoped to elude the persons who were hounding her. She wanted the terror to stop. And she felt confident it would.

After six months on short-term sick leave, the "new" Cindy finally felt strong enough to return to work. But on November 17, 1986, her first day back, she was asked to resign as director of Blenheim House. Given a year to "retire," she was told she could continue receiving long-term sick benefits until then.

"She took it very poorly," Sue Fisk recalled. "She must have felt betrayed." Fisk had run the facility during Cindy's long periods of absence and was appointed director when Cindy officially left Blenheim House.

"I asked her to leave Blenheim for her own safety," Fisk explained, adding that staff tried to convince her to move overseas to escape the torment. Cindy's employer even found her a job in Europe and offered to help pay her moving expenses.

Fisk felt extreme anguish at having to carry out the firing. She had visited Cindy often during her stay at St. Paul's, where her boss had confided that she had had a very hard childhood.

Fisk said Cindy was very good at compartmentalizing the terrorizing parts of her life, but not very good at expressing her emotions. At various times, Cindy would form an alliance with one staff member, confide in him or her, then cut that person off and move on to someone else.

Dr. Carl Rothschild, a child psychiatrist at Blenheim House, was an early confidant. When the decision was made to fire Cindy, Rothschild felt she was "psychiatrically impaired" and could not continue managing the facility. "Whatever was going on was having a serious effect on both the staff and the patients."

Dr. Friesen, whom Cindy was continuing to see, encouraged Cindy to get angry, to express her anger by writing letters of protest to her employer, which she did. "This totally unexpected and, I feel, unfair action on the part of administration resulted in a reappearance of many of my symptoms and I have had to remain on long-term disability pension," Cindy wrote in a letter dated January 15, 1987, to Peter Dueck, Minister of Health for British Columbia. "I have been unable to get a fair hearing by the local administrators of the [Greater Vancouver Mental Health Service]. I feel I have been wrongfully dismissed and possibly suffered discrimination as a result of having a mental illness. This is particularly reprehensible as the GVMHS purports to treat and, when possible, return to the work force, mentally ill patients."

This protest failed to get Cindy her job back. Instead, she hired a lawyer to reach a settlement and finally accepted an offer of slightly more than $28,000 in severance pay.

This money, however, mattered little. It was the job that counted most for Cindy. When it was withdrawn, the last prop of stability in Cindy's life crumbled.

ELEVEN

Cindy's Diary

P USHED out of her job at Blenheim House, Cindy had only one ready option to earn a living: a return to nursing. After almost 15 years as the director of a psychiatric facility, she was forced to wind the clock back two decades and take refresher courses to become, once again, the dutiful nurse. The cruel reality of it hit her like a blow to the head. Losing her job, in fact, rekindled her hatred of Roy.

Still, Cindy was a fighter, "a survivor, not a victim," as she would say. Determined not to accept defeat, she buckled down on her upgrading courses and scored 90 per cent on exams. With her managerial experience and glowing letters of reference, Cindy was hired in early 1987 as a nursing "student" at Richmond General Hospital, a few minutes' drive from her home on Claysmith. Although she would not officially regain her registered nurse status until February 1989, she was initially appointed nurse in charge of ward 2-South, a medical ward where patients were transferred after intensive care; there Cindy handled everything from the occasional Alzheimer patient and chronic alcoholics to cancer patients needing observation.

Cindy enjoyed her charges, but found nursing very regimented compared to her job at Blenheim House, where she had been her own boss. "It was the only job I ever had where I didn't have to fit in to someone else's philosophy or way of doing things. I was free to do what *I* believe in. Now I'm back to where I always used to be. Someone else sets the rules and you have to do things their way. That was true when I was growing up and when I lived with Roy, too. I sure gave Roy a lot of power."

She also found the physical work tiring, having to lift patients in and out of their beds, and to clean soiled diapers of aging men and women. And she began to resent the indifference with which some of the doctors treated nursing staff and patients.

Of one doctor, she said: "I could spit in his face. He didn't give a damn about Mrs. M and couldn't be bothered to even come and see her when I told him how serious her condition was. I even had the gall to ask him if he then wanted her resuscitated if she arrested – I couldn't have told him more plainly that there was a distinct possibility the way things were going with her, but he was 'too busy' and of course she arrested three quarters of an hour later and the efforts to bring her back were unsuccessful. The bastard, he didn't even give a damn. . . . "

The only way out of the dreary routine of institutional nursing, she felt, was to obtain a university degree. Although it seemed daunting, she took the first step by enrolling in a first-year English course, which she worked on in her few spare hours between 12-hour shifts.

Fourteen months went by without incident after the April 1986 fire. That peace was shattered on June 28, 1987, shortly after Cindy's forty-third birthday, when the burglar alarm sounded at her Richmond home while she was at work. Police dismissed it as only the wind, but Cindy was not so sure. It made her anxious, tense. Still, after weeks passed without a follow-up incident, she thought police were right. With a new name and her car re-painted blue, she felt that maybe, just maybe, peace was at hand.

Two months later, on August 28, the burglar alarm rang again; another break-in attempt. A back window had been broken. Three days went by before the alarm rang out once more; the same rear basement window was found pried open and the back yard floodlight unscrewed. September 6 saw another attempted break-in. This time, it appeared someone had used a glass cutter on the rear basement window. On some of the larger pieces of shattered glass that had dropped inside at the base of the door, police noticed scratches intersecting at 90-degree angles.

Cindy told the investigating officer, RCMP Constable James Johannson, that her dog had been barking for about 10 minutes prior to the alarm sounding. She had looked out her back window to see the apparent culprit running through her yard. Johannson toured the yard but found no footprints in the dew covering the lawn. He did notice the rear light was unscrewed. A dusting for fingerprints revealed only a glove impression. An off-duty police dogmaster was called in, but his dog could not detect a whiff of a track.

As suddenly as the flurry of break-ins arose, they stopped. All was quiet for five months until February 11, 1988, when police responded to the ringing burglar alarm at Cindy's residence. The window of her rear basement door had been broken again. This time electrical tape had been used on the glass to muffle the sound.

Again, the harassment stopped. Six months passed quietly. Cindy did her best to cope with the erratic rhythm of hospital shiftwork. Her social life was reduced to playing bridge with the Woodcocks and the occasional lunch or dinner with friends and family. A romantic relationship, she felt, was out of the question. Pat McBride had been her final fling.

Still, Cindy developed a platonic relationship with Ton Groenevelt, the real estate agent who sold Cindy her Richmond home. Groenevelt, who was nearing retirement age, would join Cindy and the Woodcocks for bridge. He adored Cindy, whom he thought was kind and caring. The only other men in Cindy's life were her father and the husbands of her sisters and women friends. After Roy, she felt she could never trust another man.

She continued to see Dr. Friesen regularly, hour-long sessions once every two weeks. Together, they agreed that Cindy should try to wean herself from the sleeping pills and tranquilizers she took to ease her anxiety and troubled sleep. Friesen also encouraged her to begin keeping a journal to vent her pent-up anger. Cindy searched through her house and found a blank book her sister Melanie had given her a few years earlier. Titled *A Women's Notebook*, it contained a quote on each page from prominent women of the nineteenth and twentieth centuries.

"Well, Melanie, you gave me this book a few years ago thinking it might help me to write down some of my anguish I was feeling and unable to talk about, and only now am I finally doing it!" Cindy wrote on an inside page at the front of the book. "My first thought was, 'Oh no, what if someone ever gets hold of it' – I hate the thought of exposing myself that way. But no one will ever see it and he [Friesen] must have some important reason for wanting me to go through the exercise. I so much want to feel intensely alive again – it feels like forever since I last felt that way. I don't even know who I am any more. Maybe this book will help me discover that."

Cindy's journal is full of raw emotion. No one recalls her ever discussing it, so it will never be known if it helped her discover who she was. It may have helped Cindy reflect on her feelings and inner thoughts. Then again, those thoughts may have frightened her. It appears she wrote candidly in her diary, expressing an honesty she often feared to do with even her confidants.

The diary offers startling testimony of the turmoil in her life. In the first week alone, Cindy poured out what would become recurring themes: her obsession with sleep, her vivid nightmares, her flaming rage at those she felt were responsible for her shattered dreams.

The first entry, dated April 18, 1988, reads:

"I feel so angry when Dr. Friesen says my father used to protect me. When were you ever there when I needed you Dad? What did you tell him Dad? Did you play your game of being the almighty Colonel who looked after his 'troops?' I don't know why I'm crying. I think my anger often turns to tears because I can't deal with it. But, dammit, when were you really there for me? You and Roy played the same game – when the door was open you were one person, but as soon as the door was closed, God help anyone who got too close. This journal is going to be useless if I'm just going to cry as soon as I start writing.

"Dr. Friesen said sometimes he feels frustrated with me. I wonder if that means anger. I'm so afraid I'm defective in some way, that I do something to men that changes them and brings out the anger in them.

"Today is two years and three days since the fire. The fifteenth has passed and it has stayed quiet, maybe I can sleep tonight. I'll keep the bedroom light on though, just in case. I'm such a coward.

"Ton phoned – wanted to come over. Said he could hear I was feeling sad. Said no. I hate to have people see me when I'm down."

April 19/88
"Oh God, another terrible night last night. Couldn't get to sleep and when I did I woke up after about two hours and I couldn't stop crying. Don't know if I had a nightmare, just aware that I kept thinking 'I hate you, I hate you,' about Roy over and over. Cried for several hours and took Valium and finally fell asleep again. Woke up with a pounding headache and feeling very listless. Couldn't drag myself out of bed until after noon.

"Have to get to work on my English assignments, but I don't want to. I don't think I'll ever get through the course, it is so hard to concentrate. I get so mad that I even have to be spending my time off on that. I just want to be back in my old job. . . . [Roy] said I would never survive on my own. Got to prove him wrong. The sun is shining and there is so much to do in the garden as well. Think I'll try working outside. I usually feel better when I've been working in the garden. Helps me get things in perspective. Would really like to just go back to bed and blot out everything.

". . . I don't know who I am any more. Ton came by late this p.m. with a single red rose. [He] said I still look sad and he thought we were friends and he felt shut out when I wouldn't share my sadness. I felt so ashamed and just wanted him to go away."

April 20/88

"Am much better day today. I slept better, no nightmares, though I woke up several times during the night. Still hated to get up. Spent several hours on English by bargaining with myself that I could quit at 4 p.m. and go out and cut the lawn and lime it. No tears today, but I feel generally sad. I wish I could understand and forgive the people at Blenheim [House] for refusing to talk to me. Not one has made any effort to contact me and I thought a few of them were close friends. I think of times they leaned on me and said how much they cared, but it was obviously bullshit. People use you and when they don't need you any more they slam the door in your face. I sometimes wonder how they sleep at night. I guess those 'friendships' were an illusion on my part too. What is real anyway? Who can you trust? The safest answer is: no one!"

April 21/88

"A busy day at work. No time to think about anything else, which was good. . . . Poor little Heidi, she sees so little of me when I'm working. I come home, feed her, have a bath and go to bed."

April 22/88

"Awake at 4:30 this morning and couldn't get back to sleep. Hard to get up and go to work. Had a very touching moment with a difficult patient today, who everyone avoids. He is very combative and confused at times. He suddenly grabbed my hand and said, 'You a good nurse, you have so much love in your eyes.' I told him I saw so much fear in his eyes. He cried and said he was afraid he was going to die! Remarkable – none of us guessed he was that aware of where and who he was.

"Since coming home his words keep going through my head. I feel so much hate inside sometimes that I think, if anyone could see my soul, it would be black. How can I be full of so much hate and have someone, a stranger, see love in my eyes? It's so confusing. Which part of me is real – the one I feel inside or the one other people seem to see outside? Dr. Friesen says I'm not a bad person. I don't think of myself as *bad*, I just don't think of myself as good. I'm not worthy, but I'm not sure what I'm not worthy of. It's like I've walled off so much anger & sadness that the walls have come full circle and engulfed me. For some reason this is feeling scary. I don't want to write any more today."

April 23/88

"A very restless night with a horrible nightmare around 5 a.m. and couldn't get back to sleep. Didn't panic as much. I'm getting better at reminding myself it is just a nightmare and not happening again. Stayed in bed until noon as I have to work nights tonight, but I didn't really sleep – just kept tossing and turning and fighting to keep images of the past from intruding. It's so discouraging that this keeps happening, I'm getting so tired again.

Karen phoned to remind me of her party tonight. I had to remind her I'm on nights. This time I'm glad I can't go. I don't feel like being around people and noise.

"Spent the afternoon writing letters and doing laundry and watering plants. I feel strangely tense, even my stomach feels knotted up, and at the same time, I feel such a deep sadness about everything. I don't feel like trying to figure it out right now, but I'm going to have to sometime. I've got to try to eat something. I'm losing weight again. Have to try to keep myself up for working tonight. I think my real problem is I'm wallowing in self-pity. What a jerk!"

April 24/88
"Not a bad night – busy, but not hectic. Had a hard time winding down to go to sleep and then awakened by kids next door around noon. Lay down on the couch with Heidi curled up by me, just to rest. Started to cry again. Don't really know why. It's not that I'm aware of feeling lonely, really. I sure wouldn't trade my home life now with what I had with Roy, especially that last year. At least I now have the freedom to do what I want and don't have to worry all the time about whether he is in an angry or calm mood. That last year was like living a nightmare all the time. Always tense, always afraid of saying the wrong thing, trying to anticipate when to disappear for a while and not always successful. . . . No one will ever really understand what it was like. Don't think about it. You left when you knew it was better to be dead than to live like that."

April 26/88
". . . Spent several hours scrubbing the sun deck and planting hanging baskets & planter boxes. While I was scrubbing the deck, I was working at it furiously, and realized I was aware of a lot of anger towards Roy that I was turning into physical work. I spend a lot of time and energy keeping the lid on a lot of anger – fury, really – that I just don't know how to express or get rid of. I imagined scrubbing his existence off the face of this earth. Every speck of grunge was a bit more of his filth that I had to scrub away."

April 27/88

". . . Hard to concentrate and have to force myself not to let my mind wander. For some reason images of Roy's face, contorted in anger, kept intruding. I kept seeing that one vein in his temple bulging and pulsing. . . . [An] image that was particularly persistent was of having my wrists and ankles tied so I couldn't get free and my face was covered with something rough and smothering so I couldn't see – everything was so dark and the horrible things they were doing and the pain. Oh my God, I mustn't think about it."

April 30/88

". . . Got a hang-up phone call about half an hour after getting home. Don't know if it's that, or what, but I feel kind of jittery. Hope there aren't any more over the next few days as that seems to have been a pattern before my house was broken into each time. Maybe I'll take a taxi to work on Monday night so it doesn't look like the house is empty. Christ, I'm sick of this! I'm so tired of living in fear. I'm so bloody tired period! I'm tired of feeling tired. Dammit, I'm wallowing in self-pity again. Sometimes I really irritate myself.

"Think I'll swallow my pride and take a Valium tonight. I really am tired but I feel so keyed up Why am I apologizing to myself? If I need a Valium, I need it. It shouldn't be such a big deal."

Cindy realized that she was having trouble dealing with the battered women brought into the hospital. For a woman who claimed for years to have experienced similar abuse, she had an odd reaction.

May 13

". . . In the back of my head a question keeps hovering: Why do I find it so hard to deal with battered women patients at work? I used to think maybe a good outcome of all I have been through would be an ability to counsel other women who have been abused and give them support. But I find I want to avoid them if they're admitted to the ward. I feel sick and angry when I see their black eyes and bruises. But – I don't understand this – I feel angry at them!"

Nearing the end of her first month of diary writing, a more profound anger toward Roy, toward herself and toward her current life powerfully asserted itself.

May 15

"While working in the garden I kept remembering the time . . . Roy, in a fit of anger, stomped all over the bed of seedlings, killing them all. I remember telling him those were living things he had so wantonly destroyed. . . . It hurt so much and it was so frightening. . . . "

May 17

"Anger. Such a small word and such strong emotion. I have so much trouble expressing it and so little defence against it except to withdraw. But not with everyone. I used to love the angry spirit and guts in some of the kids I worked with. It was such healthy anger and so justified. Why don't I feel mine is justified? But I do. I know I have a right to feel angry at Roy and the police and Dad and Doug and the people at Blenheim and Head Office [of the Greater Vancouver Mental Health Services] and some of the doctors I encountered and so many other people. But anger so often seems so destructive or futile. I used to scream at God, 'How could you let this go on?' but he never heard me or never cared, I guess. I was able to deal with anger in the parents I worked with; I guess I was able not to take it personally. But I always feel I frightened other people when I got angry myself, especially the people I worked with. They always seemed to back down when I disagreed strongly about something. But I didn't feel angry at those times – just strong in my conviction. Why did they back down?"

More and more, the severe exhaustion brought on by anxiety and lack of sleep became a preoccupation in Cindy's life.

May 19

"Oh God, so tired again. Didn't get to bed until after 9 a.m. and awake by 11, so less than two hours. Tried relaxation exercises but they just made me feel frustrated when they didn't work. Cut out the Valium today as Dr. Friesen felt I was taking too much, with Halcions [sleeping pills] as well. At least I had two weeks of rest. I dread the thought of dragging myself around, constantly tired again. It all seems so futile. I know I should be slowly working towards a natural sleep without pills. I feel so ashamed now that I succumbed to the seduction of using pills to get some rest. But trying to get back to a normal sleep is constantly being sabotaged by my constantly changing shifts. I think I should just give up pills altogether and fight this through until I either beat it or it beats me completely. I know my whole attitude changes when I'm tired. I used to need eight hours to feel refreshed – that seems a lifetime ago that I actually got that [much sleep]. Everything looks bleaker when I'm tired. Well, it's time to fight it out without any help. I should be used to that by now. Surely eventually your body just caves in and sleeps out of pure necessity if you wait long enough."

Friesen had been urging Cindy to try to establish another relationship, but Cindy kept resisting, feeling she was not ready. But her entry for May 25 shows her beginning to trust her friend Ton.

"Last night I did something I didn't think I'd ever be able to do. I phoned Ton and asked him if he'd like to come over and share a bottle of wine and talk to someone who was feeling really down. We talked for hours, and although nothing's really changed, I do feel better. . . . He phoned me after I got home from work tonight to say how honoured he felt that we were good enough friends for me to have called him. He knew how hard that had been, shutting out my friends a lot. I always felt they had enough problems in their own lives that they didn't need to be burdened with mine. I'm glad I phoned him, though I still feel a bit ashamed."

Cindy's fatigue, however, quickly overshadowed any positive feelings the experience may have provided.

May 28

"Too tired in the past few days to write anything. I feel like I'm going to spend the rest of my life feeling perpetually exhausted. What do I keep struggling for? There is no point in existence. You just drag yourself from one day to the next endlessly until you die."

May 30

"Slept fairly well once I got to sleep, but took a long time. . . . Suddenly realized that it's partly because I feel so vulnerable when I sleep. You're helpless, not on guard. For so long I never knew when something horrible would happen. I'd just seem to relax and think it was over, when something would happen that made it necessary for me to be alert, careful and watching again. Eventually I was tense all the time until I got exhausted. Now I think I tense up, fearing the nightmares or memories will start overwhelming me. What an absurd situation – I'm my own worst enemy now. I know I need to deal with the past and put it behind me somehow, but the horror is still so strong, and the fear. I had no control over my life and I was so stupid in trusting some of the people I did. Shit, when will I stop agonizing about it. It's over, for Pete's sake!"

Despite her disorientation, Cindy wanted to come to grips with just what was plaguing her mentally. Time and again she wrote of her changing attitude to her problems, and the reactions of Dr. Friesen and others.

June 2

". . . Felt pretty good today. Watched a [TV] special on post-traumatic stress disorder in Vietnam vets when I got home from work. I identified with a lot of the symptoms they described experiencing, especially the nightmares, anxiety, the mistrust of people and the flashbacks. As one man said, 'It's not just the memories, it's breaking down under it that is so hard.' I know what he means. Sometimes, when the memories become overwhelming, I feel as though I'm only now allowing myself to feel the terror and pain I couldn't deal with at the time. I had to wall the feelings off or I wouldn't have survived. I also understand why they find it so hard to talk about. You feel like no one will really understand, but you're also afraid of being overwhelmed by your own feelings, to the point of where you feel trapped forever in the horror of it. But I don't feel the urge to do violence that they describe, except for the suicidal feelings.

"I do feel a strong need for justice that I have to accept will never occur. Maybe that's the difference between living with having done something awful as compared to having awful things done to you. It's true I do hate Roy, but I just want to know he no longer exists. I don't want to physically hurt him myself. Having watched the program, I feel very lucky that I've had the help of Dr. Connolly and now Dr. Friesen. It *is* true that some good things did come out of it – I never would have met them otherwise. It's taught me that there are some good and caring people in this world. For the first time I really *feel* and don't just intellectually agree that I'm so much better than I was, say, two years ago. I remember how horribly raw I felt, like every nerve was stretched to breaking point and scraped bare of any protective covering. I really am getting better,

I really am. I've come a long way thanks to Dr. Friesen and it's time to let him know I recognize that. He must often be left feeling that I'm very ungrateful for all he's done for me."

June 7

"I feel really hurt by something Dr. Friesen said today. When I told him how grateful I was for everything he's done for me, he implied that I was saying it only because I'm someone who always feels they have to say something positive. . . . Like I'm an empty phoney who isn't 'real.' He's wrong. I'm not a liar. I may not always tell people when I'm upset or angry with them, but I don't tell people positive [things] unless I mean them either. . . . he said I've never expressed anger to him about Roy. I couldn't at first because I felt so responsible for Roy's behaviour. Then when I really wanted to talk about Roy, I felt Dr. Friesen didn't want me to – we ended up talking about Dad instead because it was safer, I guess. I got so much bottled up about Roy and I felt he thought it wasn't 'healthy' for me to think about it or talk about it. I feel so confused. I'm beginning to wonder if he [Friesen] is just as afraid of the strength of my feelings as I am."

June 8

". . . I feel a lot of anger towards the police. I doubt if I would ever be able to advise a woman to turn to the police for help. I feel like I was assaulted by them, too. Not physically, but certainly emotionally and psychologically."

June 16

"I wish I could talk to Dr. Friesen about all the things that happened. I wish I could talk about Roy. I wish I could understand what it was all about. I wish I could talk it all out until it was purged from my heart and my memory. I read something the other day in which a woman said she wasn't a victim, she was a survivor. That sounds so much more positive. I don't want to keep sinking into self pity. I want to be stronger than that. I wish I could forget.

"I keep remembering Dr. Choi telling me the whole thing had been in my imagination. He even asked me to define the word delusion. . . . It certainly made me shut my mouth. I've locked everything up inside until it hurts so much I think I can't stand it. I wish I could cry."

At work, Cindy grew increasingly disenchanted and resentful. She wondered if the strangulations she had suffered had left her brain-damaged. "Oh God, I'm scared," she wrote. "I feel trapped again. No options. Maybe I couldn't have done my job at Blenheim House again. Maybe I'm not capable of anything any more, except cleaning up old people's dirty diapers. . . . I feel like crying but the tears are all blocked up."

She also continued to have trouble coping with women patients who had been abused.

June 17

"I don't know what to do about going to work tomorrow. This afternoon a woman was admitted who had been assaulted. I saw her being wheeled onto the ward on a stretcher, with two policemen accompanying her. I felt my stomach heave and I thought I was going to vomit. I had to quickly look away and keep swallowing until the feeling went away. About five minutes later I had a panic attack – the first time it has happened on the ward. It didn't last long. I realized what had caused it and managed to get my feelings under control. I avoided even looking at the door of her room for the rest of my shift. Just before leaving, I looked at the assignment sheet and discovered I have . . . that room. I felt like I had been given an electric shock . . . I want to call in sick, do anything except walk in that room tomorrow. But I know I can't keep avoiding these women either. I don't know how to deal with my feelings

about what happened to me. It's as though I went numb at
the time and now the feelings are surfacing and I feel [are]
overwhelming. I'm so afraid they'll sense my feelings and
be hurt even more . . . Selfishly, I'm also afraid for myself. I
don't want to face the fact that it happened to me.''

June 18

"I did as Dr. Friesen suggested. After a night of repeated nightmares . . . I gave up and sat in the living room
listening to Zamfir's music, cuddled up with Heidi until
morning. I traded rooms at the hospital with Pat 'for personal reasons.' She looked startled and then willingly
agreed since her rooms are heavier than mine right now. It
may start questions I'll have to deal with by evasion but
right now I don't care. I kept thinking about what I'd like
to say to that woman but I know I couldn't say them – I
couldn't deal with the pain in her eyes. She would have felt
rejected by me. She would have noticed my avoidance and
she would have felt devastated. I want to help her but I
can't. I have to help myself first. The head nurse will be
surprised if she finds out. I've gained a reputation as being
sensitive and caring to the patients considered difficult to
manage. It's always, 'Give him/her to Cindy, she's good
with those patients.' I feel so badly. I knew how much she
must be hurting and I feel so guilty that I can't go in to her.
I'm exhausted tonight but still too keyed up to sleep. I've
got to start dealing with my own feelings or I'll never be
whole again. I don't feel good about what I did today, but I
have to recognize that it was necessary.''

At the end of June, Cindy spent several days at her parents' home on Vancouver Island, where her sister Melanie's wedding was held. The visit triggered her old
resentment of her parents' apparent bickering and what
she deemed her father's controlling nature.

July 5

"I cut my stay in Victoria short by a day and came back today because I was feeling so stressed out and fragile that I just had to get away from everyone for a while. I've slept so poorly over the past week. . . . Part of that was because I was sleeping on a cot in Dad's office and whenever I have to sleep there he always finds a reason why he has to barge in at 5 or 6 when he gets up in the morning. Even when I ask him the night before if he's going to need anything so he can get it before I go to bed, sure as fate, he barges in in the morning anyway. On the second night I pushed my suitcase against the door so he couldn't come in, but he just kept pushing the door until he got it open. Why can't he respect my right to privacy? I've even told him I have trouble sleeping because I find it hard to relax and let go to sleep and that his coming in unannounced is very startling. He just pooh-poohed it as nonsense and kept doing it. I feel like it's . . . a lack of respect for me. . . . Even worse was the tension in the house. Dad was constantly putting down Mom and anyone else who happened to be nearby. The two of them bickered constantly. It was interesting to see the difference between how [I felt] Dad treated the women and children in the family and the men. . . . And the battles between Melanie and Dad were incredible. Melanie was trying so desperately to make her wedding the way she wanted it to be and Dad was determined that things would be done his way. . . . And then on the day of the wedding, Dad put on his affable host act and everyone congratulated him on having done such a good job! . . .

"All the old stress symptoms came back. I couldn't tolerate noise, crowds or action. Every muscle felt painful . . . I couldn't eat, I was having nightmares every night, I felt like if I relaxed for a moment I was going to burst into tears and I was afraid to go anywhere there were strangers. But I had to hide all that from everyone because there was enough tension without adding my inadequacies to the problems.

"A couple of times my sisters and brothers and I escaped by telling Mom we were going in to town for dinner. We always chose a time when there were visitors in the house so Mom and Dad couldn't possibly join us. I guess they thought we were awfully rude, but by then none of us cared what they thought – we just had to get out. Those times were the most fun, though I had become so stressed that I found it hard to relax . . .

"The night before I left to return to Vancouver I made an utter fool of myself in front of my sister. But in a way I'm glad it happened. The house was full of people and the family were preparing for a ride up Island and a picnic the next day. We were then going to stop in Victoria in the evening to see a movie. The noise and the bustle in the house became unbearable and I went out on the back patio to sit by myself for a while. I felt like I was going to start screaming or crying if I didn't get some quiet. Marlene found me out there and asked me to come and join them making up the picnic. I had to tell her I couldn't join them tomorrow, that I had decided to go back to Vancouver. Then everything spilled out. I told her I couldn't bear the thought of being cooped up in a car for hours with all the noise and I confessed that I still wasn't able to sit in a dark movie theatre. I felt so ashamed admitting my weaknesses and I couldn't stop crying. I think the tears were finally a release of some of the tension I was bottling up. We talked for a long time about a lot of things.

"She told me I shouldn't feel ashamed, that the family felt so helpless to try to help me overcome all that I had been through. And that when I didn't tell them when things were hurting or becoming too much, they felt shut out and that I wanted them to pretend nothing had happened. She told me that the *greatest* honour I could pay her and my other sister and brothers was to say what I needed and believe in their love enough to feel comfortable in leaving without apology, if that's what I needed.

"We talked a lot about how it had been growing up in our family and she said I was always the protector of the kids. She even apologized for all the times she had allowed me to take the blame for something she had done. She said I always seemed so strong. . . . And she said she knew I would never tell on her. Then we cried. We ended up laughing, though, remembering some of the fun times we had together. We told each other how much we loved each other, and we meant it."

Cindy's nightmares intensified after she returned from her sister's wedding, and she had bouts of crying. Still, her diary records the growing influence Dr. Friesen was having on her well-being.

July 8

"No sleep at all last night. Tossing and turning and remembering Dr. Choi not believing me – telling me I was suffering from delusions! I feel so angry at him. I wish things could have been resolved so I could have proved him wrong. . . . Dr Friesen is so different. I don't think I could bear it if my trust in him is proved wrong. I wish I could feel free enough to talk to him about Roy. I need so much to talk about what happened and to express my anger towards Roy. To get out some of that black, cancerous rage that I'm holding inside. I feel outraged at what happened and at how incompetent I was in trying to cope with it. What an idiot I've been. I gave Roy so much power and I trusted him. I was such a naive, trusting fool. . . ."

Cindy's July 9 entry indicates a frequent pattern – every time she expressed anger at her mother or father, it quickly turned into rage toward Roy.

"I keep thinking of a comment Mom made to Marlene when Marlene apologized to Johanna. Mom said, 'Don't ever apologize to a child. Don't ever lower yourself that far.' I suddenly realized that it was Mom, too, not just Dad who made us feel so much like nothings when we were growing up. There was no recognition or respect for us as kids, ever. No wonder [with Roy] I so easily . . . gave up all the rights to which we're all entitled – I assumed I had no rights for respect and being treated as an equal. [I used to be told] I was nothing without [Roy] and I believed that. . . ."

Occasionally, Cindy came to a sudden realization of how memories of her past had helped shape and colour the problems that arose later in life.
July 13
   "Difficulty falling asleep and wide awake at 4 a.m. . . . Suddenly came to understand something – why I always freeze and do nothing to protect myself when I feel threatened. It's been bothering me so much. Why, for example, I didn't react quicker when the 'jogger' came through my back gate and assaulted me at the back door. But I learned from Dad when I was such a little girl that I would be hurt more if I cried out or fought back. . . . I think Roy understood that about me a long time ago. . . . And what a fool I was to trust him enough to tell him about my childhood.
   "It's so hard sometimes to believe I can trust Dr. Friesen. There are so many things I want to talk to him about, but when the time comes, I just can't get the words out. By the end of a session I feel more trusting, but by the time the next session rolls around it's been so much time that my walls are back up again."

By July 14, Cindy began to suffer physical symptoms of inner turmoil and she worried that her colleagues were beginning to notice. "They tell me I look so sad. I'm finding it harder and harder to pretend I returned to nursing by choice. I've Had a lot of physical symptoms . . . continual tingling and numbness of my lips and fingers, cramping of my left thumb, light-headedness, especially when I stand up, panic attacks, a feeling that my left leg is dragging . . . crying spells and inability to push out horrible memories and a continual feeling of tension and anxiety."

After Cindy's visit with Dr. Friesen July 29, she felt bitterness arise when he asked her if she would ever fall in love again. "How can he ask that? He said he thinks I'd sleep better if I had someone lying in bed beside me. That sounds so chauvinistic. It's like saying, 'Your problem is you need a man.' The old stereotype of the divorced woman who's lonely and needs sex. I rarely have any erotic feelings at all. I think that part of me is dead, too. . . . I'm afraid to let anyone get that close."

She pondered the question of relationships the next day after having her friends over for a barbecue. "I get so tired of people asking me when I'm going to start dating. It's as though you're not quite whole as long as you choose to remain single. I don't think I have much to offer a man and I'm so afraid of becoming a 'puppet' again."

Cindy's diary entries for the first week of August were perfunctory, noting only her troubled sleep pattern. Later that month, she joined a fitness centre to get some exercise. But slowly, relentlessly, the shadows of her past rolled in like midsummer thunder clouds.

August 17

"(Clorazepam 2 mg. and Halcion 1 mg.) Three hours sleep . . . Kept thinking of the bits and pieces of memory I have of the last time I was assaulted. I know I was sexually violated. There, I've finally said it. I just didn't know exactly what happened. The thing I remember most vividly was a terrible pain in my groin. I'm sure someone butted out their cigarette in me. I remember the laughter when I tried to jerk my legs together, but something was holding them stretched apart. Something was over my face because I couldn't see and I felt suffocated. Oh God, just block it all out."

August 21

". . . I wish I were seeing Dr. Friesen tomorrow. I want to start working on exorcising Roy from my mind. He still

feels like a black ghost . . . who keeps haunting me. I want
to destroy his impact on me even if I can't destroy him. . . ."

August 22
   "Very poor sleep last night. I'm not sure if I even got
any. Watched the clock every hour through the night, getting more and more frustrated. Kept thinking about Dr.
Friesen asking me if I was still in love with Roy. It makes
me so angry that he could even ask that question. Kept
getting vivid images of some of the more frightening
things that I still can't even talk to him about. I feel like he
doesn't even know who I am or understand the terror of
all that happened. I feel so alone right now – like if he
[Friesen] doesn't understand how much I hate Roy, no one
in the universe will ever understand. Again, I feel like I
somehow live on a different planet. . . . "

   Amid all her feelings of rage and resentment, a different, unexpected feeling arose.
August 26
   "Six solid hours sleep last night even after sleeping four
hours in the morning! Woke up feeling something I haven't
felt in a long time. Felt warm and cosy and sexy and rolled
over to the other side of the bed, wishing there was someone there I cared about, that I could cuddle with. Felt
really shocked when I realized what I was feeling – didn't
think I'd ever again want a man in my bed."

   If it was a sign Cindy's mood and health were improving, a phone call quickly brought back more familiar
feelings.
August 30
   ". . . Got the lawn cut and various chores done. Then an
obscene phone call ending with, 'You're dead meat, cunt,'
which was really scary . . . it reminded me of those phone

calls a few years ago. I'm glad I'm working tonight and won't be home. I want to run and hide, but I can't let myself give in to the panic. It was just a sick man getting his sick kicks. What a sick world."

September 4

"Must have dropped asleep around dawn and then a horrible, horrible nightmare . . . of the incident that came out under hypnosis. Oh my God, I wish I knew if it was a memory or just a nightmare. Very tired today and just anxious to get back home. Kept getting flashes of that nightmare at odd moments through the day. When I got home this evening I felt very anxious and nervous about being alone."

September 5

". . . nightmares again. The same one as last night and the disjointed bits I can remember of the last assault. Couldn't shake the memories all day. . . . I feel so angry and helpless and frightened and alone. Why did I ever trust Roy? I'm feeling the need to keep people at a distance again. I'm glad no one is here to touch me. My stomach is all knotted up and I have to keep swallowing to keep from retching. I wish I could cry or scream or something to loosen the tension."

September 7

". . . Repeated flashbacks and feeling so angry about so many things. Also kept wondering what to do about my future. I feel such a sense of futility about everything.

"Despite feeling tired and the day being very busy, I felt real contact with my patients. I think I'll take some flowers from my garden in to two of them tomorrow who rarely get visitors and never have flowers. The motive is selfish, really. I'll feel good doing something extra for them. However neurotic it may be, I do feel good when I feel I've done something to make another person feel better. I just want them to know someone cares so they don't feel so alone."

September 11

". . . A lot of flashbacks and a barely controlled feeling of panic most of the time. I wish there was someone here I could talk to. I feel frightened and sad and so alone. For the first time in a while I just really feel like giving up trying to cope. . . . "

September 17

". . . Feeling mostly relaxed, though every once in a while I get flashes of that grisly, bloody scene somewhere on the Island. I wish I could block it out entirely."

September 20

"Saw Dr. Friesen yesterday. He didn't want to hear about the difficulties I had . . . or the ensuing nightmares. He says I need to get on with my life and build a new relationship with someone. He also says I don't express anger when I talk about Roy, like it isn't there. I don't understand it – sometimes I feel so consumed with anger and I just don't know what to do with it. I have such a need to talk about some of the horrible things that happened. I feel that's the only way I'll be able to put them behind me.

"I felt so distant from Dr. Friesen when I left. Decided to call Ozzie to ask him how other women let go of the horrors of the past. He couldn't help much, but at least I feel he listened and understood where I was coming from. I debated all night whether to keep seeing Dr. Friesen. I think he's feeling frustrated and ready to give up anyway. He says he doesn't want me to come in pretending everything is fine, but that's not true – when I had something I really needed to talk about he didn't want to hear it. I guess I'll go and just follow his lead and just talk about the things he feels are important and find ways to deal with the rest on my own somehow."

With this entry, Cindy stopped writing in her diary. Was it because she was feeling so dejected? Was it because she felt Dr. Friesen, who had suggested she start keeping diary and on whom she had grown so dependent, seemed not to care about the issues that were the focal point of her diary?

Were her memories and nightmares too painful to write about? Or did Cindy feel it was simply necessary to shelve the past and get on with the future?

It appears that she wanted to block the murky memories, fearing what might be lurking in her unconscious. Soon, however, the dark, shadowy tormentors she recalled in her nightmares were to arise once more.

TWELVE

"Soon, Cindy"

A WIND AS cold and sharp as a new razor blade sliced
through the night of October 26, 1988, as RCMP
Constable Sandro Colasacco parked his unmarked police
cruiser outside Cindy James's residence. It was shortly
after midnight and the only sounds to be heard were those
of the dry, shivering trees and the fallen, brittle leaves that
tumbled down Claysmith Road.

Colasacco had been dispatched to check a report of a
silent alarm received earlier by Ozzie Kaban's company.

As the constable cautiously walked up Cindy's driveway, he noticed most of the lights were on in her house. A
blue Chevrolet Citation was parked in the carport, its
dome light illuminating the inside of the vehicle.

Walking closer, Colasacco could see bare legs dangling
from the open driver's door. He expected the person inside
to be startled by his approach. Instead, he found a woman
lying unconscious on the driver's seat, nude from the waist
down, her white pantyhose at her ankles. She lay on her
right side, facing the dashboard.

He leaned over to check her neck for a pulse. Nothing.
He checked again at the wrist. He noticed her hands were
tied behind her back, her right hand clutching the "panic
button" that had triggered the silent alarm. She was cold.
Very cold.

"I've got a murder on my hands," Colasacco thought.
He stepped back and noticed the grey duct tape covering

188

the woman's nostrils, the bashed left side of her forehead and two drops of blood on the left side of her blouse.

Constables Colin Adair and Sam Salters pulled up. Colasacco told them he was going next door to phone the watch commander and tell him he had found a dead woman. He did not want to broadcast the incident over the police radio and have the media converge on the house.

Adair secured the yard and prepared to take names of anyone entering or leaving the scene, while Salters went to check the car. Leaning over the woman to check for a pulse, he heard a faint wheeze.

"She's alive!" Salters called out, noticing something – it looked like a black nylon stocking – tied around her neck. The woman was Cindy James.

Adair got a knife and handed it to Salters, who climbed in the back seat, reached over and easily sliced through the nylon wrapped twice around the woman's neck. Finding it awkward getting the knife under the nylon tying her hands behind her back, he finally freed the wrists with two cuts, then checked the woman's breathing. Her breath was deathly still. Giving her mouth-to-mouth, Salters felt her breathing begin to rise and fall, ever so slowly. He stayed in the car, placing his patrol jacket over Cindy, until the ambulance wheeled in at 12:31 a.m., a minute after it had been called.

Ambulance attendant Scott Bailey found Cindy James's pulse rate was 48 beats per minute, considerably slower than the average 60 to 80 a minute. Also, she was breathing only four times a minute, slower than the normal eight to 12 breaths. Unconscious, at the low end of the coma scale, Cindy did not react to a pain test. Examining her injuries, Bailey noted marks around her wrists, bruises around her neck and a small cut above her left eye.

A second ambulance responded to the call. Since it contained advanced life support equipment, that unit rushed Cindy to hospital. Bailey and paramedic Clark McGuire rode in the back with the patient. Before attempting to establish an intravenous line, McGuire noticed a blood droplet on the inside of Cindy's right arm. He tried to establish the IV in her left arm, but failed. It was difficult to perform on a patient with such a low body temperature – Cindy was cold, hypothermic. Bailey administered a bag-valve mask on the way to help keep Cindy's respiratory rate up.

Bailey wheeled Cindy's stretcher into Richmond General Hospital at 12:50 a.m. Emergency had been notified by police that "we had a hanging coming in," recalled Dr. William Akeroyd, the emergency ward physician who examined Cindy. He remembered Cindy's eyes were open when she was brought in. She seemed to be looking around. Other times her eyes were closed, and Akeroyd noticed flickering eye movements beneath the lids. After Cindy was quickly undressed, the doctor examined the scrapes on the woman's arms and legs and a few on her chest and right thigh. The injuries appeared superficial.

A nurse recognized Cindy as a colleague, "which added to the uniqueness of the situation," Akeroyd recalled.

Cindy was in a coma when plainclothes RCMP Constable Jerry Anderson arrived at the hospital at 1:55 a.m. He had been called at home and briefed at the RCMP detachment beforehand. While Cindy was unconscious, he made some enquiries with medical staff, learning Cindy had worked a 12-hour shift before the attack. Her shift should have ended at 7:30 p.m., but she worked a half-hour overtime to deal with a death on her ward.

The hospital phoned Cindy's father and Anderson spoke to him, asking a few questions about Cindy's background. Hack said Cindy's ex-husband had been a suspect in past incidents.

Anderson got into an argument with Akeroyd when he requested a sexual assault examination of Cindy. "You have to seek the patient's permission," Akeroyd stressed, questioning at length the officer's justification for the exam.

With Cindy still comatose, Anderson left the hospital at 2:17 a.m., asking medical staff to call him when she regained consciousness. He drove to Cindy's home to examine the scene.

An Identification officer was videotaping the evidence scattered about Cindy's driveway. A yellow Kleenex with blood spots beside the hedge to the east of the carport. Cindy's keys on the carport floor near the rear of the car on the driver's side. Her pants, with hospital ID tag attached, and left shoe caught in the pantleg, beside the open car door. A wrist watch with a severed black strap and Cindy's blue nylon jacket near the front fender.

About two metres ahead of the car lay Cindy's right shoe; it was white, matching her nurse's uniform. At the back of the carport, a tent trailer and yellow canoe were stored. On the carport floor near the gate leading to the back yard were drops of dried blood, four Export "A" cigarette butts, a douche bottle, crumpled white tissue and a number of scattered coins – a quarter, three dimes, two nickels. Cindy's purse was found inside the front of the car.

Officers checked Cindy's house, but all doors were locked and windows secure. A police dog later tracked the property and the adjacent yards, but failed to find a scent. No fingerprints were found on the car nor was there any evidence at the scene, not even Cindy's prints.

At 3:10 a.m., Anderson returned to the hospital with a tape recorder to find Cindy awake, lying in bed, dazed. She had complained to hospital staff that she had been assaulted, but did not offer to elaborate.

"Cindy, are you still awake?" asked Const. Adair, who introduced Anderson, explaining his fellow officer wanted to ask her a few questions.

"I really don't remember most of what happened," she said slowly, quietly. She had just started to get out of her car, she remembered, and suddenly someone was there. Putting a knife on her neck, a man told her not to make a sound. Then there was another man. That's all she could remember.

"Okay. Did he touch you, you know, any place else?" Anderson asked.

"I don't know . . . I'm sorry, I don't know. I just don't remember." Cindy was not aware that she had been tied up or that she had summoned help by pushing her panic button.

"Did this guy that, uh, first came up to you in the carport, did he say anything?" Anderson asked.

"He just told me to be quiet or he would kill me. Not to make any noise."

Anderson tried another line of inquiry. "I understand that in the past you've had, uh, troubles with your ex-husband?"

"Yes," she replied, pausing a few seconds. "That was a long time ago. That's over."

"It's over?"

"That was," Cindy said, pausing again to gather her thoughts. "That stopped. A couple of years ago I got a divorce."

"Okay, so this incident tonight, uh, wouldn't involve him?"

"I don't see why. There'd be no point. It's been a couple of years now. What would be the point?"

"Do you recall anything about the clothing these fellows wore?" asked Adair.

"Uh, dark. They had, I thought he had . . . I think he had a ski mask on . . . because there were holes for his eyes. I thought, Oh my God, there's . . . " Cindy broke into tears, then continued when she had regained her composure. "I think he had a, I'm sure he had a . . . it was dark, everything was dark . . . I thought one held my arm and one put an injection in my right arm. But I must be wrong. It was my right arm."

The officers examined her arm and noted some puncture marks. Anderson felt Cindy was too groggy to continue, so he concluded the interview after 15 minutes. He would talk to her when she was more alert and responsive.

Anderson convinced Cindy, with the helpful coaxing of a nurse, to agree to the sexual assault exam. The results were slim: no signs of bruising or forced sexual assault;

and, despite a few scrapes of her perineum, the only abnormality was two grey pubic hairs, which were inconsistent with Cindy's own. No underpants were found among Cindy's clothing seized by police at the hospital.

Unable to find evidence in the X-rays of a disruption in the brain stem at the neck that would explain Cindy's unusual coma, Akeroyd felt it resulted from either a concussion or a toxic overdose. A drug screen was run on Cindy's urine, which revealed the presence of benzodiazapines, the generic term for the sedative found in such tranquilizers as Valium and Ativan.

Akeroyd twigged that the cause of the coma may be psychogenic, "but when you're working with a pack of nurses who were her colleagues, it's hard to push that [idea]," he noted.

Cindy spent the rest of the day in intensive care, a room with glass walls across from the nursing station. She was awake and responsive most of the day. Then about 24 hours into her stay, she lapsed into a second coma.

"I thought she had sustained a brain injury," said neurologist Dr. Howard Feldman, who found Cindy unresponsive to pain stimuli and her limbs flaccid when he examined her at RGH after midnight on October 27. He decided to transfer her by ambulance to Vancouver's Shaughnessy Hospital, which had the proper neurology facilities to check for brain trauma or a cranial blood clot.

"There were some unusual features to a most unusual coma," Feldman noted. The flickering eye movements observed while Cindy was comatose "raised the possibility that there was something more involved, of a functional or behavioural matter. . . . This was clearly a complex problem with many layers of difficulty."

Dr. Anne McNamara, chief medical resident of Shaughnessy's intensive care unit at the time, recalled that Cindy had bypassed the emergency ward and was admitted directly to the CT scanning unit. "You try to be sympathetic to people who work in the business," she said. "You don't want to parade her around the hospital."

McNamara examined Cindy once she regained consciousness about four hours after she was admitted to hospital. Cindy complained she disliked the tube stuck down her trachea, it was making her gag. "It feels like somebody is strangling me."

With the tube down her throat, Cindy wrote on a piece of paper: "I want to discharge myself. I know I have the right." McNamara told her she could not go home. Cindy became upset and began to cry. She asked to see her psychiatrist, Dr. Friesen. Medical staff contacted Friesen, who said he would not visit Cindy in hospital. She could visit him at his office after she was released, he said. Cindy was manipulative and hides in closets, he told Shaughnessy staff over the phone.

During McNamara's neurology exam, she scratched the sole of Cindy's foot and her big toe went up. This was an abnormal. Usually the toe should go down. If it goes up, it indicates possible nerve damage from, say, a stroke or a seizure.

Cindy's eye movements were normal and the electrocardiagraph showed nothing out of the ordinary. When first admitted, Cindy's blood-gas levels were low, likely stemming from her slow breathing during the period of unconsciousness. But her oxygen level returned to normal after she came out of the coma.

Another drug screen of her urine revealed the presence of benzodiazapines, which did not suprise McNamara; she knew Cindy had been given Valium and Ativan at Richmond General. There was no evidence of a fractured skull, only bruising and swelling above the left eye and superficial cuts. Since no medical cause for her altered state of consciousness could be found, Cindy was released from hospital at 1:50 p.m. on October 27.

That same afternoon, Otto Hack went to retrieve his daughter's car, which had been towed to the RCMP compound. Hack told Anderson that he felt the Vancouver police department had not taken his daughter's complaints seriously, and the disbelief had tainted the latter part of the city police investigation. Anderson assured Hack that his own investigation would be thorough.

Even though Anderson had contacted Vancouver police for their thoughts on the case – Law and Bjornerud both felt it likely that Cindy was responsible for the incidents – he felt he could not let the past influence his opinion prematurely. He did not contact Roy Makepeace, since Cindy was adamant that he not be contacted, though she did not explain why.

On October 28, Anderson arranged for a second interview with Cindy. But instead of Cindy, her mother came to his office. Cindy was too ill to be interviewed, she explained, and offered to provide a statement or answer questions on her daughter's behalf. She also mentioned $100 had been stolen from Cindy's purse during the carport attack. Anderson stressed the necessity of talking to Cindy directly, not getting information second-hand. The next evening, he phoned Cindy's mother, who said her daughter was up for an interview. Arriving at Cindy's home at 7:30 p.m., Anderson sat in the living room with Cindy and her mother.

The investigator started with easy questions about Cindy's regular routine, what shifts she worked. She explained she worked a shift rotation of four days on, four off, although occasionally she got five days off. She was working a 12-hour day shift on Tuesday, October 25, her third shift of a four-day rotation. She should have finished by 7:30 p.m. but did not leave until 8:05 or 8:10.

"The only thing that happened, really, was I was in charge that day," Cindy stated. "That was part of why I was late, because I had to finish up something."

"Couldn't leave it to the next shift, you mean?" Anderson asked sympathetically.

"Well, no. Somebody died, and we had to change a shift and," she paused, thinking, "it's just very busy, and because you're in charge, you have to kind of finish things."

Anderson asked if anything unusual happened on the drive home from work.

"Oh, my trip home was normal. I usually warm up my car for four or five minutes. It needs it. Just wait, and then I just drove home, the usual. . . . And, uh, I pulled into the driveway and I just felt really scared. I did what I always do. As I drive in, I look and make sure that nobody's there, and then turn off the lights and motor and then I leave, I get out. I get everything together, you know, organize them. When I get out I can just . . . close the door and go into the house. And it also gives me a minute to kind of, kind of listen and look . . . I know it sounds paranoid. I'm sorry." She began to cry.

Regaining her composure after a few moments, she continued. "I couldn't see anything unusual. So I put my purse over my shoulder, I had a panic button in my right hand and, uh, I had the keys in my left hand, and I unlocked the door. I opened the door and started to step out the door . . . " She paused, thinking, "and all of a sudden there was somebody behind me. And I don't know where he came from," she said, her voice rising as she broke into tears. She apologized again.

"I felt a sharp prick in my neck," she said, sniffing. "And he said, ah – I think I sort of turned toward him – and he said, ah, something like 'Be quiet' or 'Quieter' or something like that . . . 'We won't hurt you.' And he sort of pulled me out of the car with my left hand and I – I'm trying to remember what happened to things – I think I dropped my purse and the panic button in the car. And he closed the door, I think. And he sort of pushed me towards the front of the car. . . . And then there was another one. I know he came from somewhere on my right, but I don't know where he came from." She paused to cry. "And he started to pull off my jacket and that's when I panicked.

"I was sort of – I don't think that I believed that they wouldn't hurt me, but I couldn't react until that point. I just knew that wasn't true and I swung around. I remember swinging around into the man was behind me. I don't know what I thought I was going to do, but I was trying to push his knife away. . . . He said, um, it sounded like 'Snuff her.' Which doesn't make sense, and I think I said, 'No' or 'Please' or something. And then I felt something over my mouth and my right arm being pulled back, and I felt a sharp sting in my right arm and I remember thinking 'Oh my God!'" Her tears interrupted story once more. "And then I don't think I really remember anything else.

"I remember, at one point I think, but this doesn't make much sense either, I remember being cold and I remember trying to move my head, and my head really hurt, and I thought I heard somebody say something about a ball. But then I think I was hit on the head . . . like a terrific pain in my head, and I felt a sharp prick in my arm again. And, ah, then I was just cold and very dizzy and, uh, I think I knew I needed to get help, but I don't even remember – I just, I started to crawl, I remember that. And I wanted to get into my car."

"Where do you think you were crawling from?" Anderson asked.

"But I couldn't crawl . . . I couldn't use my hands and, where was I crawling from? Ah, somewhere in front of the car . . . sitting in front."

"Okay. How come you couldn't use your hands?"

"I don't know. I just couldn't use my hands. I had to, I had to crawl, but I couldn't support myself . . . something was holding my hands because I got to the car, but I couldn't get it open, and my hands were behind me. I couldn't get my hands in front of me. . . . I remember trying to stand up to get at the door latch, but I kept falling down and . . . I can remember getting into the car. . . . The only thing I could think of was to try and bang on the horn, but I couldn't, I didn't. I was too dizzy, I couldn't coordinate myself to do it . . . I couldn't do it and I fell over, because, um, I couldn't breathe, and I kept. . . . "

"Fell over where? In the car?" Anderson asked.

"In the car, because I remember trying to rub whatever was over my mouth off, but I couldn't get it off. I kept rubbing it and rubbing it and rubbing it on the seat, but it wouldn't come off. And then I thought about the panic button and I knew that, unless they had taken it, it had to be in the car because I dropped it in the car, and I tried to find it, but I couldn't, because I couldn't feel properly and I couldn't see. . . . I just kept wanting to go to sleep, and then I think I found it because I think I found something that I kept pushing and pushing. I wasn't sure if I had the right thing, and I wasn't sure where the panic part was. I couldn't find the part where you're supposed to push, and I just thought . . . I don't know what I thought. I just gave up."

Anderson asked if her light was on in the carport.

"No, I don't put my lights on during the day . . . because I always keep them on all night. . . . They're on all the time."

Did she remember being tied up?

"No, no."

"All right. Um, the individual that came from behind you initially, can you tell me anything about him?"

"Not really."

"Have you any idea how tall he was? How tall are you?"

"I'm almost five-four. And I would just touch his chin or something. Like, he was much taller than me."

"From that I would say, you know, he'd be about five-ten," Anderson estimated. "Anything else about him? Ah, clothing?"

"Just very dark."

"Very dark what? Clothing?"

"Clothing. I, I understand now it's all buried," Cindy said cryptically. "Very dark clothing. And I remember panicking at first because I thought he didn't have a head. But he was wearing a ski mask on his head, wearing something over his head."

"So when did you first actually get a look at him? Was it right away, almost?"

"I think I got a quick glance as he pulled me out and I came out of the car. But it was all so fast."

"Well, I don't want you to go fast right now. You can just take your time," Anderson said.

"But. I mean, what happened, all went so fast . . . It's hard to sort of slow down."

"Oh, we can do that. We'll just slow it down. Just take it step by step."

"I started to step out," Cindy explained slowly, "and he grabbed my left arm. .. . He sort of pulled me back . . . away from the car, and that's where I think he must have closed the door. . . . "

Anderson, struggling to get Cindy to provide some concrete evidence, a lead that would point to a suspect, asked if she could remember any other details about the first man. "The way he talked, you know, what he said, was there an accent or anything to give you an indication how old he might be?"

"I can't . . . "

"Okay. Was he 15 years old? That's what I mean. Just give me an idea. Or did he have the voice and appearance and sound of a 60-year-old?"

"His voice was kind of like a whisper."

"Did he sound like he was out of his teens?"

"He wasn't a kid. I'm, you know, I consider a teenager a kid. It didn't feel like it, but then I have nothing to base that on."

Anderson asked if she could remember anything else about the man's clothing. She said she recalled what he was wearing on his head was not wool. It made a noise that was like nylon, like ski jacket material. She did not see the man's hands, so could not say whether he was wearing gloves. The second man was dressed all in black or a very dark colour, and he was not as tall as the first man.

"All right," Anderson continued. "You said the second guy was the one that poked you with a needle, in your right arm?"

"Well, I felt that. I mean, I'm told that that probably isn't true."

"Who told you that? Who told you that might not be true?"

"Ah, I don't know. I think I said something to either Dr. Ghatak [at Richmond General] or I said something to one of the nurses or something. I said, 'I'm positive that I was injected with something.' . . . But what they say is, 'Well, we poked you lots of times'. . . . I know where they poked me, but. . . . There's no other place that looks like that, and it's got two pin pricks there. Two pokes there and it's all bruised," Cindy said, showing her right arm.

Anderson asked if she took any medication the last day she worked before the attack. Cindy explained she always took Halcion, a mild sleeping pill before going to bed. She took four of the little one-milligram pills. And she took two tablets of another mild tranquilizer. Those were two milligrams each.

Cindy was asked if she normally kept change in her uniform pocket or her pockets of her jacket.

"Well, in my uniform pocket. . . . I never take my purse to work. I always put it in the trunk of my car and I just put in my pocket what I'm going to need for money that day. . . . Usually I don't have a lot of change, but I think there was a fair amount of change that day and, ah, there would have been either a one- or two-dollar bill."

"Before I forget," Anderson said, "your mother told me that when we returned your purse back to you, you were missing money."

"Yes. About $100 was in there . . . I know there were three 20s, and I know there was one 10. It could have been two. I think it would be about a hundred." The money was in her blue wallet in her purse, she said. Anderson said police did not find the money when they looked through her purse.

"So I'm not going to get that back?" Cindy asked.

"Ah, it wasn't found at the scene here," Anderson replied. He continued after a long pause. "Okay, also there was found a yellow tissue. It was in the grass alongside of the car."

"You mean like a Kleenex?"

"Yeah."

"I had a yellow Kleenex," Cindy said. She had some in her purse, or maybe some in her jacket pocket, but she did not recall using any.

"Okay," Anderson said, moving on to another point. "I want to sort of account somehow for about, I would say, three and a half hours from the time you got home until the time at midnight when the police arrived. You were . . ."

"Was it midnight? That late?" Cindy asked, surprised.

Anderson explained it was actually after midnight by the time police arrived. A few minutes passed from the time Kaban's company received the alarm, phoned her residence and did not get an answer, then notified police.

"So it's a good three hours, huh," Cindy said, sighing.

"I think you said your jacket was being removed," Anderson said, moving on.

"I remember him pulling it from the front. He just ripped it open and I know it was off my left arm, ah, but that's when I was swung around," she recalled. She was surprised to learn that she was naked below the waist when police arrived. She stated she had been wearing pantyhose and underpants.

Anderson explained she was catheterized when she first arrived in the hospital, which may have destroyed any evidence before the sexual assault exam.

Cindy told Anderson she knew nothing about the 'Summer's Eve' brand douche bottle found in her carport the night of the attack. In fact, she said it did not "make sense."

Before leaving Cindy's home that day, Anderson took her neck and wrist measurements. "We have a specialist now that is in the area of knots," Anderson explained, adding the knot specialist would examine the ligatures that had been tied around her neck and wrists.

Three days later, on November 1, 1988, Anderson phoned Robert Chisnall in Kingston, Ont. The climbing instructor, who taught outdoor education at Queen's University, had more than 20 years experience studying knots and was a founding member of the International Guild of Knot Tyers. Chisnall had originated 100 knots of his own, included 20 adopted by mountaineers and spelunkers, and one adapted for surgery. He had also consulted on cases for Toronto police, Ontario Provincial Police and RCMP in Ontario, and had appeared as an expert witness in Ontario Supreme Court, testifying about the ligature knots in a strangulation case. He told Anderson his fee was $200 a day and it would likely take half a day to examine two ligatures.

Chisnall was sent the ligatures from the October attack, along with Cindy's neck and wrist measurements, and a letter giving some background on her.

"The victim in this case is a 44-year-old female. She is a registered nurse by profession and is currently working on the medical/surgical floor of a local hospital," wrote Superintendent William Dellebuur, head of Richmond RCMP. "She is right-handed. We are not aware of any activities or hobbies that she may have that involve the tying of knots."

Dellebuur added that the policeman who cut the neck ligature from Cindy's neck believed the knot was tied in the front, but he was not positive.

After examining the knots, Chisnall concluded: "It is my opinion that it is highly unlikely the victim was the tier of these ligatures. . . . There are no slip loops or other configurations that might have made the tying process easy for the complainant."

Chisnall explained that he attempted to simulate tying the wrist ligature on himself with a similar nylon stocking of equal length. "The tying was extremely awkward," he noted. "I pre-tied the knots around my left wrist using my right hand and teeth. This was performed with my hands in front of me. I slipped my right wrist into the appropriate segment by stretching the simulation stocking. I then stepped through my arms to position my hands behind me. This could have been done provided the victim was strong enough to force her right wrist into a stretched loop. Also, she would have to be sufficiently flexible to step through her arms.

"There was a discrepancy, though. Upon removing the simulation ligature, I noted that hitches #1 and #2 were tightest, whereas hitches #4 and #5 in the actual ligature are tightest. Hence, the complainant could not have tied herself in the manner described."

The tightness of the ligature around the neck, however, raised some questions in his mind. It was not tight enough to cause death. "Homicides on which I have been consulted involved ligatures that were as tight as four inches in circumference. . . . Knotted strangulation ligatures causing death are often buried deep in the soft tissue of the neck. As well, it is my opinion, the victim could have struggled free from the wrist ligature with a bit of effort. . . . Could an accomplice have tied her up?"

Chisnall included a diagram of how the knots were tied and suggested the person who tied them was right-handed. He also suggested police compare the diagram to the victim's shoe laces.

On November 11 at 8 p.m., Anderson met Dr. Friesen in his office across from St. Paul's hospital in downtown Vancouver. He wanted Friesen's opinion about the circumstances of the latest attack. The doctor felt Cindy's perceived rejection by her ex-husband was the root of her problem. Cindy felt she had to resort to abnormal tactics to get attention from her ex-husband, Friesen told Anderson.

Cindy phoned Anderson a few days later, telling him she was upset that he had been to see Dr. Friesen. She felt she was getting the same treatment as she got from Vancouver police, who did not believe her. "I told her I was looking at all avenues and speaking to Dr. Friesen was simply an avenue," Anderson recalled. "She was content with that."

Three months went by without incident until police were summoned to Cindy's home again on January 26, 1989. Cindy's friend, Ton Groenevelt, had been found dead, slumped at the steering wheel of his parked car in front of Cindy's home.

Moderately obese at 103 kilograms on his tall frame, Groenevelt had had a history of heart problems. The autopsy revealed he died of a heart attack after playing bridge the night before with Cindy and Tom and Agnes Woodcock, who had stayed overnight. He had fondly waved goodbye to Cindy at 11:30 as she stood at her front door.

Cindy recoiled in shock when she found him at 10:27 a.m., neatly dressed in his blue sweater, white shirt, grey slacks and black patent-leather shoes. Groenevelt had just turned 65 and received his first old-age pension check. He never got the chance to cash his second one.

Agnes Woodcock recalled that Groenevelt may have left Cindy's house that night with a broken heart. "He had come over and talked with [Cindy] that night." Cindy had phoned Agnes earlier in the evening to ask if she and Tom could wait an hour before coming over because Ton had dropped by and she wanted to talk to him alone.

"We didn't get over there until 10 and had a coffee with him. We talked and he seemed fine. I don't know if he proposed to her. She always wanted us to be there when they played bridge. He wanted a romantic relationship. She told me she wasn't ready for that, she just wanted to be friends."

Woodcock also recalled another tragic element of the evening. "[Ton] wanted to know when her birthday was. We'd had a birthday cake and played bridge on his birthday. He told Cindy, 'If you don't tell me I'm going to bring a present every month until I hit the right month.' And he did bring one that night. Cindy didn't open it. She said, 'Agnes, what should I do? I think I'll wait till my birthday.' So it was still unopened when she died. It was a vase for flowers, which she loved."

"Ton's death was a real shocker," Cindy wrote to her sister Marlene. "I still cry sometimes and feel so badly that he lay dead in his car all night in front of my house. I know from the autopsy report that I couldn't have done anything to help him. . . . But when I found his body the next morning I kept apologizing to him for not being there to at least hold his hand when he died. I feel so sad and so guilty that he died alone. I should have watched to see his car drive away before closing the door for the evening. I miss him so much, he was such a good friend and a caring person. He was the one who insisted on following me to work at nights. I feel he did so much for me and I let him down when he needed me.

"It was hard to pick up the pieces of getting the downstairs suite finished, since Ton had acted as the contractor. However, I finally found out who was doing what and the work was completed the day before Richard [Johnston] moved in. Mom was a big help – she stayed with me for a week and helped with the painting, choosing drapes, etc., and hemmed all the drapes for me. I would never have had the place ready on time without her help."

Feeling sentimental, Cindy asked her sister: "Do you ever think back to when we were kids and the dreams we had of what life would be like when we were grown up? Sure didn't work out like we dreamed, eh?

"There are times when I feel really depressed and despairing, and others when I try to be hopeful and positive and believe a normal life is still possible. I wish we'd had more time to talk to each other without the kids around. And yet, I'm glad I had the chance to get to know them a bit.

"Are you still planning on Kenya next year? I really hope the three of us can go."

The letter, dated March 8, 1989, was signed, "All my love and keep up the fight for yourself and your family. Cindy." It was the last letter Marlene received from her sister.

On April 8, a security guard at Richmond General Hospital was patrolling the parking lot and found a note on Cindy's car. "SOON CINDY," it said, in the familiar cut-and-paste style. At the end of Cindy's shift that night, she walked to her car and noticed someone had written a message in the dew on her windshield. It was written backwards so Cindy could read it from inside her car. "Sleep Well," it said.

Cindy did not sleep well the following night. Her burglar alarm sounded. The rear basement window was found ajar with a note slipped inside. The outside porch light was found unscrewed.

The alarm would sound three more times, the last on May 10, 1989, then quiet returned. Fifteen days later Cindy James went missing.

THIRTEEN

Cindy On Trial

FOR MORE than a month after the discovery of Cindy's body, newspaper headlines and media reports proclaimed, "Nurse Slain." Her death, the public understandably assumed, was murder. Then on July 12, 1989, RCMP announced that investigators had ruled out foul play. Given this contradiction, Otto Hack welcomed the news that the B.C. Coroner's Service would hold an inquest to probe the circumstances surrounding his daughter's death. The RCMP explanation "didn't satisfy me at all," he told a reporter. "There's a murderer out there somewhere."

The coroner's department hired investigators Pat Costello and Jim Smith to begin conducting interviews and gathering related documents for the inquest, which was set for October. It soon became apparent, however, that the Cindy James case was more complex than first imagined. The list of possible witnesses grew to more than 100, many of whom still had not been interviewed as October quickly approached. The inquest date was postponed and a new one tentatively set for early 1990.

On December 21, Otto Hack wrote to coroner Gerald Tilley to ask if the inquest could be cancelled. "The request," Hack wrote, "follows the painful thoughts of reliving the grim horrors of Cindy's death and the inevitable publicity and sensationalism of the media. I, too, fear the experience of being subjected to such horrible mental anguish again will be devastating."

Despite the family's wishes, the coroner felt the matter needed a public airing because of allegations that police had mishandled the investigation of Cindy's complaints. Coroner's inquests are held to probe the circumstances surrounding a death that has aroused public suspicion, and to cancel the inquest would have left that suspicion dangling. Since Hack did not pursue the matter through formal channels, preparations for the inquest continued.

Pat Costello, a 25-year veteran of the RCMP who had retired to become a private investigator, faced the formidable task of assembling more than 1,000 pages of police reports, confidential medical records, personal letters and summaries of witness interviews into a comprehensible package for the court.

With some of the witness testimony considered redundant, the list of witnesses scheduled to testify was eventually pared down to 80 and the inquest was set to run for three weeks starting February 26, 1990. A week-long inquest was rare, and a three-week inquest unheard of. Only an exceedingly complex case of great public interest would be scheduled for more than a few days. This one would eventually drag on for 40 days, spread over three months, to become the longest and, at an estimated cost of $120,000, the most expensive inquest in B.C. history.

Since 1982, Vancouver police and RCMP had spent thousands of hours investigating the case, running up a tab estimated at $1 million. This would not stop Otto Hack from accusing police of doing, in his words, a "non-investigation" of his daughter's complaints.

Opening day saw a standing-room-only crowd in Coroner's Court in Burnaby, a suburb of Vancouver. Reporters arrived early to get a clear view of the witness stand. Television cameramen jostled for position to capture the best shots of the eight people occupying the front row, which was marked by yellow signs with the hand-printed message: Family Only.

Otto Hack, looking stoic in a blue blazer, grey slacks and closely cropped grey hair, marched into the courtroom to occupy the seat directly in front of the witness stand. Beside him sat his youngest daughter, Melanie Cassidy, who had taken time off from her job as a liquor store clerk in Whitehorse. On her left was Tillie Hack, with her blue-grey hair set in a new perm. Next sat Marlene Weintrager, who had left her four children in her husband's care in Ottawa. She sat beside Roger Hack, who attended the inquest while on three weeks' vacation from his job with the High Commissioner's office in Nairobi. The youngest Hack son, Ken, sat with his wife Laura. And on the far end, farthest from his father, sat Cindy's brother Doug.

As if unconsciously obeying Otto's strict sense of military order, the family members would continue to assume almost the same seating arrangements day after day.

Also in the public gallery was Cindy's ex-husband, who sat in the last of the four rows of brown Naugahyde-and-chrome bench seats. Dressed in a brown sports jacket and a blue tie, Makepeace would not be acknowledged by the Hack family. He would remain the outcast, with some of Cindy's friends and colleagues casting glances of disgust his way when allegations of murder and abusive behaviour arose during testimony.

The Hacks hired Peter Leask to represent them at the inquest. A top Vancouver criminal lawyer, Queen's Counsel and bencher of the B.C. Law Society, Leask had a solid record of winning acquittals. The curly-haired advocate was known for sharp, decisive thinking in court, being able to grab a witness's testimony and shape it with clever questioning to the benefit of his client. He also had a habit of endearing himself to juries with jokes and wisecracks. Leask's court fees were proportionate to his ability – roughly $2,000 a day for court cases, not including trial preparation. His final bill was estimated to be close to $80,000.

The family would eventually sell Cindy's Richmond home, using part of the proceeds to "prove Cindy's innocence," as one relative put it. Although inquests are held only to determine cause of death, the family felt Cindy was on trial. They were determined to restore Cindy's tarnished reputation.

They believed police failed to investigate Cindy's complaints properly. Her file had been "tainted" by Dr. Tony Marcus's report suggesting Cindy had a mental problem and was staging the terror. It was their belief that Cindy was the victim of a night stalker and police had failed to protect her.

Representing the Vancouver police department was lawyer Catherine Kinahan, known for her aggressive legal wrangling on behalf of city hall, where she was employed in the law department. She was set to prove that while the James case was a difficult one, police had done everything they reasonably could to investigate Cindy's complaints thoroughly.

Makepeace's own lawyer, George McIntosh, could not attend the inquest on short notice. Instead, Alastair Wade, a young lawyer from the same large, prestigious Vancouver law firm, Farris, Vaughan, Wills and Murphy, attended, but only periodically, which put him at a disadvantage. With the Hacks' lawyer attending daily, Wade was unable fully to digest and analyse the range of testimony concerning his client.

Makepeace felt he had already spent enough money on legal fees over the years and couldn't afford the expense of having counsel present for the entire proceedings. "Had I equal finance, I would have put up equal opposition and that Coroner's Court would have been a whole different show," he said later.

Although he had his own private practice, lawyer John Bethell had served as coroner's counsel for many years and had spent a good deal of time in coroner's court, sometimes referred to by reporters as the Court of Death since it dealt exclusively with suspicious or unusual accidental deaths. Invariably thorough and well organized, Bethell was a master of empathy, leading witnesses through their painful testimony before they were cross-examined by other lawyers. Colleagues considered Bethell virtually unflappable. This case, however, would test the limits of his patience.

Sitting on Bethell's right in the courtroom was Pat Costello, a gregarious man with black horn-rimmed glasses. After spending months preparing the case, he usually had a document at his fingertips seconds after it was requested. He would also be called upon to arrange for further witnesses to testify.

Presiding Coroner Gerald Tilley was a former policeman known for his composure and good humour, even in the most trying circumstances. He would need it for this one: at one point during the inquest, Tilley, among others, would be accused of bias – slanting the proceedings toward a suicide ruling – by an angry Otto Hack.

As Tilley called the court to order, the din of conversation fell to a hush as the coroner explained the purpose of the inquest: to determine the time, place and cause of death – and by what means – of Cindy James.

He warned the two-man, three-women jury – a bus driver, a retired furnace repair company owner, a homemaker, a shop owner and a property manager – that it was not their role to try to find fault or lay blame for Cindy's death. If, however, the jurors felt that her death was avoidable, or future similar deaths could be prevented, then they could make recommendations to specific authorities.

Advising that the case would be complex and taxing, Tilley itemized the facts that were not in dispute: Cindy's date of birth; her date of marriage and separation; when she went missing; when her body was found.

The rest of the "facts," he warned the jury, would be subject to vastly different views and interpretations.

Tilley also noted the inquest would be divided into four segments: Part One would examine the most prominent incidents investigated by police over the years; Part Two would focus on the death scene and subsequent RCMP investigation; Part Three would cover Cindy's personal history and family background; and Part Four, her medical and psychiatric history. Witnesses would be called roughly in order of that chronology.

"It's laid out like a Stephen King novel," a reporter whispered to his colleagues at the media table.

Following Tilley's opening remarks, the first witness, Agnes Woodcock, was called to the stand to recount some of the puzzling details and bizarre incidents that would, as the inquest progressed, keep jurors awake at night and haunt them for months to come. The morbid testimony would even creep into the subconscious minds of reporters, who would report having nightmares involving dream-like aspects of the Cindy James case.

Woodcock, along with her husband Tom, provided sketchy, impressionistic memories of some of the earliest incidents: the break-ins, the slashed pillow, mysterious phone calls and cut phone lines.

Next up was Cindy's policeman boyfriend, Pat McBride, who explained how he first became involved with the case and with Cindy. He said he felt she sometimes withheld information from him. Even more frustrating, he added, was that after he convinced Cindy to get an unlisted phone number, she kept giving it out.

The first surprising testimony came from Vancouver police Constable Kiyo Ikoma, who told the court he was puzzled by the circular blood smears on Cindy's kitchen floor while investigating the scene of the second attack, on January 30, 1984. "It appeared as if somebody had wiped it," he said.

Ozzie Kaban thought the smearing had resulted from Cindy being stabbed through the hand in the kitchen and crawling to the hallway to use the two-way radio. Ikoma, however, noted that there was "just the odd drop" of blood found on Cindy's clothing. There were no smears on her clothes that would indicate she had dragged her body across the bloody linoleum.

There was also blood smeared on the kitchen counter, on the edge of the bathroom sink and on the rim of the toilet. Ikoma said he checked inside and outside the house for something that had been used to wipe the blood, but found nothing.

Bethell asked Ikoma to look at the police photograph of the crime scene and to note the smear line running parallel with the bottom of the kitchen cupboards. Bethell suggested it appeared that, perhaps, a sponge mop had been used to wipe the blood. Ikoma said he did not recall finding a sponge mop in the house.

"In your 10 years of service, did you ever come across an incident where an assailant cleaned up blood and locked the door behind him when leaving the scene?" Bethell asked.

"Lock the door, yes, but not clean up the blood," Ikoma replied.

One other anomaly struck the officer. With all the smeared blood in the kitchen, he was puzzled that there were no pools of blood in the hallway where Cindy had been found unconscious. "I thought there would be more blood [there]."

Bethell suggested that perhaps the blood had been smeared to make it appear as if there was more carnage than there really was. "That's one of the thoughts I had," Ikoma agreed.

Leask asked the witness: "You have no knowledge of why the blood was smeared around?" Ikoma agreed he did not.

At inquests, jurors are able to pose questions to clarify the testimony of a witness. The jury foreman asked if there were any swab samples taken of the blood at the scene to see if it was Cindy's. "Not as far as I know," Ikoma replied, adding police had no doubt that it was Cindy's blood.

Bethell thought of another question: Did police have a talk with Ozzie Kaban about the importance of not disturbing a crime scene? Yes, Ikoma said, after the can of dog repellent was noticed in Kaban's pocket – the private investigator had picked it up on his way into the house, leaving his fingerprints on it.

RCMP Staff-Sergeant Cal Hood told the court how he administered Cindy's third lie detector test on March 29, 1984, after she had failed two previous tests done by Vancouver police. At the time, he judged her to be telling the truth – she had passed the polygraph. "But in reviewing the test results now," he said, "I would consider my opinion to be inconclusive at this time." He had changed his mind shortly before the inquest, Hood explained, after looking strictly at the numerical value of the test results. His previous opinion was based at the time "on my subjective opinion of how she reacted" to questions. "She responded to me as I would expect a victim who has suffered a traumatic incident."

Vancouver police detective Gary Foster outlined his involvement investigating the August 21, 1985 arson in Cindy's basement bathroom on West 14th. The silver-haired officer thought it odd that two small screws and the latch fastener, which had held the window in place before it was forced open, could not be located by investigators. "We were wondering what happened to them."

The six separate fire starts would have taken considerable time to light, which indicated the fires were set by "someone who had a lot of time and was in no hurry." Foster's conclusion: "It would have been impossible to set these fires from the outside by reaching through the window."

Cross-examined by Leask, Foster agreed that it was possible someone could have climbed in the window, started two or three fires, then climbed out and started the rest by leaning inside. Leask knew that the lack of evidence made anything possible.

Still, Foster maintained that the undisturbed dust and cobwebs on the window sill indicated the "logical conclusion" was that the fires were set from inside, with the window closed. It was either an "inside job," with Cindy responsible, or someone had used a key to let himself in, turned off the alarm while Cindy was walking her dog after 3 a.m., then locked the door after leaving.

Foster also noted Cindy's private investigator did not tell him, at that time, that Cindy had been out walking her dog late that night. "It would have helped knowing this, to explain why she wouldn't have heard noises" of the break-in.

Detective Kris Bjornerud told the court he thought the arson was suspicious for similar reasons. He also questioned Cindy's response to the July 27, 1985 incident when she had received a package in the mail containing rotting meat – Cindy had tried calling Kaban, without success, and then had taken a sleeping pill 20 minutes later. "I thought it was odd because she would be scared and would want to be awake," Bjornerud commented.

Hypnotherapist Hal Booker, called to recount Cindy's hypnosis sessions, emphasized that it is usually difficult for a subject to pretend to be under hypnosis – if a person is telling the truth, emotional responses accompany verbal reponses. "It's very easy to tell the difference, if you know what you're looking for." If someone believes something is true, which is obviously a personal fable, and tells that story under hypnosis, it is called a "confabulation," he told the court.

Asked about Cindy's memory, under hypnosis, of the dismemberment of two bodies in July 1981 at a remote Gulf Island cabin, Booker said, "There's no doubt in my mind that it was real to her."

Bethell asked what happens when a schizophrenic person is hypnotized. "You tend to get fabrications and made-up stories," Booker replied. "You don't get the emotion you get during the memory of a real event."

During cross-examination by Leask, Booker stated that Cindy displayed a great deal of horror and terror recalling the murder allegations.

"If the whole incident was concocted, then this incident under hypnosis would be concocted, correct?" queried Makepeace's lawyer, Alastair Wade. Booker agreed.

Cindy's youngest sister, Melanie Cassidy, took the stand to recall what Cindy told her of the alleged chopped bodies incident. During her interview with coroner's investigator Pat Costello, she had said Cindy told her of the incident in February 1984, before the information came out during the hypnosis sessions, which began in August 1984 and ended in January 1985.

Under questioning by Bethell, however, Cassidy revised her recollection: it was not February 1984 but February 1985 – after the hypnosis – that Cindy mentioned the incident. Cindy had also told both sisters, Melanie and Marlene, in July 1984 that she had witnessed a murder, but Cassidy could not remember the details. "I was really horrified by what she related to me," she said.

"Did you pass that conversation along to anyone else?" Bethell asked.

"I did, but I can't remember who."

Cross-examined by Kinahan, Cassidy admitted she hadn't told Vancouver police about Cindy mentioning the alleged murders. "I believe I told Ozzie Kaban."

Cindy's brother Doug recalled the July 1981 boating trip, remembering he was asked to help sail the *Peacemaker* back to Vancouver after the motor died. Hack did not recall his sister mentioning anything about murder when he saw her briefly that day. She did not even tell him about this allegation until 1983 or 1984, Hack said, and he assumed Vancouver police knew about the story by then.

However, when Leask suggested to Doug Hack that Cindy had mentioned the dismembered bodies to him between February 1, 1985 and the end of May that year – after the hypnosis, Hack replied, "That's possible."

On June 21, 1985, when Cindy was committed to Lions Gate Hospital, Hack recalled Cindy phoned him and asked that he help get her released. As he understood it, Kaban had brought her to hospital to rest because she was not eating properly and could not sleep. The intention was not to commit her to a psychiatric ward, he told the court.

She was not crazy, she just needed a secure place to rest, he said.

Kaban's memory of Cindy's committal was that he had thought about putting Cindy in one of his "secure" apartments in the West End, but Cindy's physician, Dr. Allan Connolly, had suggested a psychiatrist friend, Dr. Paul Termansen, could look after Cindy at Lions Gate, where she would feel safe and get some rest while Connolly was out of the country.

"I was under the impression she was there of her own free will and it was not a committal," Kaban said. It was also his impression that Connolly was Cindy's psychiatrist, "but obviously he was not."

Kinahan asked Kaban why he never told Vancouver police that Cindy was suicidal at that time.

"I didn't know she was," he replied. "I just thought she was not eating and sleeping."

Kaban said he did not not recall having a "heated discussion" with Cindy about walking her dog after 3 a.m. the night of the August 21, 1985, arson. "To my knowledge, she would never go out after dark. She was scared of the dark," he said.

Kaban also denied ever having a romantic relationship with Cindy – the question arose after the coroner's investigators noticed entries on Cindy's calendar's stating "Stayed the night at Ozzie's apartment." Kaban replied: "We were friends," adding that he and Cindy sometimes went to dinner together and he would spend hours with her discussing her situation but he denied his involvement was anything more than friendly. She did stay at his "secure" apartment in the West End.

Cindy's next-door neighbours on Claysmith Road in Richmond were Ted and Maureen Jamieson. Ted, a ship's captain, testified he had been home the night Cindy was attacked on October 26, 1988. He and his wife had gone shopping at Safeway that evening, and his wife went to bed about 9:30 p.m. He took his two-year-old German shepherd out in the back yard to play, tossing the ball for the dog for about an hour, then went in the house. "It barked at anyone who approached the house," Jamieson recalled. "But it didn't become agitated or bark the whole time we were out there."

Ted Jamieson knew Cindy. They would say "hi" over the back fence. Once he remembered her looking in his window. "My wife asked if anything was wrong. She said she was looking for her cat." She had left for work shortly afterwards. Around dusk that evening, Cindy's burglar alarm went off, but Jamieson could see no damage to the house. He asked the investigating police officer if the alarm could have been set off by an animal. "It's not likely that a cat could put a hole in a patio window," the officer said. Cindy's back window had been broken.

During the winter sometime after the October 1988 attack, Jamieson remembered his wife called him into the living room and pointed out Cindy walking her dog up the street in the dark of night. "We just found it unusual to see her doing that after all the incidents at her house," he said.

FOURTEEN

Makepeace Speaks Out

BY THE END of the first week of the inquest, everyone in court was painfully aware that the proposed three-week schedule was far off the mark. It had taken five days just to get through the witness list marked "Day Number One."

As Dr. Roy Makepeace took the stand on the seventh day, there was a sense of anticipation among court observers. After hearing the testimony alleging murder had occurred in the Gulf Islands, he had whispered to a reporter: "Am I or am I not Ted Bundy?"

His lawyer asked the coroner to grant his client the protection of the B.C. Evidence Act and the Canada Evidence Act. This would allow Makepeace to testify without his testimony being used against him in future court proceedings. Tilley granted the request.

Leading off questioning, Bethell asked Makepeace about the apparent injuries Cindy's colleagues had observed before the marriage separation in 1982.

"First of all, they were not necessarily black eyes," Makepeace replied. "Whatever it was, I was not reponsible."

After years of pent-up frustration at being the suspect, of enduring "all kinds of slander, innuendo and hearsay," Makepeace wanted to set the record straight. And now, under oath, he could. In a firm, loud voice so everyone in court could hear, he declared: "I've never hit my wife, other than, I'm ashamed to admit, I have slapped her face with a flat hand on two single occasions. All of this is recorded in writing and has been up front from the beginning. I've never tried to hide the fact. But I have never battered my wife, I have never put a bruise on her, I have never caused an abrasion on her body, or broken bones or anything like that whatsoever in my life."

As for the alleged murders, "that is sheer fiction. I have my own speculations where this material gets in her mind, but it has nothing to do with reality. . . . It was just sort of a happy boating holiday."

His recollection of the trip was that he and Cindy had stayed the first night at the Thormanby Island cabin of a psychiatrist friend, Dr. Hamish Nichol. Did he go to look at property? No. They went fishing the day the motor broke down, he said. "I imagine we were out there for several hours."

They motored to a small rock island with a lighthouse, he recalled, and were fishing leisurely for salmon and enjoying the scenery when a wind came out of the west, "and that usually portends bad weather." As the sky darkened, the motor cut out – Makepeace later learned the prop-shaft had broken – and he had to sail back to Buccaneer Bay. Cindy panicked as they were sailing down the western side of Thormanby and Roy had to swing both sails by himself "at just the right moment or the wind would push the boat toward the rocks."

The next day, Doug took the water taxi over and Cindy took it back to the mainland. The incident frightened Cindy and she never set foot on the boat again, Makepeace noted.

He also recalled that the Hack family had a big reunion at their home about a week after the July 1981 boating trip, which he felt may have brought back some painful childhood memories for Cindy. Makepeace felt Cindy's family was plagued by communication problems and lingering grievances between family members.

"You're aware you were a suspect in some of the things happening?" Bethell asked.

"I think that's the understatement of the year."

Bethell asked under what sort of terms Cindy and Makepeace had parted when they decided to separate.

"Very amicable," said Makepeace, straightening in his chair. "It was a trial separation that was to last about one year. . . . If it was handled correctly, which it wasn't, I believe we would still be happily married."

Losing his composure briefly, he paused to gather his thoughts. "We had a fantastic relationship. A marriage made in heaven. . . . She was an exceptionally beautiful woman. A little bit vain, but most beautiful women are."

Recreational interests took them in different directions, Makepeace explained. Cindy did not want to take part in the activities he enjoyed. The plan was to try a separation for a year to give each other some freedom to assess the relationship, to see if they felt better apart than together. He agreed he probably griped about his job near the end of the marriage, but failing the oral exam that would have qualified him as a psychiatrist was not the end of the world. He went on to teach at UBC and head the social psychiatry division. He felt Cindy was more upset with his failing the oral exam than he was.

Makepeace added that he and his wife were close during the first 18 months after their break-up. They took dancing lessons, played bridge and racquetball, went to dinner, movies. They even double-dated – Cindy with McBride and Makepeace with Colleen Bergin, "a prize student doing post-graduate work at UBC." That was only a friendship, he noted, not a romantic relationship.

He and Cindy never really had a chance to work out a reconciliation after the reign of terror began, he felt. "It just went from bad to worse to impossible to death," Makepeace said, a tinge of anguish in his voice. "I did everything possible to be supporting, comforting, empathetic."

He described Cindy as "a quiet person who would hold things in." He denied that she abused alcohol or drugs during the marriage.

"In your years with her, in terms of sexual practice, was she interested in bondage in any way?" Bethell asked.

"Absolutely not," Makepeace replied. "Her sexual practices were extremely normal, highly conventional."

In his cross-examination, Leask asked Makepeace about his knowledge of the first attack on January 27, 1983. The doctor explained he did not learn about it until 10:30 a.m. the following day, when Pat McBride phoned him at work and asked, "Did you know she's been attacked?"

On January 29, as Cindy was moving back to the house on West 41st, Makepeace said he suggested to McBride that there should be more security precautions. McBride told him, "This is police business. Stay out of it."

"I guess he wanted to be the macho hero and save the damsel in distress and everything," Makepeace testified. He did not learn about the second attack, on January 30, 1984, until one or two days afterwards, he said. He had talked to Cindy on January 28, when they had made plans to play bridge together February 4. Cindy called February 2 and cancelled, sounding flustered, explaining she was "very busy." Three days later, Makepeace tried to call her but was unable to reach her. On February 6, 7 and 8 he called her at work but was given the runaround. Finally he phoned the head office of Cindy's employer and was told that Cindy had been attacked, she was safe, and if Makepeace wanted further details he should contact police, which he did. Bowyer-Smyth told him over the phone that he would meet with him soon to discuss the incident.

On February 14 Makepeace visited the Oakridge police substation where he was subjected to "an incredible 5½-hour discussion." Makepeace told the court he was shocked by the actions of the police, who, he said, tried to get a confession from him. He felt the officers tried to twist everything he told them.

"Frankly, my impression was, I wasn't going to leave the police station and I thought I was going to be framed," Makepeace said.

"That's the sort of thing that happens in South Africa?" Kinahan asked.

"The only place I have personally experienced it is in Vancouver," Makepeace replied indignantly.

"But it didn't happen, did it?" Kinahan countered.

"No, because they didn't have anything on me."

Makepeace noted Cindy made him throw away the pillowcase that had been slashed at her home October 19, 1982 – a fact he mentioned to police during his interrogation. "I told her it was evidence, but she insisted I throw it away. She had an almost phobic fear of it."

"You did not tell police about that for a year and a half?" Kinahan asked.

"That's correct. I saw no importance in it whatsoever."

Makepeace added that he later became interested in the pillow case when he noticed a pattern of Cindy throwing away evidence.

"When did it begin to interest you?" asked Kinahan.

When he and Cindy were trying to sell their house on West 41st Avenue in April 1983, Makepeace explained, he had been cleaning up the basement all day, except for one hour when he went to the bank. Cindy came home from work, flicked on the light switch and said, "Funny, no light." Makepeace noticed the two floodlamps that illuminated the yard had been unscrewed from their sockets, more than two metres off the ground. The lights had been smashed on the concrete below.

"It seemed to be a calling sign," he said. "Someone had deliberately done this, and it was an adult. It was too high for a child to reach." Cindy made him throw away the broken lights, he said, even though he suggested they should be saved for police to fingerprint. Cindy insisted they be tossed in the garbage.

"I think it was an unusual attitude toward getting rid of evidence," Makepeace noted. "It raised a query in my mind about her mental status." Around the same time, Cindy had asked him, "Roy, do you think I'm losing my mind?" Makepeace said he reassured her she was not. Now he wished he would have asked, "What makes you think that?"

Tilley asked about the matrimonial home being sold in April 1983 and how the proceeds were divided. Makepeace said the home sold for under $200,000 even though it had been worth about $300,000 the previous year. The real estate market had crashed after the 1981–82 economic recession. He recalled that Cindy received half the proceeds, plus he bought her half-share of the boat, so she would have received about $75,000 and he retained about $25,000.

After Makepeace's meeting with Otto Hack at a doughnut shop on March 14, 1984, where Hack told him to have no further contact with any family member except himself, Makepeace testified that he felt "banished" from the family. With virtually no contact with his only family in Canada, he was unaware of most of the subsequent incidents.

"I wasn't able to know anything about her, even where she lived."

The last time he spoke with Cindy, he said, was when she phoned him on July 2, 1985. Only later, when interviewed by Costello shortly before the inquest, did he learn that the call had been taped by Vancouver police to confront him with Cindy's "new-found" memories from her hypnosis sessions. For years, he had been baffled by Cindy's reference during the call to "the event" she remembered from four years ago. "That puzzled me and puzzled me and puzzled me."

Makepeace went on to note that at the time of the fire at Cindy's rented home in Richmond (April 1986) he was in South Africa visiting relatives. The fire occurred, coincidentally, on the day his father died in London, England. As proof of the trip, Makepeace produced his British passport.

Wade asked his client the meaning of "Hombagosh," which Cindy apparently heard one of her three assailants say during the July 23, 1984 attack in the van. Makepeace explained it was "Hamba Gashle," a Zulu term for " 'farewell, take care.' My sister in North Carolina uses it," he said, adding she had spent some time with tribes in Africa.

As the inquest progressed, Makepeace heard more and more of the allegations that had been made about him over the years. Recalling Makepeace to the stand, Leask asked him what he thought of the police investigation of Cindy's case. Makepeace, obviously wound up, answered the question with a rambling answer that continued virtually non-stop for almost 10 minutes.

The police, he said, had established "a kangaroo court" of his colleagues and Cindy's co-workers. They had "poisoned" the field and turned the Hack family against him.

When Bethell interjected to say that the court did not wish to hear "a long digression" founded on speculation and rumour, Makepeace shot back: "For eight years I've had to put up with all kinds of innuendo and accusations. I have one and one only opportunity to state my case. . . . I am under oath to tell the truth and to tell the whole truth, and if you want to muzzle me, fine."

"I'm not trying to muzzle you in any way," Tilley responded.

"That's okay, I'll respond with yes and no answers," Makepeace fumed, muttering under his breath: "Speak only when spoken to, like a child."

"You should make it clear to Dr. Makepeace that this is not a kangaroo court," Bethell urged. At this, Tilley called a 10-minute adjournment so Makepeace's lawyer could talk to his client. Makepeace returned calmer and more collected.

Asked how many firearms he owned, Makepeace listed off a .22 handgun and a .303 rifle, both of which he possessed while married to Cindy. After the separation, he had bought "for protection" a stainless steel .44 magnum handgun.

"It packs a very powerful punch and makes holes in motor cars," he said of the magnum. He bought it to use while gold panning in the woods. "I have a healthy respect for bears, the same as I have a healthy respect for lions in Africa."

Makepeace explained that he was taught to be a good soldier and a good scout. He enjoyed firearms and target shooting – he had been a member of the Vancouver-area Coast Marksmen club for more than 20 years. "I enjoy a well-designed firearm as I enjoy a well-designed telescope or any other instrument," he said.

Leask suggested that when Makepeace put a gun on Cindy's bed while they were married, he was not treating it in a safe manner. But Makepeace disagreed, saying the magazine had been removed and he kept his firearms and ammunition separate and locked away, as required by law.

"While living with Cindy, did you ever point a firearm at anyone?" Leask asked.

"No," Makepeace replied.

"At Cindy?"

"Never."

Makepeace said he would take his .303 rifle on the boat if he and Cindy were sailing to remote wilderness areas on the coast. One time, between 1975 and 1982, he recalled taking the gun out of Cindy's closet, where it was stored, for cleaning – he threw it on her bed. Later, Cindy told him, "The moment I saw it lying there, I knew you were going to shoot me." At the time, Makepeace was puzzled by her reaction.

Referring to the letters from Otto and Tillie Hack before Makepeace and Cindy were to be married in 1966, Leask asked him to recall the circumstances at the time.

Makepeace suggested Cindy felt her parent's reaction was, "'My God, you spoiled our party.' She was really upset about that." Part of her anger stemmed from her resentment of her parents not allowing her to go to university, Makepeace suggested. She also felt a strong sense of abandonment for two to three years when her parents moved to France and left her in Vancouver. "She felt they had failed her."

When Cindy first lived alone in Vancouver, she lived in a house on Wolfe Avenue. She had a "very deeply disturbed, almost phobic fear" of that house, Makepeace recalled.

Cindy subsequently accused Makepeace of abandoning her after they separated, even though she left him, he said.

"Did she ever accuse you in conversation or in writing of abandoning her?" Leask asked. Not specifically, Makepeace replied, but he got that impression from reading the clinical notes, obtained by his lawyer from the coroner, from the time Cindy was in psychiatric care.

Cindy had a profound fear of suffocation, Makepeace added, citing her recurring nightmare during the marriage of the cloud-like hands that would creep up to smother her. He remembered having trouble rousing her from nightmares. "She seemed to be in some kind of altered state of consciousness," he said. "This is where it resembled a child's night terror."

He reiterated that he had nothing to do with Cindy's persecution and eventual death.

"Perhaps that denial would carry more weight if you would not paint such a rosy picture of how you treated Cindy during the marriage," Leask suggested.

Testifying about the early days of his marriage, Makepeace began to recount some of the curious stories Cindy had told him about members of her family. He stressed he never knew whether these tales were true.

The earliest odd incident he remembered occurred in 1966, when Cindy received a letter from her mother just before their wedding. "She read it out to me and it was very, very disparaging about marrying a divorcé," he recalled. "About three days later, she told me *she* had written the letter herself. I asked to see the letter and she claimed she destroyed it."

From that point, Makepeace made photocopies of letters to permit handwriting comparisons. Cindy's admission of forgery was peculiar at the time, but it was only after her death, that it seemed to make any sense, he said. He felt it was part of a delusional problem and later wondered if the 1966 letter was the first one she sent herself.

Makepeace never got the impression Cindy was harshly disciplined as a child, only that she was "controlled and over-controlled." Cindy also felt her sister Marlene was always favoured, he added. "She felt, if anything, she didn't get due recognition." Cindy felt her father negated her desire to attend university because he believed women did not need a post-secondary education, Makepeace stated. Consequently, years later, Cindy resented the educational opportunities offered to her younger brothers and sisters who had attended university.

Otto Hack had previously told reporters he did not wish to comment publicly on the inquest while it was in progress. But he broke his silence on May 2, 1990, after Makepeace had given testimony about allegations Cindy had made about the sex habits of the elder Hack and brother Doug.

"It makes me disgusted . . . ," Hack said, his face crimson with anger. "There were assumptions, gut feelings, all kinds of assertions, but nothing based on fact."

Asked if he still believed his daughter's death was murder, he replied, "We're still looking for factual information in the other direction [suicide] and there hasn't been any."

In a democratic system, he added, you are assumed to be innocent until proven guilty, but all he had seen so far in the coroner's investigation was that Cindy was "the architect of most of the incidents, if not all." Hack charged that the inquest was "definitely slanted" toward suicide, and the media reports were reflecting it.

Recalled to the stand after the break, Makepeace was asked by Leask if failing to qualify as a psychiatrist in 1968 had made him angry.

"No," he said. "I had mixed feelings."

"Do you have a temper?"

Makepeace said he was angry enough to slap Cindy twice during their marriage. The first episode happened after Cindy had scattered his "boat stuff" in the basement. When he complained, she shrugged, which infuriated him. To give her an idea of what it was like to have something valuable tampered with, he went outside and stomped on her marigolds. He recalled Cindy had yelled and yelled at him. Finally, unable to take this, he slapped her.

The next episode occurred while Ken and Melanie were staying with him and Cindy. Cindy was angry about spilled soup or something that had happened on their just-completed boating trip. She was going on and on about it, in a high-pitched, unrelenting voice, he recalled.

At the end of his patience, he slapped Cindy with an open hand. No black eye, just a red mark. He considered both swats a "corrective emotional experience."

Makepeace recalled another time when he and Cindy became embroiled in an argument. "She was behaving like an irrational 10-year-old." She told her story for 10 minutes and repeated it over and over. "Then I got two or three sentences into my side and she just blew, and something blew inside me." He grabbed her upper arms and said, "Look, you agreed to hear me out."

Cindy put her hands over her head and shouted, "Don't hit me! Don't hit me!" Roy sat her down on the couch and explained his point of view. He did not hold her tight enough to leave bruises on her arms, he said.

"Two or three days later she accused me of hitting her. She said, 'I won't stick around and have you hitting me like that.' I thought, 'Oh my God, something's loose.' . . . It was the first time I realized she couldn't distinguish between fantasy and reality."

Makepeace also denied ever throwing an ashtray that hit Cindy in the head, as she had once claimed to police. Later, after they had separated, he did notice a gash on the left side of her forehead. Asked what happened, Cindy "looked down at the ground and said, 'You should know.' "

"I've heard various versions of these attacks to the point of befuddlement," he added. "I think it has a lot more to do with symbolism than it does with me."

"It is your honest belief that the Mafia were pursuing Cindy and perhaps you?" Leask asked.

"Yes," he said. But he had changed his mind after he talked to the coroner's investigator and had learned about all the incidents that happened after he had been "cut off" from Cindy and her family.

Shortly before the October 1989 interview with Costello, Makepeace recalled, he went on a six-week cycling trip to Santa Barbara, Calif., from Vancouver, with members of the Cross Canada Cycle Tour Society. He came back fit, his mind sharp.

That was when, for him, the key to his ex-wife's troubles was revealed. Cindy's pain did not originate outside herself. Rather, she suffered from multiple personality disorder. And he blamed her doctors for not recognizing that she was a "multiple."

"I'd say, in my opinion, the entire psychiatric interaction with Cindy in the last eight years has been a travesty," Makepeace testified. "My feeling is, 'Who's responsible for this patient?' And the answer is, 'Nobody.' "

Losing his composure briefly, Makepeace added: "There was no competent psychiatrist taking charge of her psychiatric treatment . . . Up to this time, not a single psychiatrist ever picked up the phone and contacted her significant other, which is her ex-spouse."

Commenting on Cindy's allegation that he had killed two people in the Gulf Island cabin, Makepeace said: "If one accepts that she was not lying and that I didn't do it, then she must be delusional."

He added, "Either the whole thing is true and I'm Ted Bundy, or I'm not."

"I take it you believe such a thing as multiple personality disorder exists," Leask said.

"As sure as the sun rises," Makepeace replied. He agreed it was a controversial diagnosis, but pointed out that MPD is accepted by many well-recognized, well-informed people within the medical community. It is difficult to recognize, he added, but its symptoms are two or more distinct personalities and periods of time loss, indicative of someone "switching" to an alternate personality, often with no memory of what that "alter" did.

Suggesting the theory was "too easy," Leask said it would be helpful if Makepeace could provide the court with examples of incidents that would point to Cindy being a multiple personality.

Well, Cindy was a very private person, Makepeace observed, and multiples are very guarded, especially in times of stress, which can trigger a switch. He also noted she was child-like and irrational at times, indicators, perhaps, of a "child personality." And the gun incident, where Cindy thought he was going to shoot her, may have involved an alter personality. During Cindy's hypnosis sessions, the hypnotherapist may have unknowingly tapped into another personality, who can have delusional thoughts, he said.

"I'm so resentful of the inadequacy of her psychiatric care," Makepeace reiterated. "Nobody checked the facts of her life. . . . And that is tragic. It cost her her life."

As Dr. Tony Marcus was called to the stand, he told the court that he did not wish to testify because he saw James in the hospital and claimed any conversations he had with her were part of the confidential doctor-patient relationship.

Marcus's reluctance to testify stemmed partly from one of his colleagues complaining to the College of Physicians and Surgeons about an interview he had done with *The Vancouver Sun* shortly after Cindy's body was found. In the interview, Marcus said he felt Cindy was a "borderline personality," functioning between neurosis and psychosis, although never totally out of touch with reality. He believed she was responsible for the incidents she reported to police.

Marcus's desire not to betray doctor-patient confidentiality raised a thorny legal issue. Marcus was stepped down while the lawyers presented lengthy legal arguments why Marcus should or should not have to testify. Leask suggested the court should provide the same protection of privacy to a dead Cindy James as it would a living Cindy. He also provided the court with legal precedents concerning the matter of confidential communications. However, after an adjournment, Coroner Tilley decided the benefit of disclosure outweighed the harm. He recalled Marcus to the witness stand.

The forensic psychiatrist told the court he was struck by the "chronicity" of the Cindy James case. "This case presented an incredible number of incidents over a very long duration, during which no perpetrator had been found," Marcus said. "I was struck by the elusiveness of it all."

Could Ativan, taken in normal doses, cause amnesia?

"No, not really," Marcus said. One of the factors that concerned him was that there was no evidence that the persecuting events occurred in Cindy's marriage. When a professional person – a minister, doctor or lawyer – engages in an organized campaign of terror to drive someone crazy, usually it starts in the marriage, he noted.

Marcus felt Cindy had a deep-seated psychiatric disorder stemming from childhood or adolescence, although he did not have time to explore those areas with her. He agreed it was possible she was sexually assaulted in childhood, but Cindy did not trust him enough to reveal any major trauma in her life. Marcus only saw her twice for a total of less than two hours.

He admitted it was possible for a person with a severe psychiatric disorder to inflict wounds on herself in order to take out her rage against another person. Still, Marcus could not rule out the possibility that there may have been another person who "moved in" on James and perpetrated the terror.

But supposing his theory was right – that James was initiating the events she reported to police – could one logically conclude that she might have gone too far and ended her life?

"A patient often walks a tightrope on the side of life," Marcus replied. "It sometimes happens by accident."

FIFTEEN

Death Scene Revisited

A S THE INQUEST plodded on to Part Two and the exploration of Cindy's death and subsequent police examination, the main RCMP investigator, Constable Jerry Anderson, took the stand.

In a low, soft voice, Anderson explained that after Cindy went missing but before her body was found, he spoke to her psychiatrist, Dr. Friesen. "He said he'd never seen her so happy and so positive." At the time, Friesen believed Cindy was still alive, although he had no idea where she was. Friesen also related to Anderson that his patient was fixated on her ex-husband and had pent-up anger toward her father.

Anderson told the court that he had taken the answering-machine messages received by Dr. Makepeace in fall of 1988, along with a tape-recording of Cindy's voice from her own answering machine, and sent them to the Federal Bureau of Investigation in Washington, D.C. The FBI, in turn, sent the tapes to the Psycholinguistics Centre in Syracuse, New York, for analysis.

The centre's specialist, M.S. Miron, concluded: "Although there are obvious similarities in voice characteristics of the known and questioned tapes, the distortions of the [voice] disguise and the paucity of content preclude judgment regarding the source similarities."

The eerie messages were played in court. The first, recorded on October 11, 1988, said: "Cindy . . . dead . . .

meat . . . soon." The hoarse, menacing voice seemed to savour each word, dragging out the message to 12 seconds. It sounded like something from *The Exorcist*.

The second message, recorded October 12, said: "Hey, man, more smack, more downers, another grand after we waste the cunt. No . . . more . . . deal." The voice was similar to the one on the first message.

Anderson explained to the court that "smack" was street lingo for heroin and barbiturates are often referred to as "downers".

"I believe that is Cindy on the tape," he added. Cross-examined by Peter Leask, Anderson had to admit he was not a voice-comparison expert.

Bethell asked Cindy's mother, after she had listened to the tape, if she thought it was her daughter's voice.

"Oh my God, no."

Bethell asked Tillie Hack if she recalled when coroner's investigator Pat Costello played the tape to her before the inquest. At that time, she had told Costello that the voice could have been her daughter.

"It could be Cindy, it could be anybody," she recalled saying at the time. The tape Costello played was more garbled, not as clear as the one in court, she added.

Otto Hack testified that it was "very unlikely" the voice was his daughter's. He thought it was a male voice.

Makepeace also thought it was a male voice and found it difficult to accept that it was Cindy. He originally thought the messages were "an attempt to incriminate me and frame me." He sent a copy of the tapes to his lawyer and advised that it be sent to the Vancouver police chief, but this was never done.

After Cindy's body was found in June 1989, Anderson explained, the ligatures around the neck and wrists were sent to Robert Chisnall, the Ontario knot expert who had been consulted earlier. Chisnall believed the ligatures were consistent with the theory that Cindy tied herself.

By June 29, the preliminary toxicology tests showed Cindy had an overdose level of the prescription drug

flurazepam in her system. Anderson said he was informed that she likely would have remained conscious for
no longer than 20 minutes after taking the drug.

Meeting with the Hacks July 11, Anderson told them he
was ruling out foul play. He was asked to tell the court the
reasons that led to his decision. Cindy's "supporters" at
the inquest – her friends and colleagues who believed she
was slain – sat attentively, eager to hear the explanation
first-hand.

For about two weeks prior to her disappearance, Anderson began, Cindy was in good spirits. In his experience
with suicides, he sometimes found that happy behaviour
indicates a person has set a course of action to carry out a
suicide. He also noted Cindy's "support people" – her
closest friends and colleagues – were leaving "en masse,"
going away on holidays, which may have made Cindy feel
she was being abandoned.

Anderson added that he thought he had a good rapport
with Cindy, and had maintained more than normal contact
with her before she disappeared, so he found it strange
that Cindy did not tell him she felt she was being followed,
and that "something big" was due to happen.

Anderson testified he interviewed one of Kaban's employees, Steve Cox, who said James had always been
aware of the times when surveillance was in place at her
home. Cox said that sometimes when he radioed his office
that he was heading home for the night, he would be part
way home when Cindy would call Kaban's office to report
a prowler. Anderson stated that Cox wished he had radioed in that he was leaving for the night, then stayed to
see what would happen. He also noted that when Kaban
installed a surveillance camera on one side of her home,
an occurrence would take place on another side.

Anderson explained that he had met with Vancouver
police Staff-Sgt. Kris Bjornerud on February 27, 1989, to
discuss Vancouver police files. Bjornerud shared Anderson's opinion that Cindy was staging the attacks. Bjornerud felt it was unfortunate that he could not get the

manpower approved for surveillance of her home. He wanted to catch Cindy "in the act."

Consequently, in April, Anderson secretly installed a 24-hour video camera trained on the back of Cindy's home; the camera recorded still photos every few seconds. Anderson felt he would be able to review the tape if an incident occurred. The camera, however, failed to film in the low-light conditions of night and the system was being fine-tuned right up until Cindy's disappearance, he said. It had been installed inside a garden shed of her neighbour, Ted Jamieson, who was the only civilian who knew about it. Anderson also had placed a secret C-237 entry in Cindy's file restricting RCMP access to the fact that the camera had been installed.

Anderson felt it was noteworthy that the Woodcocks were planning to play bridge with Cindy the night she went missing. They had a key to her house, which meant they could look after Heidi if, for whatever reason, Cindy disappeared.

Cindy was usually very paranoid and cautious, Anderson said, so he found it suspicious that she would have parked in the middle of the parking lot at Blundell Centre. While Agnes Woodcock had stressed that Cindy always liked to pull up to the front of the bank doors, another witness, Tracey McLean, said she saw Cindy park and she appeared fixated on parking where she did.

Cindy's bank-machine card and transaction slip were found together under her car, Anderson went on. "They wouldn't get there by dropping them." Had they been dropped, the paper would have fluttered and landed in a different spot than the plastic card. The more likely explanation, he reasoned, is that they were either tossed or placed under the car.

The blood found on the car door would seem to indicate violence or a struggle at the shopping centre, yet no one saw or heard anything out of the ordinary. "It's a very poor spot to do an abduction," Anderson added. A better spot would have been Richmond General Hospital parking lot.

Cindy's purse was found inside the locked car with two sets of keys. Anderson thought she had either locked herself out of the car or purposely left her keys inside "for whatever reason."

Anderson was suspicious, too, that no perishable products were found among the Safeway grocery bags. There was no sales receipt, so the groceries could not be traced. Investigators tried running the groceries through a cash register at Safeway using May 25, 1989 prices, but the total failed to match any of the computerized cashier records, not even with one or more pairs of black nylons added, he said.

The death scene was adjacent to a busy street near a major intersection – not the sort of place you would expect a body to be dumped, Anderson said. There were plenty more remote spots where a person was less likely to be detected. He felt it was more likely that Cindy walked the 1.5 kilometres from the shopping centre to where she was found.

Another factor Anderson considered when ruling out foul play was Cindy's coat, found at the death scene spread neatly on the ground, outer side down and the lapels up. Killers usually do not take that kind of care with their victims, Anderson said. He would have expected Cindy to be found lying face down if she had been slain.

In addition, there were no signs of struggle at the scene. Despite cuts and tears on Cindy's blouse, there were no corresponding injuries to the body. The cuts appeared to have been started with a sharp knife, then torn. Moreover, if someone had tied Cindy up, they would have shown her disregard and tied the ligatures as tightly as possible. Instead, the bonds were quite loose and easily slipped off one of her hands.

Noting the level of flurazepam was eventually determined to be 10 times that of a lethal dose, Anderson said it was difficult to believe someone would ingest that amount involuntarily.

At the conclusion of Anderson's statement of his reasons for ruling out foul play, Leask asked: "Would you agree that, based on the evidence, that it is not possible to say with any certainty that she killed herself or someone killed her?"

"Okay, I'll agree," he said.

"Were the stockings purchased at Safeway?" asked Leask.

"I don't know."

"Did anyone look into that?"

"I don't believe so, no," Anderson said, adding they were a common type.

"Were there any fresh perishables in Cindy's home?"

"I don't know. . . . I know her fridge was pretty bare, nearly empty."

"Did you ever ask the Woodcocks what sort of food and drinks they consumed during an evening at Cindy's?"

No, Anderson said.

"Why wasn't the body found sooner?" Leask continued. "You were searching for Cindy alive and her possible dead body? It seems like common sense to me to look in vacant houses and lots."

"In hindsight, maybe," said Anderson. The bodies of six to eight women had been dumped over the years along the dikes or in Richmond's blueberry fields, so it seemed logical to concentrate searches in those areas.

"Mr. Hack said he could get CFB Chilliwack forces to check vacant lots and houses and was told by Sgt. Campbell, 'Police are already doing that.' "

"I don't recall that," Anderson replied.

"Would you agree if the foot search was undertaken, the body would have been found very quickly?"

Anderson said it would have taken considerable manpower to do a 1.5-square-kilometre search, and even that would not have ensured finding Cindy.

Leask countered that with 500 or more soldiers searching, the body would have been found in a day or two and this would have made it considerably easier for the pathologist to determine how Cindy died.

"She could have been anywhere," Anderson said. "We didn't know she was in Richmond." He admitted, however, that no additional searches were done after May 29, 1989, just five days after Cindy disappeared.

Leask asked Anderson if he ever tried to find the youths who had frequented the abandoned "party house." The officer said he believed local skinheads had spray-painted the inside walls of the house.

Leask suggested the markings inside the house had occult, satanic significance. He asked if Anderson checked to see if any RCMP members had knowledge about satanic cults. Anderson replied he was not aware of any members with formal responsibility for that specialized knowledge.

The lawyer then asked if there had been a party at the abandoned house between the time Cindy went missing and the time her body was found.

"I believe there was, yes," Anderson said.

Leask noted Makepeace was in Richmond that day and he had an alibi. But did Anderson consider the woman who verified his alibi might have lied for him?

"Not from the pattern of responses [she gave]. I didn't consider that."

Cindy had not been prescribed flurazepam, the sedative that was found in massive quantity in her system. So, Leask asked, "You have no idea how Cindy got ahold of flurazepam, if she did?"

"That's correct."

Leask suggested the toxicology lab tests took four months because the case "received considerably less priority because foul play was ruled out." Anderson said he would have expected to wait that long even for a full-scale murder investigation.

As for the morphine, also found at a level 10 times that of a lethal dose, Leask suggested that drug experts could not tell if it had been injected or ingested.

"That's true." Anderson said he learned that morphine was used on the hospital ward where Cindy worked, although there is a tight narcotic-control system in place at the hospital.

"Every drop of morphine used and received is recorded?" Leask asked.

"Yes."

"Did you check those records?"

"No," said Anderson, as Cindy's friends and family sighed in disgust. "I was told by the hospital there were no shortages." He also said a "source" at the hospital, whom he would not reveal, had told him the narcotic-control system was not foolproof and a nurse could "short-change" a patient but record a full dose.

"What other sources of morphine are there?"

"Drugstores, the street, doctor's offices."

Anderson agreed with Leask he did not check to see if there had been any drug store thefts of morphine prior to Cindy's disappearance, and he did not investigate Dr. Makepeace's access to morphine.

"Where do you think she administered the drugs to herself?"

"I don't know," Anderson said.

"She'd have to be closer than No. 2 and Blundell?"

"I tend to agree with that."

"Would you agree that your reasons for why there was no foul play could cut both ways – suicide or murder?"

"Agreed."

A videotape of the death scene was viewed in court, showing close-ups of the nylons that bound Cindy James' hands and feet, as well as the nylon around her neck. The only sound on the tape was that of flies flitting about Cindy's decomposing remains. Cindy's mother sat wiping her eyes with a Kleenex in the darkened courtroom.

Knot expert Robert Chisnall testified about his conclusions regarding the ligatures he had examined for Richmond RCMP.

He explained that each of Cindy's hands and legs was

tied behind her back with a slip loop to form "a box arrangement."

The most conspicuous aspect of it was its slackness. The stocking tied around Cindy's wrists and ankles was loose enough that it could be slipped off.

He demonstrated in court how easy it was to tie himself in exactly the fashion Cindy had been found. Jurors stood to watch as Chisnall duplicated the ligatures. First, he tied the stocking around his neck before tying the slip loops and slipping his wrists and ankles into the loops, making it appear that his hands had been tied from behind.

Completing the demonstration, which took about three minutes, Chisnall lay on the floor with his hands and legs behind his back and with a black nylon tied around his neck. He used the same lengths of nylon as those that had tied Cindy, he explained, and even though his measurements were bigger, the neck ligature did not impede his breathing other than to make him a little light-headed.

His conclusion? Self-tying was the likely explanation.

Under questioning by Leask, Chisnall agreed that three scenarios were possible: that Cindy was tied up to make her murder look like a suicide; that it was a suicide made to look like murder; or that two people may have tied up Cindy.

Chisnall said he had seen a case of "auto-erotic" bondage involving two men tied up and dressed like women, but he did not have enough experience in the area to determine if Cindy's case involved sex-bondage ligatures.

Pathologist Sheila Carlyle testified that, because of the state of decomposition of the body, it was difficult to determine whether the overdoses of morphine and flurazepam had been administered orally or by injection.

The flurazepam was ingested orally, she believed, since tablets were found in the contents of her stomach. She also believed it was likely that the morphine was ingested. The needle mark was probably a "blood collection site" rather than evidence of an injection – blood might have been withdrawn from Cindy's arm and perhaps squirted on her car to make it look as if she had been abducted. The blood on the car was tested and found to be the same blood-group type as Cindy's.

Although Carlyle agreed with Leask that she could not rule out the skin puncture as an injection site for the morphine administered by someone other than Cindy, she added, "it is entirely conceivable and feasible that this could be a self-contrived event."

Carlyle had two reasons to believe Cindy had been alive where her body was found. She felt that Cindy had been kneeling on her neatly spread coat and had fallen over on her right side as she lost consciousness. Moreover, there was some mobility of the body as death neared, judging from how she was found. "Her right knee," she pointed out, "had worked its way under the natural vegetation floor, which suggested the body hadn't been dropped after death but had some mobility until death."

She also noted that she found the neck ligature unusual because it was wrapped once around underneath the hair and twice over the outside of the hair, where it was neatly tied.

Carlyle added that it was a relatively odourless scene, so it was not surprising that the nearby squatter failed to smell anything. "There was no escape of body gases."

A question from a juror: Carlyle originally thought Cindy's finger had been scraped to the bone by a finger of her other hand, perhaps an involuntary movement? Yes, Carlyle replied, that was her original opinion but she later determined the skin of the finger was split as part of the mummification and drying of the body, which was on its way to becoming a skeleton.

The Simon Fraser University entomologist, Gail Anderson, could determine from the incubation of insect larvae only that the body had been at the death scene since June 2 or earlier.

Toxicologist Heather Dinn estimated the amount of flurazepam in Cindy's body would amount to 20 30-mg. tablets or up to 80 tablets of a lower dosage. She did not know how long it would take to swallow that many tablets.

Pharmacology expert John McNeill, who reviewed the toxicology test results, testified that either of the drugs in Cindy's body, flurazepam or morphine, could have killed her. Both drugs cause progressive sedation and decrease brain activity, and an overdose would cause the person to become drowsy, then induce a coma and finally death.

McNeill concluded the flurazepam was taken orally, since it is only available by oral prescription and residue of the drug had been found in the victim's stomach. He estimated the dose in Cindy's system would have taken 15 to 30 minutes to sedate her and up to four hours to kill her.

The morphine could have been injected or taken orally, since it is available in tablet or liquid prescriptions. If ingested orally, McNeill noted, it could have been self-administered and rendered Cindy unconscious within 15 to 30 minutes and could have been taken up to 30 minutes after the flurazepam.

If injected, the morphine must have been administered by someone other than Cindy since unconsciousness would have occurred almost immediately and killed her within 15 to 30 minutes, McNeill said.

As the death-scene segment ended with another puzzling possibility, it was clear that police did not have any conclusive physical evidence that would prove Cindy James died by her own hand. Each portion of testimony seemed to be riddled with ambiguity.

After hearing months of testimony heavily laced with complex medical and psychiatric jargon that was confusing and tedious, the members of the jury looked weary. They wondered if they would ever return to their normal lives.

SIXTEEN

Code of Loyalty

A S T H E I N Q U E S T shifted to Cindy's personal background and family history, the first question posed by Bethell when Doug Hack took the stand was: "Did you attempt to sexually abuse your sister at any time?"

"No," Hack replied, smiling at the absurdity of the question. He also refuted Cindy's allegation that their father had abused alcohol at one point in his life. All in all, he said the Hacks were a pretty normal family.

Another incident Bethell wished to probe took place after Cindy's death: when family members had gathered to prepare for the funeral, a cache of prescription drugs had been found in a small make-up bag in Cindy's Richmond home. The family held a meeting to decide what should be done with the discovery.

"Did your dad ask you to flush them down the toilet?" Bethell asked Cindy's sister, Marlene Weintrager.

"Yes, he did," she replied. "I wish I hadn't now. I mean, in retrospect, I made a mistake."

She explained it was a family decision, with her father chairing the meeting of the family. The vials of drugs were mostly sedatives and sleeping pills with such generic names as diazepam (most commonly known under the brand name, Valium) and chlorazepam (Rivotril).

"We decided as a family that there was no point in having them. Apparently the police had been to the house two or three times, said they had gone through everything, so we didn't see that there was any point keeping them. I didn't feel at the time that it had any bearing on anything."

She made a list of the drugs from the information on the prescription bottles and gave that list to police, she said. The vials, when first prescribed, had contained about 900 pills. Weintrager explained that some vials were nearly full, others half empty and still others were found to contain two different types of drugs. She had started to count the number in each vial, but found some had more than they were supposed to have.

"This is ridiculous," she told her father. "I'm just putting down how many were supposed to be on the prescription."

Weintrager, her sister Melanie and her father later met with Friesen and asked him why Cindy would have so many pills stashed away. Friesen, she said, did not find it unusual.

"His comments were . . . Cindy saved things, and it could be also that she was planning on disappearing, to get away from all the harassments and start a new life somewhere else, and perhaps she was saving these pills so she wouldn't have to go and see another doctor somewhere else and explain everything again – she would have them on hand."

"Was there any suggestion at that time [that] getting rid of those drugs was hiding a potential suicide?" Bethell asked.

"We had been given the impression by the police that they felt that Cindy had committed suicide. It's very difficult when you are grieving, you don't really think clearly. . . . I guess we were concerned that this would just be something else that they could say, 'Okay, great. She had these pills so she committed suicide.'"

Asked if family members had found anything else, Weintrager said they found an unopened catheter kit and syringe in Cindy's house. "I think my mom threw it out."

She also found a glass cutter in one of Cindy's purses after she had taken it home to Ottawa. She told Melanie about it, but they did not think it had any significance. They knew Cindy loved gardening and thought she must have used the glass cutter to cut cold frames to put over seedlings.

Bethell reminded Weintrager that Cindy reported their father was very strict. "Yes, that's [a] fair comment," she said, agreeing that she was disciplined with a leather strap, her father was verbally abusive at times and he may have drunk too much at one time in his life.

Asked to recall Cindy's nightmares, particularly the one of the white hands coming up from under the bed, Weintrager explained that she and Cindy were afraid of snakes in the basement woodbox. "And as we got older, the snakes seemed to turn out to be the hands of somebody and we were always afraid we would never wake up."

She and Cindy were put in the basement, not as punishment, but to eat their meals sometimes, with the door shut behind them, she added. They ate on the stairs because there wasn't enough room at the kitchen table, she recalled. "I remember it being dark and scary."

Under questioning by Makepeace's lawyer, Alastair Wade, Weintrager recalled that her father hunted for sport.

"Did you ever see him bring back animals he had shot?"

"Yes," Weintrager replied.

"And did he butcher them at the house, cut them up for the freezer?"

"Not at our house," she said. "I think it was my uncle's or grandfather's barn."

The lawyer asked Marlene why she and Cindy were afraid of water. She replied that their family went to the beach often and "my dad used to play a game with us where he would flip us off his shoulders into the water – we were quite afraid of that because we couldn't swim and we thought we would drown."

"It was a game you didn't enjoy?"

"Not particularly."

Wade asked her when she was made aware that Cindy had been committed to Lions Gate Hospital, which occurred in 1985.

"I think probably just last year [1989]," she said, adding she asked Doug why he did not tell her sooner and he said he felt "we didn't have to know absolutely everything."

Cross-examined by Leask, Weintrager said she had seen no evidence that Cindy had multiple personalities. She also said she could not accept that Cindy would have committed suicide in the fashion she was found.

"If she was going to die, she would have Heidi with her. She was a very proud person. She wouldn't stage something like this."

"My understanding," said the coroner, "from what you were saying yesterday, there was a lot of things that you were not aware that were going on in Cindy's life. Having heard those things, does it kind of surprise you or shock you to know that these things went on in her life?"

"Yes. It was pretty horrible," Weintrager said. "I guess I was a little upset that I didn't know about most of these things. But Cindy was a very private person, and she never wanted to upset anybody else. She used to always just think about you before herself. I didn't know about the October attack until months afterwards, because she was so concerned that I was having problems of my own and she didn't want me to have to worry about her."

She added that she felt very sad. "My sister didn't seem to have a chance, even while she was alive, because it was my impression that people had the gut feeling that she did it herself, and I really don't believe that at all. And I feel really bad, because I wish I had known more of what was going on so I could have helped her. She really needed us, and I feel like so many of us let her down." At this thought, she dissolved into tears.

Bethell asked Melanie Cassidy if she believed Cindy was actually terrorized by someone. "Yes, I really believe that," she said. "When she would tell me of some of the attacks, and she would tell me what it was like and what happened to her, I really believed when I looked into her eyes . . . that she was telling me the truth."

"And you've heard evidence through the course of the inquest that many times she couldn't recall what happened to her?" Bethell asked.

"Right."

"Yet you're saying now that she told you what happened to her?"

"Not all the details, no. Many times she would say, 'I can't remember,' or 'Do you really want me to tell you?' She said, 'The details are too horrible.' And I said, 'Cindy, I don't want you to tell me the details if it's too upsetting for you. . . . I just want to know if you're okay. I want to be there for you, to give you a hug if you need it, but you don't have to tell me the details.' And many times she wouldn't. I think she really appreciated that."

Wade asked Cassidy why she did not tell police or Ozzie Kaban about the syringe found at Cindy's house.

"I didn't find out about that syringe until the fall of [1989]," she replied. "My mother told me."

"But you were in the house at the time that discovery was made, weren't you?"

"Yes, I was."

Cassidy said she had not been informed of Cindy's 1985 committal until a year later.

The coroner asked Melanie if she had anything to add that might assist the jury in coming to a conclusion.

"I feel that I've looked at her death with an open mind – I want to know the truth," she said. "Knowing Cindy, I don't believe she took her life, but I understand the possibility as it's been presented by other people, but I want the truth to be found, and I hope that we will."

Bethell began his questioning of Tillie Hack with questions raised by Makepeace, based on allegations he said Cindy had told him.

"When did you get your car licence?"

"Forty years ago," she replied, thereby refuting an earlier allegation that Tillie had been prevented by her spouse from driving.

The coroner then asked if she had a bank account of her own when Cindy was a teenager or young child. According to Makepeace, Cindy had said Otto Hack had not let Mrs. Hack do so.

"Oh, my God, no." Tillie said. "We hardly had two pennies to rub together."

She tried to clarify the details of Cindy and Marlene being put on the basement stairs, explaining that when they lived on 4th Avenue in Vancouver the kitchen was quite small "and when we had company we couldn't all sit around the table. We would open the door and the kids would sit on the top steps with their feet dangling through." She did not recall the basement door being closed.

"Can you think of anything in her childhood that was traumatic enough to leave a lasting impression on her or something that she would want to forget, anything of that nature?"

"Well, as the girls mentioned about the stairs, it could be that. I don't know of anything else."

Bethell pointed out Cindy stated in her "autobiography" that her mother had high expectations for the children.

"All of them, yes. They were darn smart kids."

"Was there little praise for success?"

"Not a lot, just enough that they deserved, no more, no less." The children were not punished if they failed to get an A in school, she added.

Bethell asked about Cindy's comments that her father drank to excess and that there were frequent verbal fights between her parents.

"We were in the service at the time," she explained. "The men on Fridays would go to TGIF, that means 'Thank God it's Friday,' . . . Sometimes they would come home, they would be a little bit tipsy, yes. If that's what you call drink to excess, okay. . . . Sometimes he [Otto] would say to me, 'Darn it, I would like to get out of here,' but that never actually meant anything."

Cindy probably misunderstood what her father meant, Mrs. Hack offered. "It used to upset me sometimes, fellows come home, sometimes he would bring them to our house and be a little bit tipsy."

Bethell asked her when she learned about Cindy's stay in Lions Gate Hospital in 1985.

"Right here [in court]," she replied. Neither Doug nor anyone else had told her about it.

Before Tillie Hack left the stand, the coroner wished to clarify a few matters. "Listening to the evidence," the coroner said, "would it make you wonder as to why Cindy would leave her home and walk her dog at 2 a.m. or 3 a.m. in the morning after some of these attacks?"

"I think there was a little confusion in that, whether she was really out walking the dog, I don't know," she replied.

"Did you not hear the evidence of one of the neighbors while Cindy lived in Richmond that she was surprised to see Cindy walking her dog . . . in the early hours of the morning?"

"I didn't know anything about anybody saying that they saw her in Richmond walking in the late or early hours of the morning."

"You didn't hear any of that evidence?" the coroner asked, surprised.

"I didn't hear any of that."

In his testimony, Otto Hack told the court that he felt the coroner's investigators, Pat Costello and Jim Smith, "were definitely influencing witnesses that it was suicide." He added that he found the questioning by lawyers, particularly Bethell, slanted toward suicide. He compared the inquest to an "inquisition" of his family. "I haven't seen a shred of fact that my daughter committed suicide. . . . The words I keep hearing are 'gut feeling' and 'opinion' but opinion has to be based on fact."

The only officers who did not try to prove Cindy was the architect of her own fate were Bowyer-Smyth and Bjornerud, he said. And the slant of the inquest, he added, was reflected in the media, which have reported only "the negative side."

Cross-examined by Wade, Hack said he did not accept that Cindy was suicidal, nor did he or the rest of the family feel she was mentally ill. "I know she was in mental, or if I can use the word, spiritual anguish."

He admitted that suicide was at odds with his religion. "A Christian will not accept committing suicide."

And he stated he was suspicious of psychiatrists and did not have much faith in them. "These experts who were treating her and dealing with her screwed her up much more," he said. "You take 10 psychiatrists and put them in a room and you'll have 10 different theories."

Hack could not recall anything particularly traumatic in Cindy's childhood, but during an overnight adjournment, he said the family had held a "brainstorming" session in which they compiled a list of incidents that might have affected Cindy's psychological state. He proceeded to read the list.

When Cindy was five, he said, his father – Cindy's grandfather – was baby-sitting when he fell and hit his head against the bathtub, knocking him unconscious, which frightened Cindy.

And then there was the scarlet fever episode. He said he and his wife were picking apples in the Okanagan for a month and they were not notified of the life-threatening sickness until 10 days after she was seriously ill. "They had a problem locating us," he explained. The Sea Island base surgeon phoned him and explained Cindy was over the critical stage and was in quarantine, so it was not going to do any good to rush home. "So it took a number of days. We finished the work we were doing and we went back home. . . . It's a possibility that they were, in punishment, locked out [by the woman looking after them], and this was a cold time of year."

In 1959, Cindy's cousin Joyce suddenly died of a brain aneurism. "Marlene tells me they were both very, very upset about this." Three years later, Hack said, his father, brother and one of Cindy's cousins were killed in a car accident. "And again, I didn't attach much to it until Marlene called to my attention that it really upset them greatly when they got that information. I think it mainly upset them because they felt that I was grieving a lot. Of course, that was true."

Then there was the young intern whom Cindy had met at Vancouver General Hospital, who was later killed in a car accident. "I know they were in love. She told us that. We got the impression she was engaged."

The last traumatic death involved Marlene's first husband, an air force pilot, who was killed in a plane crash in October 1973, while searching for a plane lost in the Coast Mountains of B.C. Cindy, he said, "liked [her brother-in-law] very much, and this death just added on to some of these others."

One other episode that Hack recalled had upset Cindy occurred in 1964, when he received a telegram from Vancouver General Hospital, where Cindy was doing her nursing training. Doctor's were asking for his permission to remove one of Cindy's eyes after an unknown medication had affected it. Hack sent back a telegram, saying "Hold fire until I get there" and immediately flew to Vancouver. Meeting with medical staff he told them their theories – doctors were worried the medication might get in her brain and cause irreparable damage – were not good enough to support the removal of an eye. Hack said he met that night with officials from the Workmen's Compensation Board and convinced them to fly Cindy to a specialist in San Francisco. This was done and the expert found it was a sex hormone affecting her eye, nothing more. After treatment, she recuperated fully within two weeks.

"Can you think of anything going back to the time when she would be three or four?" Bethell asked.

"No," Hack said. "We tried. We looked at it from every possible aspect and we couldn't come up with anything."

Bethell asked Hack about the passage in Cindy's diary in which she expressed her resentment of her father who, while she was staying at her parents' home in Victoria, barged into her bedroom and woke her up at five or six in the morning.

"Yes, I recall that," Hack said, "and I don't quite understand why she would say that because . . . I jog in the morning, and it's not five or six o'clock, it's usually seven o'clock. . . . And what I usually did when she slept in that room, where I kept my sports clothing, is I'd take them out at night, but there was one occasion where I forgot to take my joggers out and my shorts, and I knocked at the door, and I heard no response, so I'd just gone in there and picked these up. Now obviously it disturbed her, and I admit I probably should have just left it and gone jogging after she got up."

"She goes on to say," Bethell continued, "that this was a repeated occurrence, even though she said, 'Please, Dad, take this stuff out of here because it's hard for me to get to sleep.' . . . And she even recounts that she put a suitcase in front of the door to try to remind you and you still pushed the door open. Do you recall that?"

"I recall seeing that, and again, I'm a little confused because she stayed with us three days, and of those three days, we devoted a good deal of time preparing for Melanie's wedding, and I recall jogging only once during the three days, so I would have no reason to go in there. But it's her perception."

"I understand that," Bethell said. "But it seems typical of a theme that she recounts here of you somehow wanting to control her actions, or insensitive to her requests or wishes."

"Well," Hack responded, "I think she had that perception, and I think part of it may have been a mix-up in terms of the authority figure and the problems she had with her husband. I don't know. I'm not a psychiatrist."

During Hack's testimony about the matters raised in Cindy's diary, Marlene and Melanie were seen to walk out of the courtroom. They would never explain the reasons for their disappearance. Those, they said, were "personal."

Bethell went on to ask Hack if he had any further evidence that the court had not heard.

He said there was one point that kept bothering him. He wanted to know why, after Cindy disappeared and after her remains were found, Anderson had not been taken off the case, since he was so biased toward suicide. An impartial, objective investigator with plenty of experience and qualifications should have been assigned, "particularly in view of the fact that we've been told time and time again that this was a very complex, difficult case."

Called to the witness box, Dr. Carl Rothschild, a child psychiatrist at Blenheim House, testified that Cindy had told him that she had been forced to have breast surgery in 1982 because of physical damage she alleged Roy had caused.

The fact of the matter was, as Rothschild learned at the inquest, that surgery was elective and cosmetic – namely, breast augmentation – and not in the least corrective.

Well, said a perplexed Rothschild, "she told me she had been hit."

He then proceeded to recall his earliest memories of Cindy. He was a fairly "green" psychiatrist when he first worked at Blenheim House in 1976, and was initially "raked over the coals," he said.

"I was getting feedback from her that I knew didn't fit," he said. "I thought I was going crazy." With the help of a therapist, Rothschild said, he realized the problem wasn't emanating from him, but Cindy. She was an efficient director but was somewhat anxious, he said. During the first two years he worked at Blenheim House, she began to come to work appearing more anxious and depressed, and, by the late 1970s, he noticed she seemed preoccupied. "Most colleagues would say, 'That's just Cindy.'"

Various staff members were taken into Cindy's confidence at one time or another. "And if we didn't pan out, as it were, she would move on to someone else."

Rothschild's period as her confidant lasted about a year, starting in 1982. He recalled how Cindy would routinely stay at his home with his family after she separated and the harassment had begun. Rothschild recalled Cindy's nightmares were very vivid and terrifying, hands coming out from under the bed to grab her.

"She would awaken shrieking in the night," Rothschild said, adding that he recalled her having similar nightmares before she separated from Roy. "It's part of the things she would talk about – what to do with these nightmares."

After her separation, the intensity of these sleep-time disturbances went up so dramatically that even when she took a nap she would be awakened by terrifying dreams, he said.

Cindy told him she came from a strict military background and she had been put outside for the night when it was fairly cold, and she had been put in the basement, alone.

She also told him she had a fiancé in nursing school who had been killed in a car accident, and that she had to look after a disturbed child at home. "That's why you want to work with children," Rothschild recalled telling her at the time.

She also talked about how she and her sisters were mercilessly getting after one another, which she felt had been passed on from her father.

Rothschild tried to get her to release her feelings and suggested she might need outside help, perhaps a therapist. "Her character structure was based on holding back feelings," he said. Even though it was vital to share feelings in a clinical setting, he felt Cindy was not comfortable sharing those feelings with her colleagues.

"She learned to shut off her feelings and that's how she survived," Rothschild said. "She had to control her fears and feelings."

Once the terror arose in her life, he had suggested "maybe it's too bloody dangerous for you to be working here."

He recounted the incident that caused Cindy to cut him off as a confidant: he and his wife were going on a trip to Israel and their children were going to look after themselves. Cindy volunteered to stay at the house, but, given the troubles in Cindy's life, Rothschild thought her presence might endanger his daughters.

"Cindy was furious," he said. "She went on to someone else."

After the attacks, Cindy would be anxious and disorganized for a while, then things would smooth out, he remembered. But those periods of recovery got longer and longer. Near the end of her employment at Blenheim House, she was never in a recovery phase and couldn't function properly, he said.

"I remember at times, without any provocation, she would break into crying because of fear," Rothschild recalled.

He felt that Cindy's whole being was based around holding tightly to loyalties. She did not accuse anyone, certainly not her husband, because that would be breaking her code of loyalty.

At one point during his period as her confidant, Cindy turned to him and asked, "Are we having an affair?"

"No, Cindy. I'm trying to be your friend," Rothschild replied. It was, he felt, an odd question, "a misinterpretation of what was going on."

In cross-examination, Leask suggested Cindy's question about having an affair was simply a way of asking, "What's your interest in me? Do you have some interest other than a friendly interest?" Rothschild agreed that was his understanding.

Did he see any signs of the multiple personality disorder Roy Makepeace had alluded to earlier?

"Not from my experience," he said. Then again, he knew Cindy James so well that "that kind of jaded my professional ability."

SEVENTEEN

"A Danger to Herself and Others"

S NOW AND winter rains had accompanied the beginning of the Cindy James inquest. But as the hearing
entered the final stages focusing on Cindy's psychiatric
history, the trees were in blossom and warm May sunshine
brightened spirits, if only temporarily, outside the court.

Called to the stand was Dr. Wesley Friesen, who testified
that he had only just been certified as a psychiatrist in
1986, when Cindy became his patient at St. Paul's Hospital.

Cindy was very difficult to treat, he said, because it was
hard to establish trust with her during their one-hour, bi-
weekly visits.

"I could not establish rapport with her . . . because I had
talked to her parents and she felt I was in alliance with Dr.
Tony Marcus." Cindy also felt Dr. Connolly had been dis-
loyal to her in talking to police. As a result, "I was concerned about further rejection," Friesen said. "She felt
terror of being abandoned."

Cindy also felt guilty that she had not been a good wife
because she would not go sailing with her husband. When
Friesen first saw her, she was displaying symptoms of
major depression, including misinterpretations of reality.
He recalled he once found her in a closet – she feared she
had been followed. On another occasion, Cindy crawled
along the corridor past his office. And still another time he
found her in a fetal position, curled up in a chair – a
person on her ward had died alone and she felt guilty. An

odd reaction, Friesen thought, for someone in the nursing profession.

Friesen was very aware of Cindy's frequent, sleep-disturbing nightmares. One night in St. Paul's, he recalled, Cindy was given a tremendous amount of medication to make her sleep – enough drugs to make the average person sleep 36 hours without interruption. Cindy slept only eight hours and had awakened once.

He thought Cindy James a very fragile, vulnerable woman who had problems with intimacy. The intensity of attachment to her ex-husband was particularly unusual, he said. She felt she could never establish another relationship with a man, although there certainly were opportunities. "She was terrified by men in an intimate setting."

He admitted Cindy sometimes dressed in flimsy blouses, but he would not describe her as a seductress. "There was a tremendous histrionic quality to her," he said.

Cindy also had very limited ability to vent anger at her parents or her ex-husband. Friesen tried encouraging her to express her anger, which she was better able to do by 1989 before she went missing.

Cindy also made all sorts of statements, Friesen said, that he never verified. One time, she said, she had been put outside in the cold as punishment, and her father put her in the basement, where she feared the water would rise and drown her.

He also never tried verifying whether the incidents she reported to police were real. His function was therapist, not detective, and he was trying to win her trust so she would feel comfortable to talk about her past.

Still, "it was difficult to believe she could have possibly manufactured all these things," he said. "She certainly never displayed the sophistication in my mind."

Did Friesen see any evidence of multiple personality disorder?

"Not that I observed." He diagnosed her problem as borderline personality disorder, with features of post-traumatic stress disorder.

Friesen felt it was possible her psychiatric problems stemmed from being physically or sexually abused in early childhood or adolescence. But Cindy James never trusted in him enough to discuss those areas openly.

"She knew something but wasn't able to tell us," he said. "It was hard to separate what is real and what is fantasy . . . which is not unusual for someone who had been abused in childhood."

Asked to explain the meaning of borderline personality, Friesen said borderline personalities attach themselves to a person, a job, house or car. "Their identity comes from their career or a person and they regress badly when they lose those kinds of things."

Cindy's identity was built around her husband and her career, and losing her job at Blenheim was a tremendous setback for her. "That's what the problems in 1987–88 were all about."

Borderlines can function fairly well if their career is going well. "That's our aim in therapy, to get them functioning in a career."

Friesen thought Cindy was making real gains re-establishing her identity before she went missing. She had a new job, a new name. She had confronted her father and told him she did not want to have joint tenancy ownership of her house; she wanted to own it herself.

Although Friesen asked Cindy to begin writing her personal diary, he never read it, not even after her death.

Why did he not visit her in hospital after the October 1988 attack in her carport? "I didn't want to give her any secondary reinforcement for these attacks, if she was doing them herself." He was concerned Cindy would stage incidents to justify her therapy.

Bethell asked if she ever suggested she was sexually assaulted during the attacks. "Yes, the one in 1988, the last one," Friesen said.

He said Cindy was not a "reliable historian" because her memory of events would be hazy after an attack. "She is a perfect victim in that sense. . . . If she was attacked, her responses may be distorted and she appears not to be credible."

Friesen confessed he was concerned that Cindy might abuse the drugs he prescribed. "She was, at times, on large doses of Halcion, the only thing that allowed her to sleep and work the next day." The anti-depressants prescribed to Cindy would be lethal in large doses but Friesen didn't feel she was actively suicidal. When Cindy went to visit her brother in Africa, she took a suitcase full of drugs – a six-week supply. "She knew she had enough drugs to kill her, but I trusted her."

Cindy had mentioned she wanted to get off all medication, Friesen recalled, because she had renewed her mortgage in April 1989 at a higher interest rate and her prescriptions were costing her about $160 a month.

Cindy also experienced transference – responding to someone as if he were someone else. "For example, if I was authoritarian, she would say, 'You remind me of my father' and she would become uncomfortable and upset." She always felt put down by authority figures.

Another example of transference, he said, is falling in love with one's therapist – idealizing and seeing him as something he is not.

Was Cindy attracted to Friesen? "She had a great number of cognitive distortions with my body language," he replied. "Borderlines often have intense relationships with their therapist, so that's why I kept it as clinical as possible."

Friesen saw Cindy for the last time on May 20, 1989, five days before her disappearance. He felt she was doing great. She seemed happy and was sleeping well.

"I'd never seen her so upbeat and optimistic," he said. "She said she didn't feel as threatened, she felt safer with someone living in her basement."

Kinahan asked Friesen if he advised Cindy not to see any other therapist.

"Correct."

"And you weren't aware she was seeing Dr. Connolly until the spring of 1987?"

"She said she phoned him a couple of times."

Kinahan asked if he would agree that police officers could not blindly accept what came out of Cindy James's mouth.

Friesen agreed. "She was not a reliable historian. She was withholding information from me, there's no doubt about that."

In the end, Friesen could not explain Cindy's death. She was not, he felt, suicidal.

In mid-May, Dr. Allan Connolly was called to the stand. Connolly, a casual dresser with a dusting of hair over his ears and collar, was a physician with an interest in psychiatry. He testified he began to see Cindy in late 1983 and continued to see her until sometime after June 1987. He would visit her at her office, at Ozzie Kaban's safe house in the West End, or even at her home when she felt a crisis had arisen. He stopped billing her in 1984 because he felt his visits were an offering of friendly support from a colleague – they both worked for the Greater Vancouver Mental Health Services Association – rather than therapy.

Initially, Connolly felt Cindy was suffering from severe anxiety. He taught her breathing exercises that would put her in a shallow trance and allow her to relax. Eventually, Cindy could put herself in a trance by using relaxation therapy. He did not regularly talk to police investigating her problems, but felt Ozzie Kaban was an "ally" who had a "pipeline" to police and would provide information about the investigations. "That helped me make me feel more secure about my clinical judgments," Connolly said.

Cindy told him about her disturbing dreams, including the ones of dismembered bodies evoked by hypnosis sessions. "The dream material was elusive and not clear to her. She couldn't identify clearly the site where it was. She had a sense it was on an island."

In February 1985, Connolly noted that Cindy was becoming more distressed and felt her chronic anxiety was symptomatic of post-traumatic stress disorder, which was beginning to affect her efficiency at work. She got worse as the year progressed until, in June, "I phoned Dr. [Paul] Termansen and asked him . . . as a professional favour, to take on the management of this case . . . and then I persuaded Cindy to put herself into Dr. Termansen's hands and go into the hospital because I was concerned that the suicidal threat was, for the first time, a real possibility at that stage."

Asked by Leask why she was admitted to Lions Gate Hospital under the assumed name Cindy Jacobs, Connolly said there had been two reasons – Kaban's concern for security, and Cindy's desire not to be identified as a psychiatric patient.

Connolly also recalled an odd incident from that summer. He received a late-night phone call from Kaban asking him to visit Cindy at her home. "Ozzie was there and Cindy was curled up in the bedroom in a totally regressed state," whimpering like a child. "It was a totally dissociated state, quite clearly. She seemed to be almost not in touch with reality that evening and this was just another much more severe symptom than I'd seen," he said.

"Eventually, over a 20-minute period of just attempting to soothe her, just calling her name," Connolly said, "I was able to bring her back to where she was able to respond to what I was saying, respond to my instructions, and that's when I insisted that she take some of the Ativan, her medication, that she had somewhere."

He added that Cindy thought he had "almost magical powers in terms of what I could say to her" and she relied very heavily on his support, which concerned him, because he felt her problem was probably more complex than the therapy he was offering her.

Before the August 21, 1985, arson, Cindy had become convinced that her husband was orchestrating the campaign of terror against her. This idea was seeded in her mind and it took root, Connolly recalled. "She suddenly now had somebody in mind, rather than a generalized threat from people unknown. . . . It actually grounded her, if you wish, at some level and helped her in a therapeutic sense."

After the arson, Cindy knew she was being blamed by police for setting the fire. "I think the sense of not being believed was overwhelming."

Connolly went to visit Cindy about 24 hours after she was admitted to University Hospital after the December 11, 1985, attack. She again appeared to be in a dissociative, trance-like state. He did not see her again before she left for Germany to visit her brother for Christmas, but he recalled running into Dr. Tony Marcus during his rounds of visiting patients.

Marcus, whom he knew had been called in to consult on Cindy's case, "quite summarily told me this was just her unconscious that was doing it, and I knew what that meant. . . . I felt my own formulations somewhat in doubt because this had been a different sort of episode." By this time Connolly felt Cindy's problem was much more complex than he first thought and that there was really nothing more he could offer her. "I didn't have any new bag of tricks."

Asked by Leask to provide a "snapshot" of Cindy's condition in the spring of 1986, Connolly said her face was like parchment, her eyes sunken, she was thin and not gaining weight. Her life had become very isolated and she rarely went out. Constantly fearful and on edge, she took elaborate precautions for her safety. "If the phone rang, she'd jump about three feet in the air, literally."

After the second arson at Cindy's rented home in Richmond, Connolly recalled visiting her after she moved in with Tom and Agnes Woodcock in Vancouver. "She was in the bed looking like a skeleton, just a shell of her former self." Cindy acted like it was her last day of living and she was planning to commit suicide "and nothing I could say was going to stop her."

He recalled meeting with Cindy's brother Doug on the roof of the Woodcocks' apartment building so Cindy

would not know Doug was there, to discuss Cindy's problems. He said he had contacted a Mental Health Emergency Service doctor and Cindy was committed to the
psychiatric unit of St. Paul's. After she escaped from the
unit, she was taken to Riverview. Once she was returned
to St. Paul's, he visited her and was told by medical staff
about Cindy being involved in "sometimes child-like and
foolish behaviour . . . inappropriate behaviour even for a
psychiatric patient."

Friesen contacted Connolly two or three times in the
fall of 1986. "He also told me that he thought it was her
unconscious that had created this elaborate scenario that
had been stressing her out."

She gradually improved under Friesen's care and Connolly stopped seeing her around June 1987. "There was a
buoyancy in her, a sense of optimism about the future that
I hadn't seen for a long period of time. It was just a mutual
agreement, you know, that maybe the end was in sight and
there was a new life ahead, and she was going to get on
with it."

He recalled getting a phone message from Cindy late in
1987. He kept the message in his pocket for several
weeks, but he never returned her call. The last he heard
from her was a Christmas present, a bottle of Crown
Royal rye whiskey, with an accompanying note that read:
"How are you doing? Things are going well with me.
Thanks for all you've done."

Connolly added that during the entire time he saw
Cindy, "I never changed my opinion that this was a person
who was reacting to a siege of terror that she saw as being
real." He never saw evidence to prove the terror was real
or imagined, only that it was real to her. Connolly said he
never pressed Cindy to recall details of the terrorizing
incidents since that would only increase her stress. His
aim was to reduce stress, to get her to relax.

Bethell asked Connolly why he never returned Cindy's
phone call before Christmas 1987. Connolly explained
that he was concerned the terrorizing incidents were

starting again. He was worried that he was going to be back on the same "treadmill" that he had been on with her for several years. On a personal level, he was reluctant to get involved. Cindy never phoned again, so Connolly said he assumed her phone message indicated it was nothing urgent.

Connolly testified that multiple personality disorders are difficult both to recognize and to treat. He said he was not trained or experienced in the treatment of the disorder, and did not recognize Cindy as an MPD patient.

"If you did have a patient in whom you recognized such a disorder, what would you do?" asked Catherine Kinahan.

"Well, I would look at the nature and type of treatment and see if there was some person who had expertise in that regard available to that patient," Connolly said.

"You'd refer them to a more experienced doctor?"

"Yes," Connolly agreed.

One of the women jurors asked Connolly if he had ever considered group therapy for Cindy. He did not, he said, because of Cindy's need for privacy. It was very difficult for her even to develop a trusting one-on-one relationship with a therapist.

The jury foreman asked if it was possible that the trance-like state that Cindy induced at home as part of her relaxation therapy could have been self-induced in the hospital to "fool doctors and police when they're questioning her." Connolly did not believe her dissociative state in hospital was self-induced. "There was no evidence that I have to make that kind of speculation."

Questioned by Coroner Tilley, Connolly said he saw Cindy flip back and forth between a semi-conscious state and a dissociative state.

Dr. Paul Termansen, a well-respected Vancouver psychiatrist with more than 25 years experience, had committed Cindy to the Lions Gate psychiatric ward in July 1985.

Isn't it true, he was asked, that the existence of multiple personality disorder has only been recently recognized.

"Yes, I think that's true," Termansen said. It usually takes almost seven years from the time a person begins psychiatric treatment to diagnose the disorder.

Termansen's own diagnosis of Cindy was that of hysterical personality disorder. Characteristics include attention-seeking, inappropriate sexually seductive behaviour, excessive concern with physical attractiveness, displays of shallow, rapidly shifting emotion, and a style of speech excessively impressionistic and lacking in detail. When asked to describe, say, one's mother, a person diagnosed as hysterical personality disorder might be no more specific than "She was a beautiful person."

Termansen's initial clinical impression, he pointed out, was that Cindy was a borderline personality – a disorder that almost always stems from the first few years of childhood when "very significant traumas" leave permanent impressions on the individual.

Treatment of borderline personalities is difficult, he added, because the patient has difficulty establishing trust with the therapist. It involves long-term therapy over many years just to maintain the person so she can function fairly normally.

Termansen said it happens quite often that a borderline personality seems to resolve the problem and is apparently happy, but recovery is superficial and the patient "falls apart again."

Borderline personality patients "have recurrent interpersonality crises, poor impulse control, recurrent outbursts of intense emotion, particularly anger, and they have profound doubt as to their own identity, sexual or otherwise. I think for those of you who saw *Fatal Attraction*, that woman probably portrayed to a very excellent degree what I would consider to be a borderline personality disorder, somebody who is capable of intense attachment and tremendous rage and rejection that would be classical borderline personality."

Bethell, returning to the subject of multiple personality disorder, asked if a patient would recognize that he or she has the disorder.

"They may or may not," Termansen replied. Initially, when a multiple patient seeks treatment from a psychiatrist, he or she has no clear awareness that the phenomenon is ruling their lives, "because there is a period of amnesia between personality one and two and three."

"Would a person knowing that individual see the obvious changes from one to the other personality?" Bethell asked.

"Yes," said Termansen. "It includes changes in voice, mannerisms, behaviour, everything. So you would – if you lived with them, or if you knew them intimately – you would know when they were one or two or three." Termansen said he did not treat multiple personality cases, but he understood that while under hypnosis a person could switch to another personality.

"The splitting of the personality is a defensive operation," he explained, "to save them from facing up to or dealing with very painful memories, so instead of dealing with those emotions and memories, they instead split off into another personality, because the first personality hasn't been able to do the job adequately. . . . Of course, it's a solution that never really completely works because it's always just running ahead of the problem rather than actually dealing with it."

If Cindy's "support group" denied the possibility that she was mentally ill, would that have had any effect on her treatment, Kinahan asked.

"Well, I'm not clear as to how close Cindy was to her family at this time," Termansen said. "If she wasn't mentally ill, I would wonder what all the treatment was for then."

Leask suggested that perhaps Cindy's reluctance to disclose at Lions Gate the full history of her problems stemmed from suggestions made by Kaban or Connolly not to do so.

"Well, it could be, but it also deals me out of being any use to her because I can't deal with a patient who is not forthcoming about information that they are consciously aware of.... If they are deliberately withholding information, I very quickly lose interest," Termansen stated.

Asked by Leask if he felt Cindy was withholding conscious information, Termansen replied "very much so."

Leask, wanting to discount the seriousness of Cindy's involuntary committal at Lions Gate, asked Termansen if he thought she was possibly "a danger to herself and others" as was stated on her medical notes. Termansen said it was not a remote possibility – it was an imminent probablility. Cindy had clearly indicated she was suicidal.

"What about the danger to others?" Leask asked. "I mean, that's the kind of phrase one uses about a homicidal maniac. Now she wasn't in that sort of state, was she?"

"Well, it's hard to judge at that stage," Termansen said. "If you are about to lose control over your sadistic impulses and turn them against yourself, often it doesn't take much before it may be turned against somebody else.... Often the two go together." That was not the answer Leask was seeking.

Indicative of the jury's confusion about the meaning of the psychiatric terms and diagnoses being discussed, one woman juror asked if the term schizophrenic was another name for borderline personality.

"No, not at all," Termansen said. He explained that schizophrenia is believed to be a biochemical and perhaps genetic disorder, whereas a borderline personality disorder stems from personal experience, usually trauma experienced at an early age.

May 25, 1990 marked the final day of testimony at the Cindy James inquiry – and the first anniversary of Cindy's disappearance.

Ozzie Kaban was recalled to the stand to explain that the Hack's lawyer, Leask, had asked him to do a follow-up investigation during the inquest. He attended the scene where Cindy's body had been found to conduct an experiment that would test the effects of rodents and other animals on decomposing flesh. Contacting the UBC zoology department, Kaban was told that pig meat would most closely resemble decomposition of human flesh. He then purchased about four kilograms of pork chops from a supermarket and left those on April 28, 1990 where Cindy's body had been found. He then went back to take pictures every few days.

His findings? On the third day, April 30, Kaban found his purchase had been attacked by rodents or birds. "Two complete pork chops had been eaten or pecked at," he noted. On May 4, more had been eaten, and by May 13 the meat had disappeared entirely.

What did the morbid experiment prove? "That Ozzie should stick to his day job 'cause he ain't no scientist," a reporter whispered at the media table.

"I could not understand," Kaban told the court, "how a body could be in the same location for two weeks and not be attacked by rodents and small animals known to frequent the Richmond area." He mentioned he had talked to a neighbour adjacent to where Cindy's body had been found and the man said he had trapped 12 rats within a year. Also, Kaban said, the house was frequented by high school kids and there was a man living behind the house, cooking his meals just five metres from the body. "I have a hard time believing no one would have found the body."

Kaban was asked if he had been a beneficiary of Cindy's will.

Yes, he replied, his firm had been left $30,000, but he only learned of this after her death. He said he had spent that much on personal protection and the electronics installed at Cindy's homes, as well as another $3,000 in out-of-pocket expenses. "As far as I'm concerned, the account is paid in full," he said. "I am not working for the Hack family. Whatever [future] investigations I conduct will be strictly on my own."

Wade had a few final questions. Did Kaban or his employees ever photograph Dr. Makepeace?

Twice, Kaban said, adding that he wanted his operatives doing surveillance to know what Makepeace looked like.

Did he ever put an electronic tracking device on Dr. Makepeace's car?

"No I did not."

Did he ever phone Dr. Makepeace's residence?

"A phone call was made to verify whether he was home," Kaban said. "I believe it was the Dunbar [Park] incident. . . . We dialled his number, asked for a different name, apologized and hung up." He could not recall instructing his employees to call Makepeace again.

The final witness was Dr. Joe Noone, a Cary Grant lookalike originally from Ireland who is considered one of the top forensic psychiatrists in B.C. He was retained by the coroners service to provide a psychiatric post-mortem on the Cindy James case "in any way I please."

He told the inquest he spent about 60 hours on the case, beginning on January 22, 1990 with a review of the log of incidents, Cindy's diary and her complete hospital records. He also listened to a tape entitled "Reflections," by Cindy's sister Marlene, on which she spoke of her memories of Cindy. He interviewed Dr. Connolly for an hour, Dr. Friesen for two hours and twice visited the scene where the body had been found. On February 24 in Victoria he conferred with Dr. Larry Pazder, an expert on ritual abuse. On March 6 and 7 he went to California to confer with Dr. Bruce Danto, a specialist in police psychiatry and death investigations. He read Cindy's autobiography from St. Paul's and reviewed all photos, reports and exhibits. He also attended the testimony and cross-examination of Dr. Friesen.

He then began eliminating diagnoses. Cindy James did not, he believed, have a psychotic mental illness. It was a conclusion he did not arrive at until the evening before he was to testify.

"To a great extent," he said, "my objective assessment of this case . . . parallels fairly closely Dr. Friesen's testimony."

Before getting into specifics of his assessment, Bethell asked: "Generally speaking, when you're doing an assessment of somebody it's helpful, obviously to talk to that person, right?"

"Yes, it is."

"So I take it that whatever you're going to tell us has a caveat on it that you're only working from what other people have related and what has been written by Cindy or other people and their memories of those events involving her, is that correct?"

"That is correct," Noone confirmed. "Obviously my opinions in this matter are limited by the fact that I obviously didn't have a chance to interview Cindy James in this matter, so that is quite correct and, I think, an important caveat to indicate."

First, Noone agreed with Friesen's diagnosis of post-traumatic stress disorder – "a series of reactions that can occur in people when they experience frightening or traumatic experiences which are outside the realm of normal human experience . . . rapes, assaults, natural catastrophes, earthquakes, torture, things like that."

Sleep disturbance is one of the features of PTSD. "There are often frightening dreams or what other people call revivification experiences, where there can be a series of times when people entered altered states and basically do to a greater or lesser extent separate physical from emotional functioning, so called dissociation."

Noone also agreed with Friesen's diagnosis of borderline personality, which he noted is not considered a major psychiatric mental illness but an assessment of abnormal personality functioning. It is not rare: 10 per cent of the population have borderline personality disorder and up to 25 per cent of those in psychiatric treatment are borderlines.

What Noone did find rather odd was that a borderline personality disorder, by definition, would have to be estab-

lished in the developmental years of childhood and adolescence. So he would have expected to see evidence of it
throughout Cindy James' life. Prior to Cindy's separation
from Makepeace, her functioning showed problems, but
she was not a classic borderline personality. Still, he noted,
sometimes labels do not do justice to the uniqueness of
individuals. "Cindy James, my evidence would indicate,
was a warm and troubled woman, and not a label," he
said. "There is a seductive quality in sticking a label on
somebody and saying, 'Well, now we understand everything,' and I think we have to avoid that. And I think it's
very important to separate speculation from opinion. We
can speculate, theorize all we want. I think it's very important to reach opinions that we have a basis for. . . . The
standard we use in medicine is 'with a reasonable medical
certainty'. . . . I think, for that reason, the jury may have to
disabuse itself of many speculations and opinions and sort
out what's speculation and what's opinion."

The real problem in Cindy James's case, Noone said, is
that there was no evidence documented of a severe
trauma, the original cause of her psychiatric problem. "I
don't think anybody knows or will know when the traumas occurred in this case. She received trauma, I have no
doubt about it, but when and whether there was more than
one trauma, or whether she was sensitized by the normal
developmental experiences of childhood so that when she
was traumatized she regressed more, we don't know. That
is all speculation, and that makes this case, I think, very
unique."

"Do I understand you correctly that post-traumatic
stress syndrome did not cause borderline personality?"
Bethell asked.

"No, but what it may have done is brought the borderline personality to the surface," Noone said.

Bethell asked Noone to elaborate on dissociative states.

Most of us experience a mildly dissociative or altered
state of consciousness if we are distracted by the mental

activity going on in our heads, Noone said. He cited the example of leaving the court after Friesen's testimony and hitting the elevator button for "2" – he did it several times until he realized he was on the second floor and he wanted to go to "Ground." That was a mild form of dissociation and is considered perfectly normal.

In more extreme forms of dissociative states, there is a total separation of mind and body, possibly with amnesia afterwards, he said. A person may not remember what they have done for several hours, and when they do find out they cannot believe the things they did because they behaved so differently from their normal personality. That's when dissociation is an unhealthy disorder, a symptom of problems within the mind. The most extreme form of dissociative state is called multiple personality disorder, which Noone said is extremely rare.

"I could find no indications which would support multiple personality disorder in this case,' Noone said. "It can be the stuff of soap operas – though we all may have a prurient interest in soap operas. Probably some of you, like myself, were very upset when *Twin Peaks* ended so strangely Wednesday night, but that's soap opera. This is life, reality, and I think it's important to make the distinction."

Noone said he agreed with Friesen that he saw no evidence Cindy was on the path to suicide. "In fact, the opposite would appear to be coming from the data."

Asked if he would agree that rage was a dominant theme in Cindy's diary, Noone said he had made no note of it when reading the diary.

One of his concerns in looking at the evidence is that there may have been someone in collusion with Cindy James, doing some of the incidents. "But I have no evidence to indicate there was."

As an aside, Noone mentioned that he thought Friesen's treatment of Cindy James "was as good as I have seen in psychotherapy for many years."

A question from a juror: "Do you think if Dr. Friesen had more time, that the trauma incident might have come out?"

"I believe it would have," Noone said.

Noone's testimony probably baffled the jurors more than it enlightened them. But before they deliberated their verdict, the coroner agreed to allow final summations by lawyers, an unusual move for Coroner's Court.

Peter Leask urged the jury not to find that Cindy James met her death by suicide. His argument was a testament to the masterful manoeuvring for which he is well known in criminal court.

He started by refreshing the jury's memory of the testimony that Cindy was in improving spirits before she disappeared. And that certainly does not fit the suicide theory, Leask said.

At the same time, "Cindy's family believe she was killed by person or persons unknown. They believe it sincerely," he said. "But there's no evidence for it. We don't have evidence someone killed her."

Leask urged the jury to focus on the facts, rather than speculation, then reminded the jurors about the phone call to Pat McBride. "Someone out there is phoning in. It's not *Cindy*," he said, rekindling the mystery.

The jurors were told they may want to give some consideration to the possibility that, because of the mental conditions the doctors talked about, "Cindy *could* have killed herself without the kind of intention that would allow you to come to your verdict of suicide."

Leask said the easiest way to get to that conclusion was to accept the idea of multiple personalities.

"Now that's an attractive theory, except for this. There is no evidence to support it. None whatsover. The professionals, when consulted, and I lay particular weight on Dr. Friesen and Dr. Noone, in fact, the professionals are consistent. *All* rejected multiple personalities. . . . "

"These are trained observers. The people who know what the expression means, they say, 'No!' And therefore, I say to you, the proper way to consider that on the evidence is 'No!' "

"Dr. Makepeace said he believes in multiple personalities. There is no reason to think he is being *dishonest* with you about that. But on this subject, he is not an expert. It's really as though *I* had that opinion or a policeman had that opinion. He's a doctor. We can, say, give him a *little* more weight but, frankly, I think you should reject multiple personalities, primarily based on the evidence of Dr. Friesen and Dr. Noone."

Leask did not mention that Makepeace has three degrees, including two psychology degrees, and had been the acting head of a university psychology department in South Africa by 1950, long before Noone and Friesen were psychiatrists. Also, Leask did not remind the jury that Makepeace was once head of the social psychiatry division at UBC.

In conclusion, Leask suggested "the proper verdict is the so-called open-ended verdict." He urged the jury to recommend that police appoint one or more officers who had never worked on the case to try to find a solution.

In her final summation, Catherine Kinahan said: "The Vancouver police department's position is that Cindy's death was suicide or accident. It would be pointless to re-open the investigation at this stage. It's not going to solve this case. There is no more evidence to be found. . . . Enough is enough. This inquest ought to lay the matter to rest. Re-opening the investigation would be a waste of public money and public time."

John Bethell said there would be nothing wrong with an undetermined verdict, even though jurors had spent 40 days trying to come to a definitive conclusion. "It's frustrating, but there's nothing wrong with it."

On Monday, May 28, 1990, Coroner Tilley spent the morning summarizing the highlights of the case for the jury. Finally, he set aside his notes and, facing the jury from behind his raised dais, said: "Your duty, ladies and gentlemen, is monumental." He noted that "coroner's counsel, the investigator and myself have spent nearly a year on this case. . . . It has been a long, exhaustive process." In the end, Tilley said, he found the case "sad, very sad."

The jury began its deliberations that afternoon. After weighing the evidence, and supporting or discarding sundry hypotheses for close to three hours, it returned with an indeterminate verdict. Yes, the jurors agreed, Cindy James had died of an overdose of morphine and flurazepam, but there was insufficient evidence to determine if her death was a homicide, an accident, or suicide. In effect, her death was judged to have been caused by "an unknown event." No recommendation was made to reopen the investigation.

Otto and Tillie Hack appeared both crestfallen and annoyed. They had hoped Cindy's "innocence" would be finally upheld. "We were, naturally, a little more hopeful that something definite would come out of it, but obviously because of the complexity of the situation . . . this wasn't possible," Otto Hack told reporters as the Hack family prepared to leave the courtroom. "We have lost a daughter and a sister. I don't think anyone can appreciate it unless they've gone through it. . . . It's been extremely hard on the family."

As a newspaper photographer moved in for one last close-up of the family's reaction, his camera bag knocked over a vase resting on the oak rail dividing the public gallery from the inner court. It contained flowers that had been picked from Cindy's garden at her final home in Richmond.

Tears welled in Tillie Hack's eyes as she stared at the broken vase. It seemed emblematic of everything the media had done to the family – sensationalize the gritty

details of their private lives, leaving only the broken remains of cherished memories.

The next day's headline in *The Province* read, "Cindy
James: The mystery remains," while *The Vancouver Sun*
declared, "Jury gives up on James: Evidence insufficient
for decision." It was a disappointing conclusion to a story
that for months had been avidly consumed by readers. As
one Vancouverite told his brother in Toronto, British Co-
lumbians had become accustomed to "eating the story for
breakfast," baffled and horrified by each new twist in
inquest testimony. On Monday mornings subscribers
would telephone the two dailies to complain "the Cindy
James story" was missing from their paper. They were
surprised to learn that the inquest did not sit on weekends.

One reporter who covered the proceedings went so far
as to write about how the inquest's gruesome details had
infiltrated his own subconscious. He had a recurring
dream of finding a mutilated body in a garbage can filled
with water. Awakening suddenly, he would lie in bed,
hearing the words "Cindy dead meat soon" reverberate in
his mind. Another reporter claimed that she had received
death threats while investigating the case.

Throughout the inquest, avid readers were writing to
reporters to offer their own theories. It was inconceivable
to most that James could have inflicted this misery on
herself. They felt she had died at the hands of a madman.
Her friends remarked that Cindy was the kind of person
who literally would not hurt a fly: she would catch it and
take it outside.

Seasoned psychiatric and law enforcement professionals were more wary, a position best reflected perhaps in a
comment Pat Costello wrote to the coroner service before
the inquest began: "[Makepeace] has alibis for several of
the events, even to the extent that he was outside the
country during some of them. The suggestion is then that
someone was hired to do this. In several of these incidents,
we are told there [was] more than one person involved. In

the 33rd and Dunbar [attack], we have to believe at least three people are involved. Can you hire people to do this sort of thing and keep them going for year after year, particularly when police and private security people are constantly around? Where do you find such people?"

This skepticism was shown by many of the reporters covering the proceedings. They were irked by some of Cindy's friends, relatives and colleagues, who each morning would strongly criticize daily media reports. Stage whispers of "Lies, lies" were not uncommon. Some individuals clucked their tongues, rolled their eyes and gasped in disbelief during testimony they took exception to.

The inquest also attracted its share of outrageous speculation. One theorist was convinced Cindy James had been a prostitute and that he had met her; another claimed that an acquaintance of Cindy's in the medical profession had performed diabolical surgery on her son, and implicated the acquaintance in Cindy's troubles.

Ozzie Kaban left the court vowing to continue to investigate the case at his own expense. Asked months later if still believes Cindy was a murder victim, he said: "There's no question in my mind." He thought the inquest "spent more time trying to find her guilty and finding her a nut than trying to prove anything else." He is still investigating the case, still trying to "nail" a suspect.

Constable Jerry Anderson continues to investigate tips on the case. No new information has arisen to point the finger at anyone. Officially, the Cindy James file remains open.

EIGHTEEN

Multiple Choice

S O W H O *did* kill Cindy James?
   That's the question the Hack family kept asking following the inquest. "God, if the truth would have only come out," an anguished Tillie Hack lamented on the American tabloid television program, *A Current Affair*, which broadcast a segment in August 1990 on Cindy James' "mysterious" death.

"Somebody out there knows something," Cindy's sister, Marlene Weintrager said later in the fall of 1990.

Dr. Roy Makepeace says the complete pieces of the puzzle are staring the Hack family boldly in the face. As he said at the inquest and says now, the answer is clear: Cynthia "Cindy" Elizebeth Hack Makepeace James (a.k.a. Cindy Jacobs) suffered from multiple personality disorder.

Feeling the need for vindication after the agony he went through as the suspected villain, Makepeace wrote letters after the inquest to the two of Cindy's relatives he thought would be the most open-minded – sisters Marlene and Melanie.

He sent each a 100-page binder, outlining his views on multiple personality disorder, offering a powerful and persuasive rebuttal of Peter Leask's final summation that his diagnosis was worth little more than a policeman's opinion. The binders also included the latest medical literature and studies on multiple personality disorder, commonly referred to as MPD.

He also sent along a videotape of a TV program featuring Chris Sizemore, one of the most internationally famous multiples. She was the "Eve" of *Three Faces of Eve*, the book that had been made into a 1957 Hollywood film starring Joanne Woodward. Sizemore actually had more than 20 personalities, not just "Eve White" and "Eve Black."

Makepeace told the sisters that Joe Noone had not detected evidence of MPD because he never knew Cindy. He was just a "reviewer of paperwork." Moreover, Noone had to base his opinion on facts, Friesen's facts. With Friesen certified as a psychiatrist the year he began treating Cindy, he naturally did not have the experience to recognize Cindy as a multiple personality.

He felt Noone and Friesen, both of whom believed cases of MPD are rare, had not kept up with the current medical literature. They were still thinking of MPD in terms of the *Diagnostic and Statistical Manual of Mental Disorders III*, commonly referred to as the DSM-III, the classification "bible" of psychiatry published by the American Psychiatric Association in 1980, the first year MPD was recognized as a psychiatric diagnosis.

Until then, there had been only about 200 known cases of MPD worldwide. Since then, an estimated 6,000 cases have been diagnosed and thousands more are believed to have gone unrecognized by psychiatrists.

Makepeace pointed out that the current revised edition, DSM-III-R, published in 1987, states MPD is not as rare as it was commonly thought to be, and that one or more of the alter personalities can exhibit symptoms that suggest a disturbance in personality functioning that is often diagnosed as borderline personality disorder.

"Sound familiar?" Makepeace wrote.

Still, Makepeace acknowledged MPD is not easy to diagnose, unless a psychiatrist has a "high index of suspicion" for it.

Among the articles sent to Cindy's sisters was the 1988 analysis of 236 cases of MPD spearheaded by Canadian Dr. Colin Ross of Winnipeg. Keeping Cindy's psychiatric treatment in mind, it does provide amazing similarities: it takes an average of 6.7 years in psychiatric treatment before a multiple is correctly diagnosed. (Cindy had six years of "therapy" beginning with Connolly and later with Friesen.)

Amnesia is experienced in 94.9 per cent of cases when a personality switch occurs and is considered one of the tell-tale signs of MPD.

The Canadian study also found that the average age of MPD patients was 30; almost 87 per cent were women. A startling 85 per cent were found to have been victims of sexual or physical abuse.

Psychiatric professionals now realize multiples arise when, say, a child is chronically abused. The child may begin to imagine the abuse is happening to someone else initially, perhaps an imaginary playmate. But as the abuse continues, the child enters a trance-like state and a distinct personality is formed to deal with the abuse and protect the "core" personality from the horrible memories and pain. Often the alter personality is frozen at the age when the abuse first began, and the victim blocks all memory of the abuse as a defence mechanism.

Another new discovery: those who have been abused at an early age perpetuate the pain and anger by abusing other children during switches to another personality.

Of the 236 cases, 86 per cent had a child personality, 62.6 per cent had a personality of the opposite sex and 84 per cent had a "persecutor" personality, which carries the victim's tremendous rage at what happened to them. The persecutor often inflicts wounds on the "host" personality.

About 72 per cent of multiples attempt suicide, the Canadian study found, with the common methods being drug overdoses (68 per cent), self-inflicted burns or other injuries (56.6 per cent) and wrist slashing (49.3 per cent). Only two per cent, however, successfully commit suicide.

Treatment of multiples has proven encouraging. But the gurus of MPD point out that if treatment does not deal directly with the disorder, the patient may cease to show personalities to their therapist yet continue to experience them. In effect, the personalities try to hide to avoid detection.

Unlike schizophrenics, who hear voices emanating outside their heads, about 72 per cent of multiples hear voices arguing in their head, while 66 per cent hear internal voices commenting on their actions.

"Is this why they become 'very private persons?'" Makepeace asked in his letter. "Is this why such a patient may, on rare occasions, as with Cindy, question whether they are 'losing their minds?'"

Makepeace noted that about 64 per cent of MPD patients are wrongly diagnosed as Affective Disorders (Friesen's diagnosis), 57 per cent are diagnosed as Personality Disorder, including Borderline Personalities (Marcus, Friesen, Noone, with Termansen also leaning toward that diagnosis), 44 per cent are wrongly diagnosed as Anxiety Disorders (Cashmore, Rothschild and Connolly felt this was Cindy's problem) and 41 per cent are diagnosed as being Schizophrenic or having an equally serious Psychotic Disorder (Choi).

Makepeace received some local support for his theory. In November 1989, while thumbing through *The Canadian Medical Association Journal*, he came across a letter with the headline: "Dissociative Disorders: Need for Vancouver Unit?" It was penned by Dr. Marlene Hunter, then national co-chair of the Canadian Society for Studies in Multiple Personality and Dissociation.

Hunter wrote that the society was interested in establishing a Vancouver clinic specifically to treat dissociative disorders, including MPD. "At present there is no such unit west of Dr. Colin Ross' in Winnipeg. With burgeoning information on child abuse and its devastating consequences it becomes increasingly important for us to have the facilities available to help these innocent victims," she wrote.

Makepeace wrote Dr. Hunter, fully supporting her idea and explaining his belief that his ex-wife had suffered from MPD. Within a day of receiving his letter, Hunter called. "As soon as I read the reports in the media after Cindy's disappearance, I recognized a case of MPD immediately," she told Makepeace over the phone.

Contacted for this book, Hunter said she was currently treating 11 MPD cases within her medical practice in West Vancouver, a small upper-class enclave whose residents have the highest income per capita in Canada.

"MPD is misdiagnosed most of the time because it was taught in medical school that it is extremely rare," she explained. "It was also taught that child abuse is very rare. Now we know that is not true." She added that "there is almost always a conspiracy of silence in families" where child abuse has occurred.

What was the horrible, traumatic incident Cindy experienced in childhood that, perhaps, caused her problems in her final years? As Noone says, we will never know. Cindy never told anybody. Or else her sister Marlene is right when she says, "Somebody out there knows something." If Cindy did tell someone, that person has not come forward with the information.

Agnes Woodcock is one of the few of Cindy's close personal friends who would even entertain thoughts of Cindy being a multiple. "The only way I could see her doing that [her death] to herself is that she'd have to be a multiple personality. And of all the years I was with her I never saw a sign of it. Dr. Cashmore said he would have recognized it, working so closely with her. I was with her at the fire and she was certainly terrified. . . . I can't help thinking, Could it be possible?"

Friesen was baffled by Cindy's death because she had been optimistic, the happiest he had seen her in years, which he felt was an indication she was on the road to recovery. But as psychologist Ken Dercole had noted during his testing of Cindy during her stay at Riverview Hospital in 1986: "The periods of cheerfulness often prove to be temporary cover-ups to counter deeper fears of insecurity and abandonment."

In a confidential interview June 26, 1989, Richmond RCMP Cpl. Jack Henzie and Const. Jerry Anderson asked Dr. Friesen if he ever noticed Cindy "take on a different personality?"

"Other than the dramatic, you know, sort of falling out of the hospital ward, hiding in my closet, standing in the corner for an hour in an interview with me, no," Friesen said.

A few seconds later, he added, "The only thing she would do – I can't prove [this] for sure – she would often . . . leave whimpering messages on my answering service. . . . And that's the only thing you run into, actually, is a sort of 'Help' in a sort of panic sort of voice, in a little pathetic child-like voice, I've always assumed was her."

Friesen said the calls would follow an interview with Cindy in which he would confront her a bit about her problems.

Had Friesen looked at Cindy's diary, which he had asked her to write but had never read, he may have noticed cryptic messages in some of the entries. Cindy only admitted to her diary that she did not know whether her memory of the dismembered bodies on the island was a dream or a real memory. The diary indicates that Cindy's horrific nightmares became real memories to her. As Dr. Marcus stated, "she was in a living nightmare."

So where did the body-chopping dream stem from? Makepeace believes Cindy may have inadvertently witnessed her father butchering the carcass of a deer or a moose that he had shot. Possibly she peered through the barn door, saw the sight and thought a human body was being chopped up, then repressed the horror of the memory. Later in life, during the stress arising from her marriage break-up, Cindy transferred her childhood rage against her father to her husband, a natural father-figure since he was only six years younger than Otto Hack. In this fashion, Roy Makepeace became the villain, an easier target for her rage than her father.

If Cindy did have a multiple personality, one was likely a child. Friesen and Connolly were both puzzled by Cindy's childlike behaviour at times. But they never made the connection to MPD.

Was it one of Cindy's "alters" who told so many people so many lies? Was it this "alter" who told Rothschild that Cindy's breast surgery was to correct damage from Makepeace's alleged abuse, when the truth was she elected to have her breasts enlarged with silicone implants? Makepeace says he tried to talk Cindy out of the operation, but Cindy felt she needed fuller breasts. She had always strived to be perfect.

One of the last remaining questions: What symbolism, if any, can be read into the black nylon stockings, which were a motif in Cindy's life and death?

The case of Ruth Finley perhaps provides a hint of their significance. Finley, of Wichita, Kan., experienced a similar campaign of terror starting in 1977. She was 47 at the time. She said a man had phoned her claiming to have found a 1946 newspaper clipping with a headline reading, "Sex Maniac Uses Flatirons to Brand Local High School Girl."

"That's you, isn't it," the man asked? "I want money to keep this quiet, Ruth." She hung up on him.

Finley told police the man called her several times, then tried to jump her in an alley a year later. A few months went by until she reported that she had been snatched off the street by the man, but had managed to flee.

Police put Finley under 24-hour surveillance for five weeks without a sign of her abductor. Then threats, in the form of poems, began arriving in her mail. Nine months after the abduction, Finley was alone at a shopping mall, about to get in her car when, she said, the man stabbed her, driving the knife in her back to the hilt. The knife was wrapped with a red bandanna. Her husband also discovered an ice pick wrapped in a red bandanna left outside their home. Eggs were smeared on the house, the phone lines of Finley's home were cut and more letters signed by "The Poet" were sent to police, the local newspaper and a TV station.

It became a sensational mystery in Wichita – until police began round-the-clock surveilance of Finley, who was finally caught in 1981 mailing a letter from "The Poet." After many sessions of therapy, a repressed memory emerged: as a 3½-year-old, she was left by her father at a neighbour's farm where the neigbour had raped her and stuffed his red bandanna into her mouth to stifle her cries.

Just as the bandanna was the "calling card" of Finley's tormentor, the black stockings may have represented an assailant Cindy James had known in childhood. Maybe Cindy was molested by someone she trusted. Maybe that is where her inner rage, directed toward her parents, stemmed from.

Did Cindy James kill herself? Not exactly. If one subscribes to the MPD theory, it's possible that her persecutor personality, likely a male "alter" – remember Cindy was found wearing a man's work boot and rubber glove during the December 11, 1985 attack – took Cindy James from this world.

In a sense, Cindy James' death could be described as murder by misadventure on the part of one of her personalities.

In future, if Dr. Marlene Hunter and her colleagues successfully establish a clinic for dissociative disorders, including MPD, the chances of another Cindy James dying may be greatly reduced.

One can only hope that psychiatrists, police and families of similar victims learn the sad lessons of this tragic case.

"Who Shall I Say is Calling?"

C INDY JAMES'S death put an end to long, lonely years of suffering and misunderstanding. It also may have brought her the attention she seemed to crave in life. The torment, however, continues for those she left behind.

The national publicity generated by the prolonged proceedings resulted in the family of Cindy's sister Marlene receiving unnerving calls at their Ottawa home. In one of them, a person asked, "Are you enjoying the inquest?" Marlene and her husband wrote it off as a cruel prank. The calls persisted for many months, leading Weintrager to wonder if something more sinister was afoot.

Roy Makepeace, who had taken leave from his medical practice during the inquest, never did return to work. He decided to retire at age 64. "I just couldn't go back. I couldn't take on other people's problems."

Makepeace, of course, had been receiving strange and crank calls for years. One that remains most prominent in his mind was recorded on his answering machine shortly after Cindy's body was found. A woman's faint, tiny voice is heard to ask, as if calling from the grave: "Why did you do it, Roy?"

But none was as strange as the series of calls he received on his answering machine from a man calling himself "Ken Green" several days after the airing of the Cindy segment on *A Current Affair*.

On the night of August 19, 1990, "Green" told Makepeace that one of the Hack sons had approached him on Saltspring Island and arranged a Hack family "get together" with him to discuss "action" against Makepeace. He alleged that the family had given him an advance sum of money to find the "hitman" who killed Cindy.

"Are the kinds of things they're envisioning illegal things?" asked a dumbfounded Makepeace. "Green" confirmed that was the idea. The Hack family, "Green" said, assured him money was no problem and they were in no rush. They just wanted to remedy the image of Cindy as mentally unstable. She was no suicide. She was murdered.

The next morning, Makepeace met with his lawyer for almost three hours. After listening to the taped conversation, the lawyer advised Makepeace not to have anything to do with the man and to hand the matter over to Vancouver police.

After informing the authorities, Makepeace learned that "Ken Green" was a phoney name. Detectives subsequently took the man, a drug addict, into custody, and found there were outstanding arrest warrants in eight provinces for him.

The Hack family had paid the man $400 after "Green" intimated he knew the underworld killer who murdered Cindy, Otto Hack later confirmed. The money was to be used by "Green" to fly the killer from Winnipeg, the Manitoba capital. "We were looking at any possibilities," Hack said. "Of course, the decision was made by the family, not by myself. I was skeptical right from the start. . . . He didn't convince me at all."

After the "Green" episode, Makepeace got an unlisted phone number that is now known only to his lawyer, the Vancouver police department, three of his closest friends, and his daughter in South Africa. The harassing phone calls stopped.

The Hack family is still recovering from the aftershock of Cindy's death, the inquest and subsequent publicity. In the meantime, Hack says, the family still believes Cindy's killer is on the loose "unless you can show me something to the contrary." The Tilley inquest was "total speculation."

In his letter to Cindy's sisters outlining his multiple personality theory, Roy Makepeace said that he had one final request of his former in-laws.

"My last obligation is to quietly pay my last respects at the graveside of the woman that I loved very dearly, and to whom I was faithful throughout our married life. I purposely avoided the funeral so as not to embarrass the family when I was still perceived as an 'outcast' and major suspect. Unfortunately, I do not know the spot where Cindy now rests in peace. Maybe you could enlighten me by a postcard when you have time?"

Marlene, who began corresponding with Makepeace after the inquest, sent him the address of the well-kept memorial garden in the suburb of Surrey where Cindy's ashes have been scattered.

After 16 months of working through his grief, Roy drove to the site on September 29. He knelt in front of Cindy's memorial and loudly wept there for a long, long time. Speaking to the spirit of Cindy, he told her that he held no grudge against her. "I know this was not of your making."

After eight long, torturous years, the nightmare was finally over.

AFFLICTION
by Russell Banks
"Everything about **Affliction** is impressive . . . [it] will not let go of you, I swear, until you turn the last page." — Elmore Leonard
A disturbing novel about a desperate man's violent quest for respect and redemption.
0-7710-1055-9 $6.95

DEADLY ALLIES
Canada's Secret War 1937-1947
by John Bryden
"Reads like a spy novel . . . amazingly well written." — *Globe and Mail*
0-7710-1726-X $6.95   8 pages b&w photos

MINDFIELD
by William Deverell
"Deverell's lean-mean style gives off sparks." — *Publishers Weekly*
With two men dead, hard-boiled Montreal cop Kellen O'Reilly finds himself ensnared in a web of conspiracy and cover-up. As the body count increases, he is racked by nightmarish flashbacks.
0-7710-2660-9 $5.95

RANSOM FOR A GOD
by Tony Foster
Rumours are flying in Bangkok about a Chinese plot to steal an immense golden statue of the Buddha. American pilot Mike Carson looks like the only one prepared to derail the scheme — or pull it off.
0-7710-3233-1 $6.95

More Great Titles from M&S Paperbacks...

VICTORY AT SEA
Tales of His Majesty's Coastal Forces
by Hal Lawrence
"Good rousing stuff." — *The Vancouver Province*
0-7710-4726-6 $6.95   16 pages b&w photos

CANADIAN CRYPTIC CROSSWORDS
Volume 1
by Bob Blackburn
Your mind will be in knots as you try to solve these 70 pun-packed, delightfully devious puzzles.
0-7710-1526-7 $5.95

MAPLE LEAF BLUES
Harold Ballard and the Life and Times
of the Toronto Maple Leafs
by William Houston
"An incredible tale . . . Were it not for Houston's believable easy-reading journalistic style, one would think it came from the *National Enquirer*." — *The Winnipeg Free Press*
An up-to-date look at the team as well as a sharp account of irascible owner Harold Ballard.
0-7710-4242-6 $6.95   16 pages b&w photos

RUNNING WEST
by James Houston
"An honest and haunting fictional treatment of the harsh realities of the fur-trade era." — *The Edmonton Journal*
0-7710-4268-X $5.95

PLAYING FOR KEEPS
The Making of the Prime Minister, 1988
by Graham Fraser
"The best book yet written about any Canadian election campaign." — Peter C. Newman
0-7710-3211-0 $7.95